PUBLIC PARTICIPATION AND INNOVATIONS IN COMMUNITY GOVERNANCE

Public Participation and Innovations in Community Governance

Edited by
PETER McLAVERTY
School of Public Administration and Law
The Robert Gordon University

ASHGATE

Published by
Ashgate Publishing Limited
Gower House
Croft Road
Aldershot
Hants GU11 3HR
England

Ashgate Publishing Company
Suite 420
101 Cherry Street
Burlington VT 05401-4405
USA

Ashgate website: http://www.ashgate.com

British Library Cataloguing in Publication Data
Public participation and innovations in community governance
1. Political participation 2. Community organization
I. McLaverty, Peter
323' .042

Library of Congress Cataloging-in-Publication Data
Public participation and innovations in community governance / edited by Peter McLaverty.
p. cm.
Includes bibliographical references and index.
ISBN 0-7546-1566-9
1. Local government--Citizen participation. 2. Political planning--Citizen participation.
I. McLaverty, Peter.

JS211 .P83 2002
323'.042--dc21

2001053603

Reprinted 2003

ISBN 0 7546 1566 9

This book is printed on acid free paper.
Typeset by Owain Hammonds, Bontgoch, Talybont, Ceredigion, Wales SY24 5DP.
Printed and bound in Great Britain by Biddles Limited, Guildford and King's Lynn

Contents

List of Tables

List of Contributors

Nils Aarsæther, is a Professor at The Institute of Planning and Community Studies, University of Tromso.

Georgina Blakeley is a Lecturer in Politics at the Huddersfield University.

John Diamond is a Research Fellow, in The Centre for Local Studies at Edge Hill College of Higher Education.

Arturo Flores is a PhD student at the University of York.

Cornie Groenewald is a Professor in the Department of Sociology, University of Stellenbosch.

Erik-Hans Klijn is Senior Lecturer in the Department of Public Administration, Erasmus University, Rotterdam.

Joop F.M. Koppenjan is a Senior Lecturer in the Faculty of Technology, Policy and Management at Delft University of Technology.

Daniel Kübler is a Research Fellow in the Institute of the Built Environment of The Swiss Institute of Technology.

Torill Nyseth is a Førtesmanuensis at The Institute of Planning and Community Studies, University of Tromso.

Ciaran O'Faircheallaigh is a Professor at Griffith University.

Asbjørn Røiseland is a Researcher at The Nordic Research Institute.

Antoinette Smith is a Senior Project Co-ordinator, Matie Community Service, University of Stellenbosc.

Sonja Wälti is Visiting Researcher, Georgetown Public Policy Institute, Washington DC.

Acknowledgements

As editor, I would like to thank all those who attended the Public Participation and Innovations in Community Governance conference in June 1999, especially those who gave papers. I must also thank my two co-organisers of the conference, Andy Asquith and John Dickens. As my Head of Department at the University of Luton, John Dickens was always supportive and gave maximum encouragement, even during the difficult times the Department of Politics and Public Policy faced as I was trying to complete the editing of this book. Finally, I would like to thank Claire O'Neill for helping me to cope with the intricacies of word processing and Sue Morris for her help with the index.

John Diamond would like to thank Carole Brocken for help in preparing his chapter. He would also like to thank Anne Kearney, Andy Nelson and Stuart Speeden for discussing the points raised in his chapter.

Chapter 1
Introduction

Peter McLaverty

Over the past ten to fifteen years, nation-states across the world have become interested in, and committed to, increasing the participation of citizens in 'public affairs'. This general interest in increased public participation has been accompanied, according to some writers, by a move from systems of government to what those like Rhodes (1997) call 'governance'. It was to investigate the ways in which developments in public participation related to ideas of 'community government' that the Centre for the Study of Public Participation at the University of Luton, in collaboration with the Political Science Department at Gotburg University, decided to host an international conference. The conference took place in June 1999 at the University of Luton's Putteridge Bury site and attracted participants and paper givers from the continents of the globe. Over forty papers were presented at the conference. The chapters in this book represent some of the papers discussed at the conference. Unfortunately, not all the papers could be included in this book and some papers of a high quality have had to be excluded. In all cases, the papers have been significantly amended since the conference. In a few cases, new papers have been written for this book. In this introduction, I want to place the chapters in some analytical context. I will start by considering some of the key ideas behind the concept of 'governance'. In the following section, I will suggest that states have become interested in public participation for a variety of reasons, including the 'fiscal crisis of the state' (O'Connor, 1973) and for reasons of legitimacy. I will go onto introduce some of the arguments concerning the relationship between initiatives in public participation and democracy. Finally, I will say a few words about the chapters that follow this introduction.

Governance

Governance, for Rhodes, involves a number of changes from traditional patterns of liberal democratic government. Applying his analysis specifically to Britain, Rhodes (1997, pp. 4–5) contends that important changes have taken place in three broad inter-linked areas: the development of policy networks; the development of 'governance'; and accountability. In the specific area of governance, Rhodes (1997, p. 4) argues that the development of policy networks has necessitated changes to the way in which government 'confronts self-steering interorganiozational networks'. While the state ultimately has more power than the networks, it has to allow the networks some independence. The growth of policy networks, it is argued, leads to unintended policy consequences, implementation gaps and 'policy mess'. Attempts by the state to directly control or manage the organizational and social complexity which is created by the growth of powerful policy networks, only adds to unintended policy consequences. The state undergoes a process of hollowing out. As a result, it is argued: 'Indirect management is the central challenge posed by governance for the operating code of central elites' (Rhodes, 1997, p. 5). For Rhodes (1997, p. 9), policy networks can take five forms. These are: tightly integrated policy communities; professional networks; intergovernmental networks; producer networks; and issue networks which are loosely integrated.

On this analysis, the state has lost its overall directing and controlling role within society. The state now has to work with policy networks, which contain representatives of a number of social interests. Such networks are important, according to writers like Marsh and Smith (2000) because as well as limiting participation in the policy process, they define the role of actors, decide which issues will reach the policy agenda, and they privilege certain actors and interests by controlling access and by supporting certain policy outcomes. In addition, within the rules of the game, policy networks shape the behaviour of actors and reduce accountability by increasing private government (cf. also Marsh and Rhodes, 1992). The impact of policy networks is not just felt at central government level, it is argued, but is also found at regional and local levels of government. Moves to governance and away from government have resulted in governments (at different levels within states) working in partnership with interests and groups in society.

However, it can be questioned whether the developments that are suggested really represent a significant change in the workings of government and the state. From a Marxist perspective, there are writers, such as Ralph Miliband (1973), who argue that the state in capitalist society has always been constrained in its actions due to the political power that the capitalist class is able to exercise, on the basis of its ownership of the means of production, including its control over the media of mass communication. Moreover, for Miliband (1973), the state has always been predisposed to listen to the demands of capital, not least because of the background of those who run the state. The state, at least in Western Europe and countries like Australia and New Zealand, has tried to work with, and through, groups in the post-war period, especially those of capital and labour, during the heyday of corporatism, with varying degrees of success in different countries. This was a period in which the scope and functions of government increased considerably (cf. Maier, 1987). The power of groups of professionals, trade unionists, and business interests, to frustrate government intentions, has been commented upon by a number of writers over the years. Of course, from the mid-1970s, the idea of the state trying to work closely with 'the two sides of industry' has become unpopular in many parts of the world. And in a number of countries over the past 25 years, the state has shed responsibility for some of its activities and has gone into partnership with groups to carry out, at least, some of its functions. The point of contention is between those who argue there has been a fundamental move from government to governance, with the growing importance of policy networks, and those who read the changes differently. For some, with the growth of 'globalization' associated with the policies of neo-liberalism, which have been adopted by a number of governments, the workings of the nation-state have undergone important changes. Indeed, Philip Cerny (1997, p. 2) has argued that 'The rediscovery of governance ... has come about not because "self-organizing, interorganizational networks" have expanded through a wholesale or ineluctable process but because the wider (global) structural context has itself changed'. Moreover, writers, such as Pierre and Peters (2000 pp. 17–18) argue that hierarchies within government and the state are still important. While they do not deny that networks have increased their power in recent years, they argue that networks have not usurped the power of state hierarchies. Such hierarchies should be considered, they contend, as a form of governance. And, for Kooiman (1993), the state has not lost its ability to steer society. Recent developments, however, it is argued, have resulted in changes in the ways in which the state steers (cf. Pierre, 2000).

Fiscal Crisis

James O'Connor (1973) argued that western capitalist states faced a major crisis from the late 1960s onwards. The crisis was the result of growing pressures for increased state expenditure on social welfare and the military. However, the demand for increasing state spending faced problems in respect of funding. State finance comes mainly from the taxation of people's income, their spending, their property or the profits of business. The taxing of profits is generally opposed by business, however much businesses may benefit from the resulting state spending. Some, like Michael Mann (1995), have argued that western states have faced problems in recent years because of the unwillingness of their populations to pay the taxes to enable states to carry out their functions effectively. It is argued by some that the state, therefore, faces contradictory pressure: to increase spending, while at the same time holding down, or reducing, taxation (Offe, 1984). Such pressure have been seen to result in the state facing a crisis of legitimacy (cf. Habermas, 1988). In addition, in the 1980s and 1990s the state sector was seen as inflexible, inefficient and expensive. As a result, changes were called for in the way states and governments operated, including the introduction of market or market-type structures (cf. Pierre and Peters, 2000, p.5). There were also approaches which stressed that the people should have greater access to, and influence over, governments and the process of governing. This has lead some western European writers to view 'governance' as relating to the development of forms in which society is more fully involved in the process of governing (cf. Kooiman, 1993).

If the analysis has validity, then one way in which the state may try to cope with the fiscal and legitimacy crises is by attempting to get 'closer to the people'. This may be a particular imperative for the state, if the growth of networks is seen to be undermining the legitimacy of traditional representative democracy. I would suggest that it is against this background (of reduced government legitimacy and 'fiscal crisis') that the interest in increased public participation, which has been expressed by governments in different parts of the world, might be understood.

Initiatives in Public Participation and Democracy

Initiatives in public participation, which have been advanced by governments, are often seen as promoting democracy. For example, the Labour government in Britain, in its policies associated with local government, has pursued a commitment to 'democratic renewal' and 'modernisation'. Each commitment is associated with efforts to increase public participation in council affairs and to bring councils closer to the public (Stewart, 1999). However do efforts to increase public participation necessarily have any connection with democracy? To an extent it depends on what is meant by democracy.

Some argue that democracy is an 'essentially contested' term. The meaning of democracy is not clear and is open to a number of interpretations. While not all interpretations are necessarily equally valid, on this approach, there is no one definition of the concept that is correct, above all others. However, this general position is rejected by Beetham, for whom there is only one approach to the definition of democracy that is valid. For Beetham democracy concerns the making of collectively binding decisions and rules, in which all who are subject to the decisions have an equal control over the decisions. He has put it as follows:

> If democracy, then, belongs to the sphere of the political decision-making for an association or collectivity, then a system of collective decision-making can be said to be democratic to the extent that it is subject to control by all members of the relevant association, or all those under its authority, considered as equals (Beetham, 1999, pp. 4–5).

For Beetham, therefore, democracy can only be said to exist where decisions are made collectively and where there is equal control over the making of collective decisions. The forms, or institutions, in which the principles oaf democracy are embodied are less important then the principles themselves. Beetham (1999, p. 4) has further argued:

> Democratic institutions are so termed to the extent that they embody democratic principles; democratic principles in turn require practical institutional form for their relaization. Of the two, however, it is the principles that are central to the question of definition; institutions are secondary and derivative, and may take different forms in different contexts.

While the definition advanced by Beetham, and his supporting arguments, would not be accepted by all writers on democracy, those who analyse democracy in terms of different models would not, for example, agree with Beetham (for example, Macpherson, 1977, Held, 1996), his position is sufficiently convincing for this writer to use it as the criterion for judging whether initiatives are democratic. Broadly supporting Beetham's approach to the definition of democracy does not, of course, mean that the ways in which all those concerned have equal control over collective decisions is unimportant. Nor does it mean that the consequences of collective decisions, either for individuals or for the collectivity, in which all concerned exercise equal control, are viewed as unimportant. What is does mean, however, is that issues of whether decisions are made on the basis of deliberative procedures in which all are able to participate equally, for example, or whether decisions are made on the basis of binding referendums, are secondary to the questions of equal control over collective decisions. Moreover, broadly supporting Beetham's approach to the definition of democracy means that the focus is placed on actual decision-making. Again, focussing on decision-making does not mean that what happens before decisions are made is seen as unimportant; nor does it mean that formal voting is viewed as the only, or even the main, democratic procedure. Focusing on equal control over collective decisions does not mean that one should not be concerned, from a democratic perspective, with the cultural, economic or general social background against which people make decisions. Questions of how inequality in the boarder society influences those areas of society in which democracy operates remains an important issue for democratic theory and practice. Defining democracy as each having equal control over collective decisions, obviously raises important questions about the relationship between direct and representative democracy. There have always been writers who have regarded representation as incompatible with the essence of democracy (cf. Burnheim, 1985). And if one goes back to the roots of democracy in Ancient Athens, the procedures adopted were very different from what we regard as 'representative democracy' today. In electing representatives, there is no reason why all affected should not have an equal amount of control. However, issues arise about what should be the relationship between those elected as representatives and the broader electorate.

The idea of representation, as it has developed in advanced capitalist 'liberal democracies', involves the idea that those elected as representatives to parliament and so on should have the freedom to decide what they think is best for those they are representing. The argument is most elegantly developed by Edmund Burke. However, one can question the extent to which that view of representation is compatible with notions of equal control. If elected representatives are only loosely connected to the wishes of those they represent, in what sense can we say there is equal control? One may argue that the practicalities of the modern world, and the need to make decisions that cover a large geographical area, reduce the extent to which those who are elected can act as direct delegates of the wider electorate. And certainly once you get above a certain size or beyond a certain geographical level, treating the elected as delegates becomes very difficult. However, if one takes ideas of equal control over collective decisions seriously, one cannot be happy for those who are elected to make decisions which bare little or no relation to the views of those who elected them. On way round that problem, some argue (cf. Saward, 1998), lies in making more use of referendums, where the vote of each is equal. Yet, whatever use is made of referendums, it seems implausible to argue that all decisions that are taken within a modern polity should be decided by a binding referendum of 'the people'.

Another way in which some argue the gap between representatives and electors can be reduced, or closed, relates to the development of information and communication technologies (ICTs). For a number of years, writers have argued that 'new technology' makes the development of direct democracy possible. Whether the mechanism that is considered is the television set, the internet on the computer or something else, the argument is put forward that, through technological advance, individual citizens can gain control over decisions that are currently taken by their elected representatives. Sitting in front of their television or computer screens, the argument runs, citizens could not only make the decisions that are currently made by representatives in parliaments, regional or local assemblies and so on (Wolff, 1970). In addition, citizens could actively take part in debates among themselves, in an open but structured way, on the issues on which they would subsequently vote. Alternatively, citizens could listen to the debates in parliaments and assemblies, in which elected representatives take part, and cast their votes having heard those debates (Budge, 1996). In that way, it is suggested, not only would the quantity of democracy be increased but so would the quality.

However, a number of criticisms are made of these arguments. Even supporters of participatory democracy, such as C.B. Macpherson (1977), argue that such citizen involvement is unrealistic and undesirable. Many issues that modern governments have to address are seen as so complex that they could not be left to popular initiative. Areas which are often suggested in this respect, are those relating to the economy, such as levels and types of taxation, public spending and interest rates. Moreover, a common criticism made of direct democracy is that it demands too much of people. How many of us, it is asked, would be willing to spend large portions of our spare time listening or contributing to 'political' debates or voting on propositions? 'Politics' is an important aspect of our lives, it is contended, but it is not the only important area of our lives and should not override everything else. However, whatever the strength of the criticisms of some of the arguments in favour of direct democracy, there seems little doubt that the growing interest in public participation is being fuelled, in part at least, by the development of ICTs. Whether technological advances will lead to a major extension of public participation or whether the issues surrounding participation are much more structural, cultural and motivational than technological, remains an open question.

Taking the definition of democracy as equal control over collective decisions, what might we make, in general terms, of the initiatives that have been introduced by a number of governments and public bodies, in recent years? How do they relate to ideas of democracy? Might they be seen as advancing equal control over collective decisions? In general, it can be said that in so far as the initiatives which are discussed in this book are not directly concerned with decision-making they can only be, at best, tangentially connected to the development of democracy. In as much as the mechanisms analysed are advisory or consultative, again, they have little direct connection to the advancement of democracy. Moreover, the measures which are introduced to increase or develop public participation may be introduced for reasons that have little to do with the enhancement of democracy. For example, a public body may decide that efficiency can be increased if there is greater public participation. Those who run a public body may decide, on the other hand, that public participation may be a way of reducing opposition to, or increasing support for, its policies. Yet again, those who run a public body may decide that the cost of carrying out the public body's tasks may be reduced if public participation is increased. There are a number of other reasons why those who run public bodies may decide that greater public participation is desirable, which have nothing to do with democracy.

Even where an initiative in public participation is introduced with the aim of increasing democracy, as defined above, problems may well arise, in practice. If democracy is about achieving equal control, of the relevant population, over collective decisions, what does that mean? Who comprises the relevant population? If one is looking at health care, for example, is the relevant population simply existing patients or does it include potential patients and those of us who fund the health care system in some way? If some people will be more seriously effected by a particular decision than others, who will be effected to a lesser extent, should those more seriously effected have greater control over the decision than those who are less effected? The problem of where you draw the line as to who can participate in a democracy and to what extent they should be able to participate is, in practice, a desperately difficult issue which confronts the democratic process. It is an issue which those in public bodies who genuinely want to see an enhancement of democracy, through public participation, cannot avoid. Who is the collectivity, is often far from clear.

The Structure of the Book

The chapters in this book examine a number of initiatives in public participation which have been introduced in specific countries in recent years, except for the final chapter, which contains a consideration of the approaches of different writers and institutions to public participation. Some chapters take an historical approach to the developments under scrutiny, while other writers are able to analyse specific initiatives with less historical background. An effort has been made to avoid an exclusive concentration on advanced capitalist countries, those in Western Europe, North America, Australia and New Zealand. As a result, as well as chapters on Western European countries, like the United Kingdom, Switzerland, Norway, The Netherlands, there are chapters dealing with Mexico and South Africa. The chapter on participation in Australia deals with the efforts of the indigenous population to gain control over the areas where they live. Each of chapters 2–9 concentrates on specific initiatives or initiatives covering a particular geographical area.

In Chapter 2, Ciaran O'Faircheallaigh analyses how the Aborigine people in a particular part of Brisbane, Australia, Cape York, have tried to use environmental impact assessment procedures to gain greater control over the territory where they are based. O'Faircheallaigh shows how the conventional environmental impact assessment procedures have been radically reformed by the Aborigine people. Taking an historical approach to the position of indigenous people in Australia, and focusing on their treatment under successive governments, O'Faircheallaigh explains how Aborigines have had to fight for participation in the control of their land. The chapter assess the progress that has been made and outlines the problems which the strategy adopted by the aborigines faces.

Cornie Groenewald and Antoinette Smith analyse the experiences of an initiative to increase citizen participation in local government affairs in the West Coast Development Region of South Africa. The initiative is placed within the context of the development of non-racial rule in South Africa and developments since the end of apartheid. The chapter reports empirical research conducted by the authors into the workings of one aspect of the participation process. While the authors show that some progress has been made in increasing citizen participation, they also conclude that progress has been limited and draw attention to some of the reasons for the lack of progress.

The chapter by Arturo Flores, which follows, presents an analysis of efforts by the led local council in a municipality in Mexico City, Tlalpan, to increase citizen participation, through the implementation of provisions of the Citizen Participation Law. Flores shows the problems that the state faced in trying to introduce a system of community participation in public affairs. The prevailing system of 'community involvement', which was dominated by strong individuals often with little respect for democratic procedures, has proved very resilient. The new participation procedures have, in many ways, continued the clientelism, which remains an important part of politics in Mexico.

In Chapter 5, Georgina Blakeley analyses developments in Barcelona, in the areas of decentralization and citizen participation, since the ending of the Francoist dictatorship. Blakeley outlines the different periods of reform and considers the extent to which the changes have increased citizen control. While accepting that progress has been made, Blakeley argues that the results of the developments have been ambiguous. The dangers of participation being limited to an agenda controlled by the local state and the related danger of citizens being excluded form major decisions, are raised in Blakeley's analysis. Blakeley considers what citizens loose by participating on the state's terms and raises questions about the limitations of the forms of participation that have been developed in Barcelona and the consequences for citizen involvement.

Daniel Kübler and Sonja Wälti, in Chapter 6, consider the increasingly important issue of the changing position of metropolitan politics and governance. Arguing that metropolitan areas are no longer confined to the core of cities or towns, they contend that this has important implications for the way in which social and public policy is developed in the metropolis and for the decentralization of local government. Looking at the situation in Switzerland, they show how the issue of drug taking has forced local governments covering cities and those covering surrounding areas to work together, along with other 'stakeholders' in the development of policy. Kübler and Wälti analyse the tensions that have arisen and raise important questions about the best ways to extend democracy in an era of metropolitan governance.

In chapter 7, John Diamond focuses on the moves towards the decentralization of services and activities in certain left-Labour local councils in Britain in the 1980s. Diamond argues that the commitments to extending democracy and increasing public participation were overcome by a 'managerialist agenda' which gained supremacy. For Diamond 'managerialism' has become very strong in British local government. Currently 'top-down' approaches are strongly embedded. Diamond argues that the stress on improved service delivery, makes it difficult for local groups to question the structures within which services are delivered. Despite the talk of 'citizen involvement', Diamond contends that initiatives are led by council officers and professionals who, thus, define the local agenda. Diamond considers a model of decentralization which might offer an alternative to the current situation.

Erik-Hans Klijn and Joop Koppenjan, in chapter 8, evaluate a number of developments in the Netherlands and especially in Amsterdam. The heart of their paper looks at the re-development of the Bijlmermeer in Amsterdam. Klijn and Koppenjan detail the different stages of the re-development and evaluate the use of a process of interactive decision making. The Blijlmermeer experience shows that, for interactive decision making to work, elected politicians need to move from being the ex post selectors of policy from different options, to becoming the initiators and facilitators of public debate with citizens, out of which policy options will emerge. As well as considering the Biljmermeer re-development, Kiljn and Koopenjan also evaluate five projects which attempted to implement a scheme of interactive decision making developed by the Institute for the Public and Politics in Amsterdam. The results of the projects, in terms of the success of the interactive scheme, were mixed.

The chapter written by Aarsæther, Nyseth and Røiseland reports the findings of research into the development of neighbourhood councils in Norway, below the municipal level. The authors analyse the development of two types of neighbourhood council in Norway, what they tern 'the top-down' and 'the bottom-up'.'Top-down' councils are initiated by the municipal authority, while 'bottom-up' councils are initiated by communities themselves. The research shows important differences between the types of councils, in terms of their composition, their concerns, their funding and how actors perceive their purposes. The reported research raises important questions about the nature of public participation and feeds into the debate about the respective merits of state promoted initiatives and community inspired initiatives.

Finally, in chapter 10, McLaverty, rounds off the book, with an analysis of a number of different approaches to public participation. The positions of a number of writers on the subject, both positive and negative, are compared and contrasted. McLaverty concludes that approaches to public participation necessarily reflect writers' conceptions of human capabilities and possibilities. They also reflect the type of society which writers regard as desirable and possible.

References

Beetham, D. (1999) 'Defining and Justifying Democracy', in D. Beetham *Democracy and Human Rights*, Polity Press, Cambridge, pp. 1–29.

Budge, I. (1996) *The New Challenge of Direct Democracy*, Polity Press, Cambridge.

Burnheim, J. (1985) *Is Democracy Possible?*, Polity Press, Cambridge.

Cerny, P. (1997) 'R.A.W. Rhodes, "The New Governance: Governing Without Government"', *Political Studies*, vol. 45, no. 1, pp. 1–2.

Habermas, J. (1988) *Legitimation Crisis*, MIT Press Cambridge, MA.

Held, D. (1996) *Models of Democracy*, second edition, Polity Press, Cambridge.

Kooiman, J. (1993) *Modern Governance: New Government-Society Interactions*, Sage, London.

Macpherson, C.B. (1977) *The Life and Times of Liberal Democracy*, Oxford University Press, Oxford.

Maier, C.S. (ed) (1987), *Changing Boundaries of the Political*, MIT Press, Cambridge MA.

Mann, M. (1995) 'As the twentieth century ages', *New Left Review*, 214, pp. 104–124.

Marsh, D. and Rhodes, R. (1992) *Policy Networks in British Government*, Clarendon Press, Oxford.

Marsh, D. and Smith, M. (2000) 'Understanding Policy Networks: Towards a Dialectical Approach', *Policy Studies*, vol. 48, pp. 4–21.

Miliband, R. (1973) *The State in Capitalist Society*, Quartet Books, London.

O'Connor, J. (1973) *The Fiscal Crisis of the State*, St. Martin's Press, New York.

Offe, C. (1984) *Contradictions of the Welfare State*, MIT Press, Cambridge, MA.

Pierre, J. (ed) (2000) *Debating Governance: Authority, Steering and Democracy*, Oxford University Press, Oxford.

Pierre, J. and Peter, B.G. (2000) *Governance, Politics and the State*, Macmillan, Basingstoke.

Rhodes, R.A.W. (1997) *Understanding Governance*, Open University Press, Buckingham.

Saward, M. (1998) *The Terms of Democracy*, Polity Press, Cambridge.

Stewart, J. (1999) *The Nature of British Local Government*, Macmillan, Basingstoke.

Wolff, J.P. (1970) *In Defence of Anarchism*, Harper and Row, New York.

Chapter 2

Overcoming Severe Obstacles to Public Participation: Indigenous People and Impact Assessment Procedures in Australia

Ciaran O'Faircheallaigh

Introduction

This paper addresses attempts to achieve participation in governance by Australia's indigenous people, a group which has, for much of the last 200 years, been deliberately and systematically excluded from involvement in political and administrative decision-making by the Australian state. This context of exclusion is critical in understanding the particular problems and issues which arise in relation to indigenous participation in governance, and it is a context which is fundamentally different from that which shapes the possibilities for participation faced by most groups in developed countries. Substantial attention is devoted in the early sections of the paper to exploring the reasons for indigenous exclusion and the mechanisms used to give effect to it.

The particular aspect of governance which provides a focus for the paper involves public appraisal of large-scale development projects and in particular the statutory social impact assessments (SIAs) utilized as part of appraisal processes. This area is of great significance to indigenous people because major development projects have the potential to dramatically affect indigenous communities located nearby and because the participation of those communities is critical if public policy decisions are to be properly informed and if effective mitigative strategies are to be identified and pursued. Despite the importance of public appraisal processes to indigenous people, their general exclusion from participation in government has, until very recently, been reflected in this area also.

Later sections of the paper outline the way in which some indigenous groups in Australia have sought to enhance the extent and impact of their involvement in project appraisal processes in the face of continuing and serious barriers to their effective participation. These barriers include the difficulty of achieving active participation from communities which for many decades have been marginalized from decision-making process and subject to highly paternalistic administrative regimes. The paper draws on the experience of Aboriginal communities on Cape York Peninsula in far north Queensland to outline the strategies which indigenous leaders and organizations have used in seeking to overcome obstacles to participation. These strategies are based on the development of community-controlled impact assessment procedures which interface with mainstream statutory processes but allow communities a high degree of indigenous autonomy in conducting impact assessments.

The Historical Context: Dispossession and Marginalization

It is impossible to understand the contemporary context for indigenous participation in governance without having a general sense of the history of relations between Australia's indigenous and non-indigenous populations over the two centuries or so since European settlement of Australia commenced. It is of course also difficult to provide an understanding of this history in a few pages, and it is critical to stress the enormous diversity of the indigenous experience arising from the uneven nature and timing of European settlement and the variety of responses adopted by different indigenous groups (Lucashenko, 1996). Nevertheless there is also a great deal of commonality in the indigenous experience, and what follows seeks to identify critical components of that experience.

Five points are particularly important to note. First, the vast majority of Australia's indigenous population were dispossessed from their tribal lands. Dispossession took place at different times, at varying speeds and with varying degrees of violence depending on, for instance, the nature of the resources sought by the colonisers and the suitability of the land for European agriculture (Goodall, 1996, Reynolds, 1987). However with the exception of the desert regions of central Australia and the monsoonal regions of the coastal north, indigenous dispossession was almost total and was inevitably accompanied by major population decline due to shootings, introduced diseases and destruction of social structures (Beckett, 1988a). By the 1960s virtually no land remained in the possession of indigenous people in the states which contain the bulk of Australia's population (Victoria and New South Wales), in Tasmania, or in the more fertile southern regions of Queensland, South Australia and Western Australia (Goodall, 1996).

The dispossession of Australia's indigenous people continues to this day. In 1992 Australia's High Court overturned the doctrine of terra nullius (which assumed that Australia was an 'empty land' in 1788 when it was claimed for the English Crown by Captain Cook), and recognized that indigenous Australian's possessed rights in land prior to colonization, referred to as 'native title'. The Court also stated that native title survives where it has not been validly extinguished by the Crown and where indigenous people have maintained a continuous association with their traditional lands. However since 1992 federal and state governments have legislated to extinguish much of the native title which remained. For instance in September 1998 the Queensland government legislated to extinguish native title on one category of leasehold land which covered about 13 per cent of the state's land area.

The second point to note is that indigenous Australians were denied basic human rights, including political rights, and that this made it impossible for them to participate in governance even at the most basic level (Pettman, 1992). The denial of human rights reflected the generally held view that indigenous people were sub-human and so neither deserved, nor were capable of exercising in a rational manner, the rights enjoyed by other Australians. In the words of a contributor to one of the first debates in Australia's Commonwealth Parliament, established on federation in 1901, indigenous people were 'less than human'.

Such attitudes were used to justify exclusion of indigenous people from the franchise, severe constraints on their personal movement, and bans on any form of organized political activity. Denial of economic rights also inevitably had political consequences, particularly during a period in history when property ownership was frequently a precondition for the effective exercise of political rights (Beckett, 1988a). As well as being deprived of their ancestral lands, indigenous people were paid much less than whites for equivalent work or forced to work without pay, and when they did earn wages their money was taken from them and controlled by police and missionaries (Beckett, 1988b; Larbalestier, 1988).

Third, indigenous people suffered from deep-seated racism in relation to every aspect of their lives. At a group level, they suffered the ignominy of being constantly told that they were less than human, 'backward', capable of doing nothing of value without the assistance of missions or government, and belonging to a worthless culture which would inevitably disappear under the influence of the superior white race (Beckett, 1988a; McConnochie, *et al.*, 1988). At an individual level, racism was experienced in myriad forms, for instance through the segregation imposed on indigenous people when they shopped, went to church or to social or sporting events; through the denial of access to employment opportunities or to rental accommodation; and through the countless jibes and insults dealt out in school yards, bars and work places (Pettman, 1992). As with dispossession, such experiences by no means belong to the past, and indeed there has been an upsurge of racism associated with the rise of Pauline Hanson's One Nation Party and the backlash which has followed the (very limited) recognition of native title rights.

A fourth part of the historical context, and one of particular significance in relation to the issue of public participation, is the fact that many indigenous people were born into settings which were highly institutionalized, leaving them very little room for the exercise of any individual freedoms, let alone of political expression. Dispossession was accompanied by the creation of reserves, government or mission, on which the remnants of indigenous populations were located. In some cases the motive of government authorities was simply to keep indigenous people out of view and out of the way of farmers and industrialists (Larbalestier, 1988, Morris, 1991). In others it was to try and provide them with the basic training which would allow them to be absorbed into the ranks of the industrial work force. For missions the motive was often to 'save souls' and in some cases (especially in the remote centre and north) to protect remnant indigenous populations from destruction and exploitation by ruthless miners and pastoralists (Beckett, 1988a).

However while the motives of those running institutions varied the forms of organization and the methods of control they embodied were very similar. They were all premised on the assumption that indigenous people were incapable of looking after themselves and that the whites who operated institutions had a superior understanding of indigenous needs. Thus institutions were run with iron discipline and without any consultation with their indigenous inhabitants. Any refusal to accept the discipline imposed by whites or any questioning of the dominant regime met with instant and usually severe punishment. The reserve system was backed up by legislation which made indigenous people wards of the state and so effectively allowed government officers to control almost every aspect of their lives (Beckett, 1988a; Morris, 1991).

The ultimate manifestation of the state's total control over its indigenous subjects, of the racist underpinnings of state policy and of dominant social attitudes was the practice of permanently removing children from their Aboriginal families and either placing them in institutions or, in more recent times, having them adopted by white people. Children were removed forcibly and from a very early age. In contemporary Australia attention focuses on what is referred to as the 'stolen generations', those individuals who are still alive today and who were removed in the period between the 1930s and the end of the 1960s, when the practice ceased (Edwards and Read, 1989, Read, 1984). However, removal of children, and particularly of lighter-skinned children of mixed descent, was a part of state policy from the earliest period of settlement and was intended to hasten the destruction of indigenous society by removing young people from its influence (HREOC, 1997). It was a policy which failed (see next point), but the extent of human misery which the policy created over a period of some 150 years beggars the imagination.

The fifth critical point to make is that the sustained attempts by the dominant society to destroy indigenous culture and social forms failed. Even in those parts of Australia where settlement occurred first, and where the impact of dispossession and hostile government policies have been felt most strongly and for the longest period of time, indigenous people have maintained vibrant and distinctive social forms and cultural practices which mark them off from the non-indigenous population. In seeking to define what is distinctive about indigenous society it is again important to stress the enormous diversity which characterises indigenous Australia (Attwood, 1989, Pettman, 1992). For example in some areas indigenous languages and cultural practices are still dominant, and while the Australian legal system is in force traditional 'Aboriginal law' plays a central role in determining individual behaviour and social practice. In major urban centres English is the language of indigenous discourse and a casual observer might perceive little on the surface to indicate the survival of distinctly indigenous social or political forms. However despite this diversity two distinctive and inter-related elements remain central to virtually all indigenous groups. The first is the importance of links to their ancestral lands in defining identity, culture, law and spirituality, links which maintain their force regardless of whether indigenous ownership is recognized under Australia's legal system. The second element is the primacy of kinship in defining social and political identity and in the formation and pursuit of political interests (Beckett, 1988b).

While their culture and social identity has not been destroyed, indigenous Australians have suffered greatly from the historical circumstances and state policies outlined above. They have much higher infant mortality rates and much lower life expectancies that non-indigenous Australians and their health status is poor (Pettman, 1992). Their average income is much lower than the Australian average reflecting their poor access to the labour market and, ultimately, their exclusion from many educational opportunities (Daly, 1993, 1995). They are much more likely to be arrested, and much more likely to end up in prison, than other Australians, and are also more likely to commit suicide (Royal Commission into Aboriginal Deaths in Custody, 1989, 1990, 1991). In general their access to public services is poor, especially in the small rural towns and remote regions in which some two thirds of Australia's indigenous people live.

Barriers to Participation

The factors discussed in the previous section create formidable barriers to indigenous participation in governance at all levels of the Australian political system. Some of the major ones are:

Indigenous Australians attach little or no legitimacy to the state, which provides the primary forums in which, and the mechanisms through which, participation in governance can occur. The Australian state has either itself taken, or allowed settlers, missionaries and corporations to take, actions which have stripped Aboriginal people of their land, treated them as sub-human, denied them basic rights, left them in parlous economic and social circumstances, and stolen their children. Obviously a group of people who have been treated so badly by the institutions of the state can hardly be expected to be enthusiastic about seeking to participate in those same institutions.

Racism continues to permeate many aspects of Australian life. If indigenous people do seek to participate they are often met with suspicion or hostility by other participants in the political process.

The Australian state has been built on the dispossession of indigenous Australians. It is to be expected that state actors and state institutions would display a profound ambiguity about the prospect of participation in governance by precisely those people whose dispossession is fundamental to the existence of the state.

At a general level, their disadvantaged social and economic status and their lack of numerical strength (about two per cent of the Australian population) means that indigenous people find it difficult to win the support of key political actors. In more specific terms, indigenous people often lack the resources to participate effectively in political processes which occur in distant state capitals or in Canberra and often require participants to have access to substantial legal and other technical expertise.

Their formal exclusion from political processes over a period of 200 years means that indigenous people have limited experience in developing explicit, agreed policy positions or in identifying strategies and establishing political structures designed to pursue these policy positions. Yet effective participation requires the group concerned to have a clear understanding of its goals and of the appropriate means of achieving these.

There are very real differences in cultural, social and spiritual understandings between indigenous and non-indigenous people and in some cases they do not even share a common language. Thus indigenous people find themselves trying to participate in processes based on assumptions, values and perspectives which are quite different to the ones which they hold. This situation represents a barrier which would be very significant even if non-indigenous people and institutions were more favourably disposed towards indigenous participation.

These barriers are formidable and very real. However, to gain a full appreciation of the wider political context within which indigenous people operate two additional general points must be made.

First, indigenous Australia has never accepted its exclusion from mainstream political processes and there have been, at least since the 1930s, continuous attempts to win a right to participate in these processes and to shape the policy outcomes which affect indigenous people. These attempts involve both the creation of indigenous political organizations, mobilization of indigenous voters during elections, and many forms of direct action including protests, strikes, sit ins and re-occupation of traditional lands, though not, to date, political violence (Attwood, 1989, Evans *et al.*, 1988, Reynolds, 1987).

Second, the nature of mainstream responses to indigenous demands have not stood still. Since the mid 1960s there have been a series of constitutional changes, judicial decisions, policy and budgetary initiatives and institutional changes which have enhanced the economic, political and social status of Australia's indigenous people. It is impossible to review these here but they include the 1967 constitutional referendum which empowered the federal government, for the first time, to make laws on behalf of indigenous Australians; the initiatives of the Whitlam federal government (1972–1975) in greatly expanding expenditure on programs designed to benefit indigenous people; the High Court decisions in relation to the Mabo (1992) and Wik (1996) native title claims which embedded the concept of native title in Australia's common law; and the creation in 1989–1990 of the Aboriginal and Torres Strait Islander Commission (ATSIC), an unusual 'hybrid' organization which has an elected national Board and regional councils representing indigenous people throughout Australia and an administrative arm which manages the provision of some key federal services to indigenous communities.

Each of these initiatives has been followed by considerable backsliding by subsequent governments and in the case of the High Court's Wik decision by a substantial winding back of indigenous rights by state and federal legislatures. It is also the case that all of the initiatives just mentioned arose from federal jurisdictions and institutions, and that state governments have been much less concerned to counter indigenous disadvantage and exclusion. Nevertheless progress has been made and of course the indigenous refusal to be excluded from participation has been critical in ensuring that this is the case.

Major Project Developments and Impact Assessment Procedures

The remainder of the paper focuses on a particular area of governance from which indigenous Australians have until recently been excluded but which has increasingly become a focus for their demands for participation.

This involves conduct of impact assessment procedures undertaken by governments as part of project appraisal processes. During recent decades most Western countries have introduced processes designed to allow the systematic appraisal of development activities such as large-scale resource exploitation and construction of major infrastructure items like dams, power transmission lines and highways. Australia is no exception with national legislation being introduced in 1974 and a range of state government legislation being enacted in the 1970s and 1980s.

The introduction of legislation requiring impact assessment of large-scale development activities recognizes the fact that these activities can have huge impacts, negative and positive, on the social, economic, cultural and environmental circumstances of affected populations, and especially on the living conditions of those people living adjacent to the projects concerned. Equally important is the realization that it is both possible and desirable to mitigate negative effects and enhance positive ones, given an understanding of a project's likely effects and of the characteristics of the affected population and given appropriate policy responses.

It has also been widely recognized that to be effective social impact assessment must be based on the active participation of affected populations. Without such participation, it is extremely difficult to accurately identify likely impacts, to achieve a full understanding of the needs and aspirations of local populations or to develop policies and strategies which are likely to be effective in reducing negative effects and increasing beneficial outcomes. Increasingly, effective social impact assessment has been equated with participative social impact assessment (Blishen *et al.*, 1979; Coombs *et al.*, 1989, Finsterbusch, 1985, Gagnon *et al.*, 1993).

A capacity to participate effectively in impact assessment procedures is of particular significance to indigenous people for two major reasons. First, indigenous communities can experience negative impacts from major development projects which are unusually severe and indeed in some cases are completely destructive of indigenous society and culture. Restrictions of space prevent a detailed discussion of this point. It is sufficient to note that in recent decades major development activities have resulted in the destruction of tribal hunting lands; large-scale environmental damage; relocation of whole communities; destruction of spiritually-important sites or landscapes; a decline in social cohesion, social control and community autonomy; and a range of cultural, social and economic problems associated with in-migration of non-indigenous people seeking employment opportunities (for a detailed discussion see O'Faircheallaigh, 1991).

The second reason arises from the fact that large-scale development activities also create economic opportunities for indigenous people whose cash incomes tend to be low in comparison to those of the non-indigenous population. However these potential benefits do not normally flow automatically. There is a need to establish relevant policies and implementation frameworks in relation to areas such as employment and training of local workers, local business development and infrastucture development. Indigenous participation in social impact assessment is critical if relevant economic opportunities are to be identified and policies implemented which will ensure that those opportunities are made available to indigenous people.

Thus effective indigenous participation in social impact assessment procedures is essential. However indigenous people face formidable barriers in achieving effective participation. To some extent this reflects, in the Australian context, the general factors outlined above. There are also some specific barriers which arise in the area of social impact assessment or, perhaps more correctly, the general barriers to participation outlined earlier arise in specific forms in this case.

To appreciate this fact, it is important to have a general understanding of the way in which statutory social impact assessments tend to be organized. Usually they are initiated by developers and controlled by state agencies which have an interest in promoting ‘development’. (There are of course exceptions to the rule, which receive a great deal of attention in the literature precisely because they are exceptions. A case in point is Berger, 1988). Typically, the project proponent will initiate an SIA procedure (or more usually an environmental impact assessment procedure which has a social component) by requesting state authorization to proceed with a project. The proponent and the relevant state agency will then negotiate terms of reference for the impact assessment, with other government agencies and interested third parties usually having some right to comment on (though not to amend) draft terms of reference. The proponent retains consultants who undertake impact assessment studies designed to address the terms of reference and who report at least initially to the proponent. Public hearings and other forms of consultations typically occur either as part of the social impact assessment or as part of the government's response to draft social impact assessment reports. The proponent revises draft reports in light of comments from government agencies and the wider public. Relevant state authorities then decide whether to approve project development on the basis of the final impact assessment and also, of course, on the basis of a range of wider political and economic considerations.

In some situations indigenous people have simply been excluded from statutory impact assessment procedures. Chase has shown how developers, state government officials and consultants denied the right of Aboriginal people to participate in impact studies of a proposed silica sand mine at

Shelburne Bay in Queensland, despite their traditional associations with the area involved (Chase, 1990, pp. 16–17). Other, similar situations are discussed by Justus and Simonetta (1982), Michalenko and Suffling (1982), and Ross (1989).

In other cases, indigenous people have been admitted at a formal level, but have been unable to participate effectively in SIA and so have been powerless to influence its outcomes. This may be because the time allowed for SIA and for project approval more generally is excessively short, particularly given that indigenous decision-making processes may be protracted. Indigenous groups often lack the financial resources and the access to 'technical' information and expertise required to ensure effective participation. The use of culturally alien forms of inquiry (such as highly formalized and legalistic public hearings) can also create problems.

More fundamentally, SIA and project approval procedures may fail to acknowledge the values and perspectives of indigenous people where these conflict with the ethos of the dominant society. Edelstein and Kleese (1995), for example, show how native Hawaiian perspectives regarding the spiritual and religious significance of volcanoes and the land surrounding them were rejected in the assessment of proposals for harnessing geothermal energy. The result was that native peoples affected by these proposals were marginalized from the project approval process. Edelstein and Kleese argue that the stress on supposedly 'rational' and 'scientific' approaches to impact assessment which usually characterize project approval processes are in fact far from value neutral, because they promote developmental agendas and deny the validity of perspectives and evidence put forward by indigenous peoples (Edelstein and Kleese, 1995, pp. 20–22; see also Craig, 1989, pp. 2, 5–6, Howell, 1983, pp. 346–47).

In the face of such formidable barriers, how is it possible to achieve effective indigenous participation in impact assessment procedures? The remainder of the paper sets out the approach adopted in the Cape York region of north Queensland.

Cape York Peninsula: The Region and its People

Cape York Peninsula occupies the most northern part of the state of Queensland. During recent decades the indigenous population, decimated after European settlement by disease, dispossession and the violent attacks of settlers, has grown rapidly, and today indigenous people account for just over half of the total population of 25,000. This population is tiny in comparison to Cape York's land area.

Despite the impact of settlers, governments and missionaries, Aboriginal people retain important aspects of their traditional culture, spirituality and social structures. Census data indicate that two out of every three Aboriginal residents speaks at least one Aboriginal language; hunting and fishing is still an important source of food for many people; associations with particular areas of land are critical in defining identity and in creating a framework for social relations; and family or clan-based systems of kinship and reciprocity still constitute the core of social structures and the basis for much of economic and political life.

In the past, the mineral resources of Cape York have been developed with scant regard for the interests of its indigenous inhabitants. For example, reserves covering huge areas of land allocated for the use of Aboriginal people were revoked in the 1950s to make way for exploration and mining. As late as the mid 1970s, exploration and mining leases were being granted over Aboriginal reserve land against the express wishes of traditional landowners.

During the 1990s Aboriginal communities have been determined to ensure that they have a much greater degree of control over, and achieve substantial benefits from, resource development on their tribal lands. In pursuing these goals they have been assisted by a regional organization, the Cape York Land Council (CYLC), which is governed by a council comprising a male and female representative from each Aboriginal community on Cape York and two people representing traditional landowners who do not reside in the region. The CYLC was initially established in 1989 as a result of grass roots opposition to proposals to develop a space base on Cape York Peninsula without reference to the concerns and aspirations of Aboriginal people. It now plays a variety of roles in assisting its constituents to achieve recognition of their rights in their tribal lands and an effective say in the development and management of those lands.

Achieving Indigenous Participation: The Cape York Model

Fundamental to the approach adopted by the Cape York communities is a realization that the barriers to involvement in mainstream project appraisal processes are so formidable that it is pointless to pursue conventional approaches to participation. This realization has increasingly led communities to refuse to become involved in conventional social impact assessment processes and to negotiate with government and proponents to 'internalise' those processes to the communities themselves. Rather than seeking to influence the outcomes of appraisal processes dominated by proponents and government agencies and operating on the basis of assumptions rooted in non-indigenous world views, communities have sought to themselves take control of large components of the project appraisal process and in particular of social impact assessments.

The mechanisms used to pursue indigenous control have varied from case to case. Some communities hold their traditional lands as Aboriginal reserves and under state legislation introduced in 1989 developers wishing to obtain mining leases must seek the consent of the trustees for the reserve (usually the elected community council) before state authorities will consider granting leases. In these cases the trustees have refused to take part in any discussions about providing their consent until community-controlled social impact assessments of the proposed developments have occurred. Even where companies already hold mining leases granted prior to 1989, they usually require additional leases from community councils to undertake ancillary activities such as construction of transport corridors and this provides the community with a degree of leverage. For example in 1996 Alcan, the Canadian aluminium company, wished to develop a bauxite mining lease granted in 1965. The company needed a lease on the Napranum community's reserve to construct a haul road from the mine to a port, and the Napranum community council, with the support of the CYLC, refused to consider granting the lease until Alcan and the state government agreed to support a community-based social impact assessment not only of the road and port but also of the proposed mine.

In other cases resource development companies, seeking to implement corporate policies which require them to establish positive relationships with indigenous people whose tribal lands they mine, have been prevailed upon to support impact assessments of existing mining operations as a prerequisite for discussions on development of co-operative arrangements.

To understand the significance of community control for indigenous participation it is necessary to explain in some detail how community-based social impact assessment works and how it differs from conventional SIA.

The first step involves the creation of management structures which will provide overall direction to the SIA. Discussions are held between the CYLC and leaders of community organizations and with individuals who are identified by the CYLC, on the basis of its existing knowledge, as senior traditional owners of the lands affected by the project concerned. A Steering Committee or similar structure is created with representation from the key organizations and traditional owner groups. For instance one Steering Committee comprised five senior owners of the land area involved; the chairpersons of the community council and the outstation support organization; and representatives of a range of specific community organizations, including the elders' group, the cultural resource management group, and the educators' group (the latter included in an attempt to ensure that the interests of younger people received specific consideration).

The composition of the Steering Committee reflected an acceptance that, while traditional owners of land subject to mining are most directly affected by a project and so have a right to substantial representation, major projects affect all the members of a community located nearby and so it is appropriate to have a broadly-based representation. It also reflects a melding of conventional European concepts of 'stakeholder' representation and the influence of Aboriginal custom and contemporary political reality. For instance, in the example just cited, the Steering Committee included three people whose formal designation was as representatives of broad groups within the community. However while they certainly fulfilled this role, they came from tribal groups whose traditional country was far from the impact area but which have been, since well before the arrival of Europeans in Australia, close allies of the group whose land would be directly affected by mining. Their presence on the Steering Committee re-affirmed that alliance and ensured that it could be brought to bear in a contemporary context.

The Steering Committees, advised by the CYLC's professional staff, plays a critical role in controlling the overall direction of the SIA, in ensuring indigenous participation, in part by conferring political legitimacy on the process, and in guiding and facilitating the work of researchers and consultants retained to assist with the SIA (see below).

The second step is to conduct anthropological work to identify the full range of indigenous interests affected by a project and the indigenous people who can 'speak for country' in Aboriginal law and custom. This is essential to ensure that all of the interests affected are adequately represented in the Steering Committee and, if necessary, membership of the Steering Committee is expanded once the anthropological work is completed. Just as importantly, it identifies for the consultants who will conduct community consultations the estate groups affected by the project, the membership of these groups and the identity of key individuals within them. This information is critical in allowing the consultants to identify the population which should, ideally, be consulted; to identify key individuals who must be consulted; and to develop consultation strategies which can be effective while also recognizing constraints of time and money (see below).

The third step is the conduct of the community consultations which are designed to establish the impacts associated with, or likely to be associated with, a project and to express the aspirations and concerns of the Aboriginal community in relation to that project. The process involved is set out in detail elsewhere and only a brief summary is provided here (Holden and O'Faircheallaigh, 1995, Howitt, 1996, O'Faircheallaigh, 1999).

The consultants who will carry out the community consultations are appointed by the Steering Committee with the assistance of the CYLC. To date the consultants have been non-indigenous people with expertise in social impact assessment, although usually a number of community members will be selected to work with the consultants both to facilitate their work and to allow the transfer of skills into the community. In some cases the Steering Committee will appoint people who have worked in the community before and have demonstrated their capacity to operate effectively and in a culturally-appropriate manner appropriately. In others a formal selection process will occur, and the outcomes are frequently not those one would expect from a conventional European selection process. For instance in one recent case a Steering Committee selected a less experienced applicant with a short curriculum vitae to join a consultancy team, because it believed that this person was less likely to dominate meetings, and more likely to allow community members to articulate their points of view, than a more experienced but more personally assertive candidate.

The Steering Committee maintains management control over the consultants throughout the SIA process, both in relation to the overall direction of the work and, if it feels necessary, in relation to the conduct of research in the community. As an example of the latter, on one occasion a Steering Committee was unhappy at the way in which certain sensitive issues were being addressed by one consultant, and it required that a different approach be adopted. (For a general discussion of the issue of indigenous control over social impact assessment processes, see Ross 1990; O'Faircheallaigh 1999.)

Draft terms of reference are drawn up on the basis of the consultants' prior experience. They are discussed with the CYLC and the Steering Committee (and possibly also with the proponent and with relevant state agencies), amended as required and then approved in final form by the Steering Committee.

Desk-based research and fieldwork are undertaken to develop a profile of the community, and in particular to identify categories of people who may be affected differently by the project. Government and company documents are used to establish basic information in relation to the proponent, the project and its existing (or potential) impact. This work can be critical not only in providing information to community members, but also in placing the CYLC in a position to offer advice in relation to alternative negotiating positions and strategies.

Community consultations then begin, using a variety of approaches and methodologies which are appropriate to the specific context. The sorts of approaches utilized in conventional SIA (formal hearings, large public meetings, opinion surveys) are rarely employed because they are not culturally appropriate and so are unlikely to elicit indigenous participation. Much more emphasis is placed on small group meetings which often occur on people's traditional country, and especially on areas which will be the subject of project impacts, rather than in offices or halls. Typically, meetings will be held with clan groups associated with particular areas of land but also, for example, with Aboriginal mine workers, partners of mine workers, young people, and community rangers whose responsibilities in relation to cultural heritage and environmental management give them a specific interest in certain development impacts. In many cases individual discussions are held with key people within clan groups. The guiding principle in organizing consultations is to ensure that their nature and timing reflect indigenous preferences as closely as possible, given the available resources. As discussed below, limited availability of resources does currently represent a real constraint on the extent to which preferred consultation models can be applied in practice.

The consultation meetings and discussions are used to document the actual or likely effects of project operations, as experienced or anticipated by community members. Frequently people's experiences are being documented for the first time because they have previously not been involved in project appraisal processes, and the information they provide is often profound in terms of the insights it offers into the effects of development projects and activities. The consultations are also used to identify people's concerns and aspirations and to establish their priorities in relation to the project concerned, and to provide them with the information gained from desk-based research and initial field work. Provision of information by the consultants often elicits requests for further information from community members, and triggers provision of additional information by them to the consultants. Thus the consultations tend to involve an iterative process, rather than a 'one off' presentation of information and documentation of views and opinions.

Additional desk-based research may be undertaken in response to specific requests for information or to issues raised by community members and not included in the original terms of reference. Initial proposals are developed aimed at maximizing benefits and minimizing costs associated with the project. These are discussed with groups and individuals in the community, and in some cases alternative approaches are devised which appear more likely to satisfy the (at times conflicting) aspirations of various groups. Identification of such alternatives may create further demands for information required to establish their feasibility.

A draft SIA report is prepared, workshopped in the Steering Committee and discussed in community meetings to ensure that it accurately and fully reflects community perspectives. A final impact assessment report is then provided to the CYLC and the Steering Committee. This includes a community profile, factual information about the company and the project, an extensive and detailed discussion of impacts to date and of people's concerns and aspirations, a series of recommendations which offer concrete strategies for dealing with concerns and pursuing aspirations and a summary of advice to the negotiating team. The report will usually also suggest a monitoring program for ongoing measurement and review of social and economic impacts (see for example Holden and O'Faircheallaigh, 1995, Howitt, 1996, O'Faircheallaigh, 1996).

The final SIA report is then provided to the proponent and to relevant government decision-makers. It is thus 'inserted' into the conventional project appraisal process, providing critical information which would otherwise be entirely absent or replacing information which would have been collected by non-indigenous agencies using conventional, Euro-centric assumptions, approaches and methodologies.

Community-Controlled SIA: An Evaluation

The advantages of community-controlled over conventional social impact assessment are numerous. They are also to some extent self-evident in the light of the earlier discussion regarding the barriers to indigenous participation in governance in general and in SIA procedures in particular. They can be summarised briefly as follows.

Community-controlled SIA overcomes the marginalization of indigenous people from the impact assessment processes because it makes indigenous people and their interests central to those processes. Critical in this regard are the following factors:

a) SIA is conducted within management structures created by and consisting of indigenous people.
b) The terms of reference which specify the scope and focus of impact assessment studies are set by indigenous people.
c) The consultants who conduct these studies are selected by and report to indigenous people.
d) Impact assessment reports are shaped by and subject to the approval of indigenous people.

Following on from these points, there is considerable opportunity for indigenous values to find expression in the SIA process as a whole. Community-controlled SIA helps greatly to facilitate indigenous participation because it:

a) Removes SIA processes from the direct control of the state, legitimizing them and reducing the hostility and cynicism which indigenous people typically feel towards state-sponsored processes or structures.
b) Greatly reduces the danger that racism and the ambiguous attitude of state actors towards indigenous involvement in governance will act as barriers to indigenous participation.
c) Ensures that the approaches and methodologies employed in SIA are culturally appropriate and driven by the need to maximize indigenous participation.
d) Create important opportunities for indigenous people to gain experience in developing explicit, agreed policy positions and in identifying strategies designed to pursue these policy positions. This experience has ramifications well beyond the specific area of social impact assessment.

The end result is that the information fed into government decision-making processes is much more likely to reflect indigenous realities and indigenous interests. This does not of course ensure that the outcomes which emerge from government decision-making processes will favour indigenous people, a point we return to below. However outcomes favourable to indigenous people will be extremely difficult to achieve in the absence of information which they regard as accurate and appropriate.

In addition and very importantly, if government decision-makers choose to ignore indigenous interests then communities have very well established policy positions, derived from SIA processes, to provide a basis for taking political action designed to place pressure on government. Further, participation in the social impact assessment process tends to raise the political awareness of indigenous people, increasing their willingness and capacity to engage in political processes. Thus in one recent case a community developed, as part of the SIA process, concrete and detailed strategies to pursue direct political action in the event that public officials ignored the positions they had articulated in the SIA report. It is difficult to imagine such outcomes resulting from conventional project appraisal processes.

Nevertheless some major issues and problems remain. The first relates to the willingness of governments and proponents to allow indigenous communities to control impact assessment processes. Cape York communities have enjoyed considerable success in this regard, because they have been able to exploit some legislative opportunities; because they have displayed a substantial degree of cohesion at a community and at a regional level; and because both governments and resource developers have felt increasing political pressure to be seen to involve indigenous people in appraisal of projects which affect them. It must be acknowledged that other indigenous peoples may not be in as strong a position.

The second involves the issue of resources. Community-controlled impact assessments of the type outlined above are resource intensive, as a result of the logistical costs of organizing consultations and of the need to retain SIA specialists and ensure access to relevant information. In Cape York some resources have in most cases been provided by the proponent; in only one case by the Queensland government; in a number of cases by the Aboriginal and Torres Strait Islander Commission; and in all cases by the CYLC, community councils and individual indigenous people who often have to dig deep into their limited personal resources in order to participate. Almost inevitably resources have been severely strained and this has meant that consultations have been more limited than communities would have wished. Resource constraints will remain a severe barrier to community-controlled SIA until government accepts that provision of resources to indigenous communities represents a fundamental prerequisite for their meaningful participation.

A third issue involves questions of timing. Implementation of SIA procedures which are culturally appropriate and comprehensive can be time consuming, which can create problems when developers are working to tight time frames or where statutory project appraisal processes specify brief time lines. Indigenous communities may be in a position to negotiate extensions of time frames based on their capacity to create major problems for government and developers by refusing to participate in community consultations required before statutory project approvals can be given. However where this is not possible their capacity to implement appropriate procedures is obviously constrained.

A final and critical issue involves the extent to which information produced by social impact assessments have an effect on public policy decisions. As mentioned above, while community-controlled SIA processes mean that government receives accurate information on impacts and on indigenous aspirations and concerns, it does not follow that public officials will implement policies which seek to minimize negative effects and maximize positive effects on indigenous people. In fact non-utilization of findings is a chronic problem affecting social impact assessment in general and not just SIA which involves indigenous people (Armour, 1989, 1991, Craig, 1989, p.51, Howell, 1983, p. 347).

In CapeYork indigenous communities have utilized a negotiation-based approach to try and ensure that governments and projects developers do make use of SIA findings. This approach is described in detail elsewhere (O'Faircheallaigh, 1999). In summary, indigenous communities have sought to organize SIA as one stage in negotiation processes involving proponents and government. The information derived from community-controlled SIA is used to formulate policies and strategies which then form the basis for negotiating positions adopted by communities in relation to project developments. Communities have had considerable success in prevailing on proponents to enter contractually binding agreements which seek to minimize the costs and maximize the benefits experienced by indigenous people as a result of major development activities. Their success in this regard reflects the need of project developers to reach an accommodation with indigenous people, either because of their need to receive indigenous consent to the specific actions such as the issue of leases, or their desire to avoid the adverse publicity arising from conflict with indigenous people.

Indigenous communities have had less success with government, which has been willing to endorse agreements struck between developers and indigenous communities but has been less willing to participate in agreements in an active manner. This results from the fact that governments are generally under less pressure than proponents to secure approval for any specific project and that they wish the costs of mitigating programmes to be borne by the proponent. At a broader level it may also reflect the point made earlier in the paper regarding the reluctance of state agencies to allow substantial indigenous participation in governance and more generally to accommodate indigenous interests. As noted above, community-controlled SIA does however enhance the capacity of communities to undertake political action designed to overcome this reluctance.

Conclusion

Indigenous people in Australia face formidable barriers in seeking to participate in governance, both generally and in the specific area of project appraisal processes. Indeed those barriers are so substantial that the only viable means of participation may involve indigenous people adopting a substantial degree of control over the relevant processes, pursuing them independently of government, and then later negotiating with government regarding the terms on which a re-engagement with 'mainstream' processes can occur. Such an approach, while certainly not without its problems, has brought significant advantages to indigenous communities on Cape York, allowing them a say in decisions which greatly affect their lives and from which they have previously been entirely excluded.

References

Armour, A. (1989) 'Integrating Impact Assessment in the Planning Process: From Rhetoric to Reality', *Impact Assessment Bulletin*, vol. 8, pp. 3–15.

Armour, A. (1991) 'Impact Assessment and the Planning Process: A Status Report', *Impact Assessment Bulletin*, vol. 9, pp. 27–33.

Attwood, B. (1989) *The Making of the Aborigines*, Allen and Unwin, Sydney.

Beckett, J. (1988a) 'Aboriginality, Citizenship and the Nation-State', *Social Analysis*, vol. 24, pp. 3–18

Beckett, J. (ed) (1988b), *Past and Present: The Construction of Aboriginality*. Aboriginal Studies Press, Canberra.

Berger, T.R. (1988) *Northern Frontier, Northern Homeland: The Report of the Mackenzie Pipeline Inquiry*, Douglas and McIntyre, Vancouver.

Blishen, B.R., Lockhart, A. Craib, P. and Lockhart, E. (1979) *Socio-Economic Impact Model for Northern Development*, Department of Indian and Northern Affairs Canada, Ottawa.

Chase, A. (1990) 'Anthropology and Impact Assessment: Development Pressures and Indigenous Interests in Australia', *Environmental Impact Assessment Review*, vol. 10, pp. 11–23.

Coombs, H.C. *et al.* (eds) (1989) *Land of Promises: Aborigines and Development in the East Kimberleys*, Centre for Resource and Environmental Studies, Australian National University, and Aboriginal Studies Press, Canberra.

Craig, D. (1989) *The Development of Social Impact Assessment in Australia and Overseas and the Role of Indigenous Peoples East Kimberley*, Impact Assessment Project Working Paper No 31, Centre for Resources and Environmental Studies, Australian National University, Canberra.

Daly, A.E. (1993) 'The Determinants of Employment for Aboriginal People', *Australian Economic Papers*, vol. 32, pp. 134–51.

Daly, A.E. (1995) *Aboriginal and Torres Strait Islander people in the Australian Labour Market*, Cat. No 6253.0, Australian Bureau of Statistics, Canberra.

Edelstein, M.R., and Kleese, D.A. (1995) 'Cultural Relativity and Impact Assessment: Hawaiian Opposition to Geothermal Energy Development', *Society and Natural Resources*, vol. 8 pp. 9–31.

Edwards, C. and Read, P. (1989) *The Lost Children*, Doubleday, Sydney.

Evans, R., Saunders K. and Cronin, K. (1988) *Race Relations in Colonial Queensland*, University of Queensland Press, St. Lucia.

Finsterbusch, K. (1985) 'State of the Art in Social Impact Assessment', *Environment and Behaviour*, vol. 17, pp. 193–221.

Gagnon, C. Hirsch, P. and. Howitt, R. (1993) 'Can SIA Empower Communities?' *Environmental Impact Assessment Review*, vol. 13 pp. 229–53.

Goodall, H. (1996) *Invasion to Embassy: Land in Aboriginal Politics in NSW 1770–1972*, Allen and Unwin, St. Leonards, NSW.

Holden, A. and O'Faircheallaigh, C. (1995) *The Economic and Social Impact of Silica Mining on Hope Vale*. Aboriginal Politics and Public Sector Management Monograph No 1. Centre for Australian Public Sector Management, Griffith University, Brisbane.

Howell, B.J. (1983) 'Implications of the Cultural Conservation Report for Social Impact Assessment', *Human Organization*, vol. 42, pp. 346–50.

Howitt, R. (1996) 'Napranum: Part of the Damage or Part of the Healing?, The Economic and Social Impact of Bauxite Mining and Related Activities on the West Coast of Cape York Peninsula', Confidential Report, November.

HREOC (Human Rights and Equal Opportunity Commission) (1997) *Bringing Them Home: National Inquiry in to the Separation of Aboriginal and Torres Strait Islander Children from their Families*, Human Rights and Equal Opportunity Commission, Sydney.

Justus, R. and Simonetta, J. (1982) 'Oil Sands, Indians and SIA in Northern Alberta', in C.C. Geisler *et al.* (eds), *Indian SIA: The Social Impact of Rapid Resource Development on Native Peoples*, University of Michigan, Ann Arbour, pp. 238–57.

Larbalestier, J. (1988) 'For the Betterment of these People: The Bleakley Report and Aboriginal Workers', *Social Analysis*, no. 24, pp. 19–33.

Lucashenko, M. (1996) *Policy and Politics in the Indigenous Sphere: An Introduction for Bureaucrats, Aboriginal Politics and Public Sector Management*, Research Paper No. 1, Centre for Australian Public Sector Management, Griffith University, June.

McConnochie, K. Hollingsworth, D. and Pettman, J. (1988) *Race and Racism in Australia*, Social Science Press, Wentworth Falls, NSW.

Michalenko, G. and Suffling, R. (1982) 'Social Impact Assessment in Northern Ontario: The Reed Paper Controversy', in C.C. Geisler *et al.* (eds), *Indian SIA: The Social Impact of Rapid Resource Development on Native Peoples*, University of Michigan Press, Ann Arbour, pp. 274–89.

Morris, B. (1991) 'Dhan-gadi Resistance to Assimilation', in I. Keen (ed), *Being Black: Aboriginal Cultures in Settled Australia*, Aboriginal Studies Press, Canberra.

O'Faircheallaigh, C. (1991) 'Resource Exploitation and Indigenous People: Towards a General Analytical Framework, in P. Jull and S. Roberts (eds), *The Challenge of Northern Regions*, North Australia Research Unit, Darwin, pp. 228–71.

O'Faircheallaigh, C. (1996) 'Aurukun: Mining Is Here Already, The Economic and Social Impact of Bauxite Mining and Related Activities on the West Coast of Cape York Peninsula', Confidential Report, November.

O'Faircheallaigh, C. (1999) 'Making Social Impact Assessment Count: A Negotiation-Based Approach for Indigenous Peoples', *Society and Natural Resources*, vol. 12, pp. 63–80.

Pettman, J. (1992) *Living in the Margins: Racism Sexism and Feminism in Australia*, Allen and Unwin, Sydney.

Read, P. (1984) *The Stolen Generations*, Ministry of Aboriginal Affairs, Sydney.

Reynolds, H. (1987) *Frontiers: Aborigines, Settlers and Land*, Allen and Unwin, Sydney.

Ross, H. (1989) 'Aboriginal Control and Participation in SIA'. Paper presented to the International Association for Impact Assessment Conference. Montreal, June.

Ross, H. (1990) 'Community Social Impact Assessment: A Framework for Indigenous Peoples', *Environmental Impact Assessment Review*, vol. 10, pp. 185–93.

Royal Commission on Aboriginal Deaths in Custody (1989), (1990), (1991) *Reports of the Royal Commission into Aboriginal Deaths in Custody*, Australian National University Press, Canberra.

Chapter 3

Public Participation and Integrated Development Planning in Decentralized Local Government: A Case Study of Democratic Transition in South Africa

Cornie Groenewald and Antoinette Smith

Introduction

This paper investigates the integrity of the process of public participation as reflected within a decentralized integrated development planning. The democratic transition in South Africa forms the backdrop of the study with special reference to the effects of this transition in decentralized local government. A case study approach is used. The democratic transition in the field of local government and its application in a specific rural development region are selected as case material. The West Coast Development Region in South Africa has been chosen as a testing ground of the study. The two most important reasons for selecting this region are firstly, that it has taken the lead implementing the newly passed policy of integrated development planning in South Africa and secondly, that the population has been subjected to systematic and sustained development and capacity building inputs by the state since 1994. This year was also the year of the first democratic elections ever in this country. An empirical study of the effects of public participation within integrated development planning that was completed recently, is described. In addition, some qualitative experience in the field of development planning is discussed. The simple question that the chapter asks is: How successful was the input from outside agencies, together with the efforts made by local government in ensuring the integrity of the democratization process?

Transition to Democracy and its Link to the Global Trend

In the past few years, South Africa has undergone one of the most phenomenal processes of political transformation (Wessels, 1998, p. 66). According to Huntington (1986, p. 344) transformation is ‘a change in the direction of greater social, economic or political equality, a broadening of participation in society and polity’.

In South Africa, the transition to democracy is characterised by the simultaneity of two democratic traditions namely that of traditional parliamentary or representative democracy and that of grassroots participatory democracy (Pillay, 1996, p. 325). Participatory democracy is practised through the forming of sectoral interest groups or stakeholders who draw their members from the different organizations within that sector. This corresponds with the notion of modern pluralism that means extensive participation in the political process through competing and autonomous groups (Wessels, 1998, p. 71).

A further trend in the transition to democracy was the negotiation of a decentralization of power that resulted in the much-debated tripartite (national, provincial and local) structure of government. The Constitution, which prescribes relations between the three spheres of government, encourages co-operation and co-ordination and provides areas of exclusive competence and areas of shared or concurrent competence (Constitution, 1996).

The resulting pattern of the transition to democracy is a social pluralistic society where, as is the case in post-independent African states, an intricate pattern of associations prevail in the public sphere (Chazan, 1982). It consists of voluntary associations filling the middle ground between the family and the state and thus appears as potential building blocks for an emerging civil society (Du Toit, 1995, p. 31). This implies that some form of institutionalization must exist between the state and the informal groupings in society. It can also be argued that the democratization of society is not possible in the absence of civil society, provided that citizens who actively involve themselves in public affairs, do not enter the public domain in the pursuit of private interests only but to the benefit of society as a whole.

The policy that was to give impetus to the social participatory democratization in South Africa is the Reconstruction and Development Policy (RDP) as adopted by the 1994 Government of National Unity and contained in the *White Paper on Reconstruction and Development* (RSA, 1994, p. 4). The RDP refers *inter alia* to the development of strong and stable democratic institutions and practices characterised by representativeness and participation.

This policy advocates two very important principles or values of democracy, namely participation and representation that are inter-linked and interdependent. According to Wessels (1998, p. 72) this implies not only direct political representation and participation through the political process, but also indirect representation through interest groups. He considers representation as the very essence of both direct and indirect democracy.

An important issue that was central to the transition process, was that of land reform which was addressed by, amongst other, the *Development Facilitation Act* (Act 67 of 1995). This act was intended to speed up reconstruction and development programmes and projects relating to land by creating a new land-use planning system (Pycroft, 1998, p. 153).

As this process was perceived as 'unfinished' (Bernstein, 1997, p. 21; Levin and Weiner, 1996) a participatory democratic alternative was proposed to gear up 'genuine popular participation' (Levin and Weiner, 1997, p. 264). This would include the facilitation of the process through local and community development forums where land committees and interest groups can be established (Levin and Weiner, 1997a, p. 265). Public forums were part of the RDP strategy and could, in our view correctly, facilitate broad-based participation at a grass-roots level.

The notion is underpinned here that democratization must be embedded in institutions that have the capacity to manage the process of participatory governance and development. It also suggests that all aspects of development must filter through to the lowest level of grassroots participation. The question that comes to mind is whether this suggestion is realistic and feasible.

The two values of democracy that are prominent and of central concern in the transition from apartheid, representation and participation, are included all aspects of transformation. In this chapter we will focus on participation and investigate processes of participatory democracy in an institutional field and geographical region where it has been advanced most. The aim is to assess whether this process is delivering authentic participation. In what follows, the concept of participation, and subsequent representation structures, will be further explored.

The Notion of Authentic Participation

Following De Beer (1996), participation in public affairs could be directed towards two different outcomes in relation to the transformation process. The RDP rhetoric implies the so-called strong interpretation of participation as a system-transforming process. This means that participation must aid social empowerment, in contradistinction to the weak interpretation of participation as involvement, which is also referred to as a system-maintaining process. The ultimate result of empowerment is the release and transformation of the self-help skills of the community, something that is reiterated in the RDP. According to De Beer (1996, pp. 67–68) through empowerment human needs are addressed, problem-solving skills are acquired, people are mobilised to act collectively and according to mutual interest, and self-awareness is created and internal potential within the community is mobilised. Empowerment refers to action at grassroots level. These are central concerns in the RDP, conceptualised as an approach of people-centred development.

Literature explaining people-centred development does not only assume a focus on people as objects of development but also sees them as active partners in the development process. Since the 1990s, this approach to development has been systematically and actively promoted as *human development* (Ul Haq, 1995). The notion of community participation seems to be a necessary condition for these partnerships. This is supported by authors such as James Midgley *et al.* (1986, p. 21) and the United Nations (1975) who define popular participation as follows:

> participation requires the voluntary and democratic involvement of people in
> (a) contributing to the development effort,
> (b) sharing equitably in the benefits derived therefrom and
> (c) decision-making in respect of setting goals forming policies and planning and implementing economic and social development programmes (as quoted in Midgley *et al.* 1986, p. 25).

In order for public participation to become an instrument of empowerment, it needs an infrastructure from where it can be initiated. It implies the notion of institution building and representation. The notion of institution building denotes:

> ...the creation of procedures for democratic decision-making at the local level and the involvement of people in these procedures to the extent that they regard them as the normal way of conducting affairs (Midgley *et al.*, 1986, p. 29).

Decision-making bodies should be fully representative, democratically elected and accountable, which implies that representation forms an equally important building block in the success of participation. The people who participate, should represent the grouping they belong to and be accountable to them. The importance of institution building is, therefore, to ensure that all people in the community are represented through participation.

The way that government sees and responds to community participation will be most decisive for attaining authentic participation by the people. Authentic participation in community development will be optimal under conditions where the state supports a participatory mode of response to its constituency (Midgley *et al.*, 1986, pp. 38–44). Authentic participation involves all three criteria specified in the United Nations (1975) definition of community participation quoted above. It is also to be distinguished from pseudo-participation which limits community involvement to the implementation or ratification of decisions already taken by external bodies (Midgley *et al.*, 1986, p. 26).

In the next section the policy directions for local government development in South Africa and the degree to which community representation and participation should be sought, and relevant approaches in this regard, are introduced.

Policy Framework for Local Government Development and Participation in South Africa

The local government transformation process in South Africa followed three well-defined phases, starting with a pre-interim phase that began in 1993 with the enactment of the *Local Government Transition Act (209 of 1993, Second Amendment Act, 1995)*. Representatives from the established local government bodies (statutory) and those groups that had previously been excluded from local government but represent local people (non-statutory) were constituted as local forums that performed local government functions during this phase. The interim phase was ushered in by municipal elections in November 1995 and June 1996. The final phase followed an extensive process of research resulting in the *White Paper on Local Government* (MPA, 1998) and will introduce the final form of local government (Pycroft 1998, p. 154) which was expected by November 2000. The final phase and local government structures are guided by principles provided for in the Constitution of the Republic of South Africa that is mandating local government, among other, to promote local social and economic development (MPA, 1998, p. 15).

Development at the local level is seen as linked to the democratization process and the inclusion of citizens and community groups in the design and delivery of municipal development programmes (MPA, 1998, p. 20). Four key development outcomes of local government are aimed at: (1) provision of household infrastructure and services, (2) creation of liveable, integrated cities, towns and rural areas, (3) local economic development, and (4) community empowerment and redistribution (MPA, 1998, p.22). The tools and approaches for achieving these outcomes require a process of integrated development planning and budgeting, performance management, and working together with local citizens and partners. We, therefore. need to look more closely to the process of integrated development planning (IDP), as it has developed in South Africa (MPA, 1998, p. 26).

Municipalities are required according to the *Local Government Transition Act* to produce IDPs. A specific methodology is prescribed for an IDP. Local authorities need to understand the various dynamics operating within their area of jurisdiction, develop a concrete vision for the area, and strategies for realizing and financing that vision in partnership with other stakeholders (MPA, 1998, p. 27). IDP is therefore a process through which a municipality establishes a development plan for the short, medium and long term. A specific sequence of steps in producing an IDP was proposed and operationalized.

IDPs should be viewed as incremental plans that need to be reviewed annually and adapted as priorities change. It is a normal and required municipal function – 'IDPs are not "add-ons" and should not be 'farmed out' to consultants' (MPA, 1998, p. 28). They help municipalities to develop a holistic strategy for poverty alleviation, and need to be comprehensive and, therefore, multi-sectoral. IDPs should lead to institutional and financial plans that are intended to guide municipalities in delivery and in transformation.

Furthermore, the White Paper (MPA, 1998, pp. 33–35) sees building local democracy as a central role of local government and states that municipalities should develop strategies and mechanisms to continuously engage with citizens, business and community groups. Active participation by citizens is required in the following respects: as voters, as citizens (for example, who express via different stakeholder associations, their views before, during and after the policy development process in order to ensure that policies reflect community preferences), as consumers and end-users, and as organized partners involved in the mobilization of resources for development via business, non-governmental organizations and community-based institutions (MPA, 1998, p. 33).

With regard to participation in the policy process, municipalities are encouraged to develop mechanisms to ensure citizen representation and participation in policy initiation and formulation, and the monitoring and evaluation of decision-making and implementation. Five approaches to achieve this are proposed namely, *forums* to initiate and/or influence policy-formulation, structured *stakeholder involvement* in council committees, participatory *budgeting initiatives*, *focus group* participatory action research and *support* for the organisational development of associations in marginalized areas (MPA, 1998, pp. 33–34).

According to Pycroft (1998, p. 153) the attempt to institute development planning from the centre in South Africa, has proved to be difficult, if not impossible. He discusses the following constraints on the implementation of the newly assigned role of local government (1998, pp. 154–157):

a) Democratizing local government does not necessarily mean it is equipped to perform the developmental role ascribed to it like managing its own administration, budgeting and planning process.

b) It is not geared to overcome the inadequacies of the past as expected from it, due to the fact that under apartheid it performed a narrow range of traditional local government functions and played a minimal developmental and redistributive role. Often these functions were performed in a paternalistic, non-consultative way.
c) The expectation of the local council to co-ordinate the development activities within its jurisdiction that are undertaken by other spheres of government, both provincial and national are mostly far beyond its capabilities.
d) Local, provincial and national government operate as equal partners in a given municipal area in contrast to the more traditional hierarchy of government tiers. This does not mean that it happens without difficulties, as local government is in certain instances entirely dependent on subsidies from provincial government.

It is expected that these factors will effect the ability of the local government to create an atmosphere where public participation can take place without constraints. In the case study that follows, the majority of these concerns surfaced in practice and it becomes apparent that even under the most favourable circumstances, the process does not take place without a fair number of problems. A question that remains unanswered, is even if the representation and participation works according to plan, will the standard of governance be adequate to see this process through to delivery?

The Case Study: West Coast Development Region

The West Coast Development Region is selected as a case study for the following reasons:

First, both authors have been involved in social development activities in the West Coast over a prolonged period of time and have gained an intimate knowledge of local conditions and communities in the region.

Second, the West Coast has been designated as one of eight 'Spatial Development Initiative' (SDI) locations in the country (WCII, 1997). The intention of the initiative is to focus interest, effort, and investment in a specific location which has developmental potential, with under-utilised infrastructure and resources. The initiative is managed under the name *West Coast Investment Initiative* (WCII) and has as its focus the opportunities created by the mini mill of Saldanha Steel as well as the under-utilised opportunities in agriculture, tourism and fishing in the region. The SDI programme is driven by the national Departments of Trade and Industry and Transport and has specific aims, job creation, realisation of growth potential, encouragement of small, medium and micro enterprises, and the development of the export potential of the region. One of the key aspects is public-private partnerships meaning a participatory mode is intended. The focus includes agriculture and tourism and, therefore, the WCII is regarded as important for the rural development of the region.

Third, the West Coast is a development region with a rural profile. It is demarcated as a development region in terms of the *Provincial Development Council Act* of the Western Cape Province and it comprises two sub-regions, a southern part and a northern part. Industrial activities are concentrated in the Saldanha-Vredenburg area in the south. The hinterland's economy is based mainly on agriculture with products such as wine, grain, deciduous fruit and vegetables. Other industries include fishing, forestry, mining and tourism. The population is spread over the two sub-regions with stronger concentrations in the southern sub-region (76 per cent) and in the local towns and settlements. The population (total 290,957) is made up of coloureds (77 per cent) and whites (19 per cent). Blacks (or Africans) are still a minority (4 per cent) but it is expected that this group will grow in future. The dominant language is Afrikaans.

Fourth, the West Coast has been earmarked, in the previous dispensation as well as in the current period, for special projects. Important for the purposes of this paper are two initiatives: a) capacity building of RDP forums and b) timeous commencement with integrated development planning of the region as a whole as well as that of the different towns and rural districts and settlements. Both of these matters relate to the institutional infrastructure of the region. This is considered as an important factor that impacted on the results of this study and is briefly discussed below.

With reference to the first initiative, RDP forums, it should be noted that they have been actively promoted in the Western Cape since the national election of 1994. The idea of forums is not novel. In fact, forums have proved to be a vehicle for representation and promoting democracy and to assist in the process of transformation during the interim period of local government as mentioned earlier. Based on the relative success of forums and their widespread occurrence, a forum culture has been created in South Africa (Bekker, 1994). Forums are seen as frameworks for managing information, opinion-formation, diversity, convergence of contrasting ideas, and for consultation, negotiation and participation regarding planning and development.

During the post-1994 period, immediate steps were taken to install forums in national, provincial, regional and local levels of government. In the Western Cape Province this seemed to be a necessary instrument at the provincial, regional and local levels in order to institutionalise consultation and negotiation with civil society. RDP forum formation did not prove to be an easy process, due to past divisions in local communities, and because knowledge and expertise was lacking regarding the role, functions and responsibilities of RDP forum participants (see Groenewald, 1997, pp. 379–399). Accordingly, the Western Cape provincial government started a pilot project of training and capacity building of RDP committee members. The West Coast Development Region was selected as the target area for the pilot project. The project comprised a number of consecutive phases. An initial training and capacity building phase was presented first during 1994. A follow-up programme was installed after the lapse of about one year with training sessions based on a needs assessment. Fifteen RDP committees were included in these training sessions. Training modules included aspects such as leadership and organisational processes, strategic planning, conflict resolution, and so on. These RDP forums did not become the effective vehicles, as was envisaged and with the demise of the RDP office in 1996, the rug was pulled from under the forums in terms of national and provincial support. The work that was done to empower the different communities was not lost, however. The remains of the RDP forums served as the basic structures for consultation in the establishment of the Provincial (PDC) and Regional Development Councils (RDC) according to the Western Cape Development Council Act (No. 5 of 1996). The functions assigned to the PDC according to the Act are that of co-ordinating, facilitating and initiating consensus amongst stakeholders on provincial, regional and local development planning, policy objectives and development strategies of the PDC (PDC, 1998, p. 7). In the West Coast, the RDP forums, as well as the RDC, served as a point of departure in terms of representation for the integrated development planning process that followed during 1997/8. The PDC established a framework in terms of stakeholder representation that was adopted by the West Coast region. The framework lists a wide arrange of stakeholder groups to be included in the development consultation process (PDC, 1998, p. 12).

Regarding the second initiative of integrated development planning the Provincial Administration of the Western Cape initiated during the latter half of 1997 the IDP process in the province. It issued a guideline (PAWC, 1997) and held training workshops on how to conduct the process at local authority level. With reference to the non-metropolitan areas, three local authority levels were involved:

a) Regional level government structures – District Councils.
b) Transitional Local Councils for urban areas (TLCs).
c) Transitional Rural Councils, for non-urban communities (TRCs).

District Councils were servicing TRCs and small TLCs. All councils, regardless of their level and scope, were expected to complete their IDP in due course and to serve as the basis for the budgeting of the next financial year. District Councils were responsible for the IDPs of TRCs and smaller TLCs. Again the West Coast Development Region was seen as a region to serve as a model for other development regions in the province. Accordingly, the West Coast District Council was instructed by the Province to manage the IDP process for the region and the smaller TLCs and TRCs.

Guidelines for the IDP process were presented at workshops at different venues. It consisted of a ten-phase planning process.

With reference to public participation the guideline suggested that RDP forums or similar bodies be used as vehicles for public consultation as it was presumed that these bodies were representative of the communities they served. Because of the sustained input into the functioning and capacity building of RDP forums in the West Coast Region over a period of more than two years, it may be assumed that the consultation process would have been relatively successful and legitimate in delivering an integrated development planning output. In practice, the composition of stakeholder groupings coincided with the requirements stated by the PDC.

The aim of the IDP process' intent is to deliver a five-year development plan for a specific local government area. The five-year cycle started for the financial year 1998/99 (midyear). The plan was to be revised (upgraded and refined) every subsequent year. This should be based on proper public participation in all phases of the planning process, as explained above. The process should be driven by the relevant local authority (or its service agent) and assisted by officials, 'experts' and facilitators.

In the case of the West Coast, the practical mode for public participation was to conduct so-called community-liaisons (called workshops) that consisted of invited representatives of all local interest groups and stakeholders. A facilitating agency was contracted through a public tender procedure to lead the community-liaison.

An empirical monitoring process was conducted in eight instances during the final series of public consultation workshops. The aim was to measure the effect of such public consultations on the integrity of the process followed, as perceived by the participants in the workshops. Both authors were also part of the organisation that was contracted to facilitate the first and the last of the workshops held in that specific region. This involvement offered the opportunity to do qualitative research during the course of the process. A description of the research and its outcomes follows.

Research Design

It is assumed for the purposes of this study that the community-liaison or workshop constitutes the heart of the issue of participation. Assessment of whether the process has been perceived as authentic will accordingly focus on the functioning of this aspect of the process, but also on the issue of representation. The research has been driven by the question to what extent the people to be affected by the outcomes of the IDP have been participating in the process of development planning and to what degree they have experienced such participation as authentic participation.

For the purposes of this study, a selection of the following local authorities and community liaisons were made:

a) West Coast District Council (WCDC), representing three subdivisions or community liaisons.
b) Five TRCs (councils for rural districts) representing one community liaison each.

These community liaisons represent, firstly, the total region and its population as serviced by the WCDC as well as all rural districts under the auspices of the relevant TRCs but exclude all towns governed by TLCs. Furthermore, the selection of local authorities covered the total region and the rural districts, which by nature consist of dispersed populations. It is assumed that the most difficult conditions for participation are represented in this sample. Should a favourable outcome be recorded by the research in these instances, it may be concluded that the process, as driven by the above-mentioned authorities, indeed passes the test for creating a process of authentic participation.

The measurement of the integrity of the process of participation was carried out at the various community liaisons or workshops. These workshops were the last in a series of workshops that were held since October 1997 over a period of twelve months. The authors started the quantitative research at the first workshop in the series that was intended for orientation of the participants and to constitute a sound base of representation at the workshops. The local authority officials working to include all the relevant interest groups in their area of jurisdiction, put in a great amount of effort. The people who attended the first workshop were then requested to indicate if any interest group were left out. Lists were compiled and used to conduct the next round of invitations. The second phase consisted of a number (four to five) workshops that had the aim to produce the basic framework of the plan that would enable the officials and experts to complete the development plan and give input to the budget procedure. The authors were again involved in the final phase that comprised one workshop each for the various local authority areas to finally accept and endorse the development plan (or framework as it is called) as *their product.* It was during this last round of workshops that the empirical measuring of participants' representation profile and perceptions were made, that is after the completion of the first round of IDP.

A structured questionnaire was compiled, to be completed by participants at workshops, and to be tested at one workshop. The same questionnaire was administered twice during the same session, first at the beginning of the session and later at the end of the session. On average the workshops' length were about two to two-and-a-half-hours.

The workshops' programme included the following items:

a) a detailed explanation of the IDP process, a submission of the development framework (document) and a detailed explanation of its contents,
b) an opportunity to debate the document and to correct the community profile, and, finally,
c) to accept the framework as a true reflection of the community's input and participation.

Observations made at the workshops that could have impacted on the responses were:

a) Attendance at workshops was affected by long distances, the absence of public transport and the constraints of obtaining leave from work to attend meetings. Workshops were scheduled according to the circumstances of the majority.
b) The explanation of the process was long, technical and not interactive. People were given time to ask questions.
c) People indicated that the process was time-consuming and questioned its cost effectiveness and its potential to deliver.
d) A cynicism was expressed by the community members about the ability of the local authority to fulfil its role as development agent, while councillors had concerns that expectations for delivery were not aligned with fiscal abilities.
e) This was the first round of the process which was under pressure due to the time frames of the budgeting process. The participants had doubts about the feasibility of the process to align the spending of the budget with the needs expressed.

Table 3.1 Key to Statements

Question 2: Contribution to the Process
2.1 I understand all the steps and the contents of the process.
2.2 I had full opportunity to participate in the process.
2.3 I have contributed to process up till where it is now.
2.4 I was part of the process of budgeting.
2.5 My interest group has been served through the participation.

Question 3: Needs Assessment
3.1 The community had a say in the assessment of the needs.
3.2 The process brought forward the real needs of the community.
3.3 The community will gain from this process.

Question 4: Decision-Making
4.1 The community participated in decision-making about the goals.
4.2 The community participated in decision-making about planning.
4.3 The community will participate in decision-making about implementation.

Question 5: Representation/Responsibility
5.1 The group that participated in this process was representative of the community.
5.2 The group that participated in this process will be accountable to the community.
5.3 The community is in control of this process of integrated planning and implementation – not the consultants.

Question 6: Local Authority as Development Agent
6.1 The local authority is the body that should *facilitate* the process of development planning.
6.2 The local authority is the body that should *manage* the process of development planning.
6.3 The local authority is the body that should *implement* the process of development planning.

Question 7: The Nature of the Process
7.1 This process of integrated development planning is exceptional and above the normal.
7.2 This process of integrated planning is normal and ought to be like this.

Question 8: The State's Motive with the IDP
8.1 The state is sincere in its advancement of participation on the local level – there are no hidden motives.

The attitudes reflected in these observations can relate to the argument by Botes (1999) that initiatives by the state are sometimes met with distrust and suspicion and lead to apathy on the side of the community.

We measured variables to test people's perceptions of the process, on two levels. On the first level, twenty specific aspects of the IDP process have been developed. This was done according to statements to which the respondent was supposed to express an answer on each item with a choice of four possible answers (see below). These 20 statements were divided among seven broad areas of the IDP process. Five items dealt with respondents contribution to the process (Question 2); three with needs assessment (Question 3); three with decision-making (Question 4); three with representation and accountability (Question 5); three with the role of the local authority as a development agent (Question 6); two with the characteristics of the process (Question 7); and one with the state's motive in respect of the IDP (Question 8).

Statements were developed from the criteria or indicators of participation in the IDP process, reflected in the theory of authentic participation and the policy framework, as outlined above. The indicators that were measured were the following:

a) Empowerment to participate (2.1) as primarily advocated in the White Paper on Reconstruction and Development (RSA, 1994) and supported by others (De Beer, 1996, pp. 67–68).
b) Opportunity to participate (2.2) and
c) Participation in the budgeting process (2.4) as prescribed to local authorities by the White Paper on Local Government (MPA, 1998: 33–35).
d) Participation through interest group (2.5) (see Levin and Weiner, 1997a, p. 265) and
e) Participation in identifying needs and gaining from it (3.1–3.3) (see e.g. 'Sharing Equitably in Benefits' in United Nations, 1975 in Midgley *et al.*, 1996, p. 25).
f) Contribution to development effort (2.3) and
g) Decision-making about goals, planning and implementation (4.1–4.3) according to the United Nations (1975) definition of popular participation.
h) Qualities of decision-making bodies (5.1-5.2) and
i) Participation as a normal way of conducting affairs (7.1–7.2) as stated by Midgley *et al.* (1986, p. 29).
j) The community must be in control and not consultants as prescribed by the White Paper on Local Government (MPA, 1998, p. 28).
k) The motive of state is sincere and it advances participation relating to the typology by Midgley *et al.* (1986).

Items in the questionnaire took the format of a statement to which the respondent answered by marking one of four answers: (a) I do not know, (b) Uncertain, (c) Yes, or (d) No. This answer set was chosen after a pre-testing was completed with ordinal answers ('strongly disagree', 'disagree', 'agree' or 'strongly disagree'). Because respondents could not understand or relate to those answers, the answer set was changed and interpreted as below.

All respondents were required to answer according to this answer set. All items were put to the respondents twice, first in the beginning of the session and second at the end of the session.

On the second level of measurement respondents who answered by endorsing 'I do not know' or 'Uncertain' were taken as persons who did not have information or knowledge about the item at the time. (A few respondents who did not offer a response were also included in this 'no information' category after close inspection of the response patterns).

Those who answered 'Yes' or 'No' were seen as persons with the necessary knowledge to express an opinion on the item, whether positive or negative. Thus, the item carried a knowledge dimension that was measured by two response sets respectively. On the one hand, 'I do not know' and 'Uncertain' (as well as 'No response') indicated no knowledge or not enough knowledge about the item to express an opinion while 'Yes' and 'No' on the other hand indicated enough knowledge on the part of the respondent to express an opinion.

It was therefore possible to establish firstly whether the respondent had knowledge about the matter referred to in the item.

Secondly, because two measurements were taken, it was also possible to establish whether a certain respondent had changed from a position of no (or not enough) knowledge in the first measurement to a position of definite knowledge about the matter in the second measurement. These cases will be indicated by a change from either 'I do not know' or 'Uncertain' (as well as 'No response') to either 'Yes' or 'No' in the second measurement. The Sign test for two related samples (Bryman and Cramer, 1997, pp. 137–8) compares the number of positive and negative differences between two scores from matched samples but ignores the size of these differences. This test was applied to measure the change from a position of 'No knowledge' to 'Knowledge' (a positive difference) or vice versa (a negative difference), or a 'tie' (where no change was recorded between the two measurements.

Thirdly, it was possible to determine a change in attitude with respect to each item among those respondents who have had already knowledge about the item at the first measurement. For example, a respondent who changed his/her answer from 'No' in the first measurement to 'Yes' in the second measurement, did not only have the necessary level of knowledge to express an opinion but also changed that opinion from a negative to a positive during the interval between the two measurements. For the purpose of this study, attitude is considered to be reflected by the expression of an opinion about a particular subject. Therefore, through selecting respondents with the necessary level of knowledge about an item during the first measurement the change in opinion or attitude about the item could be determined by comparing the first and second response on the same item. The McNemar test for two related samples (Bryman and Cramer, 1997, pp. 127–9) is considered to be an appropriate test to determine the significance of such changes in the level of knowledge about the various items and was applied accordingly.

The following classification variables were included in the questionnaire. This could also give an indication of the representation in the sample:

a) The relevant IDP workshop (this referred to the local authority that the workshop pertained to) [Local authority].
b) Age of the respondent [Age].
c) Sex of the respondent [Sex].
d) Race group of the respondent (three categories were applied: Black, Coloured and White) [Race].
e) Language of the respondent (home language was implied; three categories were suggested: Afrikaans, English and Xhosa; an open category "Other" was provided as well) [Language].
f) The interest group represented by the respondent (this was an open category and responses were classified after completion of the questionnaires by the researchers) [Interest group].
g) The number of workshops attended since October 1997 by the respondent in the IDP series [Number of workshops].

The number of workshops attended since October 1997 by the respondent in the IDP series, served the purpose of giving an indication of the representation in the sample as well as determining the origin of the knowledge before the first measurement. It is assumed that exposure to workshops will contribute to a better knowledge level. Further analysis of the link between those with knowledge and the number of workshops could, therefore, be determined by firstly re-coding those who have never attended workshops as 'no workshops' and those who attended one to five workshops as 'attended workshop'. Respondents with knowledge were those who could answer YES or NO and those with no knowledge were those who could not answer YES or NO. A cross-tabulation was then made of those respondents with knowledge and the workshops they attended. This was done for both measurements. This indicated the influence of prior attendance of workshops on the respondents' knowledge as well as the workshop during which the measurements were made.

Findings

Altogether 137 questionnaires were returned at eight workshops; 77 (56 per cent) were collected at West Coast District Council workshops and 60 (44 per cent) at TRC workshops. Not all respondents stayed throughout the workshops to complete the second round of measurement. There were 18 questionnaires which were not completed fully. A total of 121 questionnaires were therefore available for comparing the two sets of answers to the two measurements.

The sample gained showed the following characteristics (based on N=137).

a) The mean age of the group is 44 years (SD=12.37 years). The age distribution for the region as a whole was not available according to the age intervals used for the study but it appears that all age groups were fairly equally distributed according to ratio.
b) 79 per cent are men. Men are over-represented in this study, as the men constitute 51 per cent of the region's population.
c) 56% are white and 42 per cent coloured; only 1 person each was black and Asian. Whites constitute 20 per cent, and coloureds 73 per cent of the region's population. The sample, therefore, does not correspond with the race profile of the region.
d) The majority are Afrikaans speaking (98 per cent). The region's population is 91 per cent Afrikaans speaking.
e) 57 per cent were representing NGOs and 43 per cent government organizations. The latter comprised government departments and local authorities (including councillors).
f) 31 per cent were attending these workshops for the first time, the rest have attended one or two workshops (27 per cent) or more (42 per cent) in the past.

An overview of responses that portray the distribution and changes of answers to the statements put to the participants in the workshops, follows below.

First, the spread of responses to the statements in both measurements is provided (Tables 3.2 and 3.3). The first level of creating a new variable – the level of knowledge about integrated development planning – will also be indicated. Two measures are possible and shown in the two respective tables. Secondly, the change in the level of knowledge is indicated and assessed for statistical significance according to the Sign Test (Table 3.4). Finally, the change in opinion about the integrated development planning process, among those who have claimed to be knowledgeable from the outset, is detailed and assessed according to the McNemar Test (Table 3.5). In all cases the total sample is used.

Table 3.2 Responses to First Measurement

Q	N–R %	DK %	U %	Y %	N %	%K
2.1	–	2.9	16.8	75.2	5.1	80.3
2.2	.7	3.6	4.4	70.1	21.2	91.3
2.3	.7	2.9	8.0	59.1	29.2	88.3
2.4	.7	2.2	11.7	22.6	62.8	85.4
2.5	.7	5.8	21.2	64.2	8.0	72.2
3.1	.7	10.2	20.4	63.5	5.1	68.6
3.2	1.5	8.0	27.7	56.2	6.6	62.8
3.3	–	8.8	15.3	73.7	2.2	75.9
4.1	.7	9.5	23.4	57.7	8.8	66.5
4.2	.7	8.8	27.0	51.1	12.4	63.5
4.3	–	12.4	31.4	51.8	4.4	56.2
5.1	.7	10.9	32.1	44.5	11.7	56.2
5.2	.7	6.6	21.9	69.3	1.5	70.8
5.3	–	6.6	31.4	49.6	12.4	62.0
6.1	–	3.6	5.1	85.4	5.8	91.2
6.2	.7	3.6	2.2	87.6	5.8	93.4
6.3	1.5	2.9	8.0	83.9	3.6	87.5
7.1	.7	6.6	32.8	38.7	21.2	59.9
7.2	1.5	3.6	16.8	73.0	5.1	78.1
8.1	–	4.4	24.1	65.0	6.6	71.6

Explanation: The percentage of respondents with knowledge is calculated by adding the percentages in the Yes and No columns.

With respect to Table 3.2 – showing the responses of the first measurement – the low percentage of no response (N-R) is noticeable and possibly an indication of a high motivation among the participants to give their support to the research. Secondly, the highest percentages are found among the Yes-responses (Y), except for item 2.4 where a percentage of 62.8 per cent was recorded in the No-category (N). This item refers to the budgeting process to which the participants did not contribute directly.

Generically their input into the planning process is interpreted as a part of the budgeting process as the item claimed. If the respondents understood this, their answers will be yes on this question. In that particular phase of the process, no explicit budget process took place, which could explain the high percentage of No answers. Their input into the planning process could, however, be interpreted as a *part* of the budgeting process, as the item claimed. A number of items drew fairly large percentages of responses under the Uncertain-column (U).

Table 3.3 Responses to Second Measurement

Q	%RESPONSE, N=121					%K
	N–R	DK	U	Y	N	
2.1			1.7	93.4	5.0	98.4
2.2			5.8	82.6	11.6	94.2
2.3			6.6	79.3	14.0	93.3
2.4	.8		14.9	31.4	52.9	84.3
2.5	.8	2.5	14.9	78.5	3.3	81.8
3.1	.8	2.5	11.6	83.5	1.7	85.2
3.2	2.5	1.7	13.2	76.9	5.8	82.7
3.3	.8	3.3	9.1	86.0	.8	86.8
4.1		4.1	16.5	75.2	4.1	79.3
4.2	.8	4.1	19.0	68.6	7.4	76.0
4.3	.8	5.0	13.2	72.7	8.3	81.0
5.1	.8	4.1	21.5	62.8	10.7	73.5
5.2	.8	1.7	12.4	81.8	3.3	85.1
5.3			18.2	79.3	2.5	81.8
6.1	.8	.8	7.4	84.3	6.6	90.9
6.2		1.7	5.0	86.0	7.4	93.4
6.3	1.7	.8	5.0	90.1	2.5	92.6
7.1		3.3	19.8	51.2	25.6	76.8
7.2	2.5		9.1	86.0	2.5	88.5
8.1		3.3	14.9	79.3	2.5	81.8

Explanation: The percentage respondents with knowledge is calculated by adding the percentages in the Yes and No columns.

The level of knowledge that was calculated from the responses in Table 3.2 indicates fairly high levels across the list of items. Never was a minority percentage (below 50 per cent) encountered. The lowest levels were found among items in Question 3 (Needs assessment), Question 4 (Decision-

Table 3.4 Changes in the Level of Knowledge from the First Measurement to the Second Measurement

Q	%K1 N=137	%K2 N=121	–D (N)	+D (N)	TIES (N)	SIG
2.1	80.3	98.4	0	20	101	.000
2.2	91.3	94.2	4	6	111	.754
2.3	88.3	93.3	4	8	109	.388
2.4	85.4	84.3	9	6	106	.607
2.5	72.2	81.8	7	19	95	.031
3.1	68.6	85.2	5	25	91	.001
3.2	62.8	82.7	5	28	88	.000
3.3	75.9	86.8	2	17	102	.001
4.1	66.5	79.3	8	24	89	.008
4.2	63.5	76.0	5	22	94	.002
4.3	56.2	81.0	4	34	83	.000
5.1	56.2	73.5	2	22	97	.000
5.2	70.8	85.1	4	20	97	.002
5.3	62.0	81.8	10	32	79	.001
6.1	91.2	90.9	6	5	110	1.000
6.2	93.4	93.4	6	4	111	.754
6.3	87.5	92.6	4	9	108	.267
7.1	59.9	76.8	5	28	88	.000
7.2	78.1	88.5	4	16	101	.012
8.1	71.6	81.8	7	16	98	.093

Explanation: A *negative* difference implies a change from 'Knowledge' in the first measurement (%K1) to 'No knowledge' in the second measurement, (%K2) while a *positive* difference means a change from 'No knowledge' in the first measurement to 'Knowledge' in the second measurement. A *tie* means that no change occurred between the two measurements.

making), Question 5 (Representation) and Question 7 (The nature of the process). The two items under Question 7 were opposites and could be an indication of the reliability of the measure. If a respondent answered No on Item 7.1 it could be expected that he/she should answer Yes on Item 7.2 (or vice versa). A test (by means of a cross tabulation for both measurements between items 7.1 and 7.2) showed that in the first measurement 27 of the 29 respondents who answered No for item 7.1 indeed responded with a Yes in item 7.2. Likewise, all 31 respondents who answered No for item 7.1 answered Yes for item 7.2. The reverse was not true. Of the 53 respondents who answered Yes for item 7.1 only 4 answered No for item 7.2. The

Table 3.5 Changes in Opinion from the First to the Second Measurement

Q	Y–Y (T) (N)	Y–N (Ch) (N)	N–Y (Ch) (N)	N–N (T) (N)	TOTAL (N)	SIG
2.1	91	1	4	3	99	.375
2.2	82	2	12	12	108	.013
2.3	72	0	16	17	105	.000
2.4	21	4	14	57	96	.031
2.5	72	0	4	4	80	.125
3.1	76	0	2	0	78	.500
3.2	61	3	5	3	72	.727
3.3	85	1	2	0	88	1.000
4.1	62	3	5	2	72	.727
4.2	58	0	5	7	70	.063
4.3	54	5	4	1	64	1.000
5.1	51	4	3	9	67	1.000
5.2	80	1	1	1	83	1.000
5.3	55	0	11	1	67	.001
6.1	95	4	2	4	105	.687
6.2	98	4	2	5	109	.687
6.3	97	2	3	1	103	1.000
7.1	37	7	5	16	65	.774
7.2	85	1	3	2	91	.625
8.1	75	2	5	1	83	.453

Explanation: YES–YES (Y–Y): Respondent answered YES in the first measurement and YES in the second measurement. No change is indicated in opinion about the item. YES–NO (Y–N): Respondent answered YES in the first measurement and NO in the second measurement. A change in opinion about the item is implied. NO–YES (N–Y): Respondents answered NO in the first measurement and YES in the second measurement. A change in opinion about the item is implied. NO–NO (N–N): Respondent answered NO in the first measurement and NO in the second measurement. No change is indicated in opinion about the item.

corresponding figures for the second measurement are 62 Yes-answers and only 2 No-answers. One could argue that, together with item 7.1, the process is indeed exceptional, and once a person endorses this fact he/she would agree that this should become the norm (along with item 7.2). All-in-all one should not deduce too much from items 7.1 and 7.2.

From Table 3.3 (concerning the response pattern for the second measurement) it is quite clear that a shift towards Yes-responses (Y) appeared. Less No (N) –, Uncertain (U) – as well as Don't know answers were recorded. Item 2.4 (about budgeting) still draws a majority No-answer (52.9 per cent). The level of knowledge (%K) about the IDP-process increased on all items.

Table 3.4 deals with the question whether the direction of the shift is a positive one, i.e. from a position of No knowledge to a position of Knowledge, and whether this shift is statistically significant (SIG). Except for item 2.4 (budgeting) and 6.1 (facilitation) all positive differences were larger than the negative differences or remained the same on item 6.2 (managing). The majority of the changes were significant on the .05 or lower level. Exceptions are item 2.2 (opportunity for participation), 2.3 (contribution to the process), 2.4 (budgeting), 6.1 (facilitation), 6.2 (managing), 6.3 (implementation role of local authorities) and 8.1 (state's sincerity). All these items reflected positive differences but they were not statistically significant. The reasons for this will become clearer in Table 4 where the significance of the change of opinion is measured.

Table 3.5 assessed whether changes occurred in the way participants with a sufficient level of knowledge saw the various aspects of the IDP-process. The majority finding is that no change was experienced. This is specifically true among the YES-YES responses. It could be argued that if a participant answered YES to an item in the first measurement, the chances are exceptionally high that the same response will be forwarded at the second measurement. Where the respondent answered NO in the first measurement, a fair chance existed that the answer would change in the majority of cases to a YES. This happened in 13 of the 20 items. Not all changes were significant. Only four of the total change patterns were statistically significant on a level of .05 or lower. They are 2.2 (opportunity to participate), 2.3 (contributed to the process), 2.4 (budgeting) and 5.3 (community control process). The reason for this will become clearer below in the integrated analysis of Tables 3 and 4. Pertaining to the change of opinion, the general finding is that among those who have a sufficient level of knowledge of the IDP-process to assess the items, only a small number of changes were brought about in their opinion about the process through their participation in the workshop.

When integrating the results in Tables 3.4 and 3.5, further analysis reflects the following:

The indication in Table 3.4 is that the level of knowledge increased during the workshops, generally at a significant degree. The high levels of knowledge in both measurements on the items 2.2–2.4 can be attributed to the nature of the question. The answer in these cases could be either based on the opinion of the respondent or on knowledge of the process or both. The changes in answers on these items do not signify a change in knowledge but in opinion (see 2.2–2.4 in Table 3.3). It can, therefore, be deduced that the input of the workshop did not change level of knowledge in this case but it did lead to change in opinions. This explains why the

Table 3.6 Percentage with Knowledge According to Workshop Attendance

Q	W0, %K		W1–5, %K	
	M1 (N=42)	M2 (N=39)	M1 (N=95)	M2 (N=82)
2.1	66.7	94.9	86.3	100
2.2	81.0	92.3	95.8	95.1
2.3	83.3	94.9	90.5	92.7
2.4	85.7	89.7	85.3	81.7
2.5	57.1	79.5	78.9	82.9
3.1	47.6	71.8	77.9	91.5
3.2	42.9	69.2	71.6	89.0
3.3	66.7	79.5	80.0	90.2
4.1	47.6	69.2	74.7	84.1
4.2	50.0	64.1	69.5	81.7
4.3	42.9	79.5	62.1	81.7
5.1	40.5	64.1	63.2	78.1
5.2	47.6	84.6	81.1	85.4
5.3	52.4	82.1	66.3	81.7
6.1	88.1	82.1	92.6	95.1
6.2	85.7	92.3	96.8	93.9
6.3	85.7	92.3	88.4	92.7
7.1	47.6	69.2	65.3	80.5
7.2	59.5	79.5	86.3	92.7
8.1	69.0	79.5	72.6	82.9

Explanation: Respondents with no prior workshop experience (31 per cent of the total sample) were divided into two categories, those with knowledge and those without. In Table 5 (columns 2 and 3) the percentage noted in each cell is the percentage of those with knowledge on that specific item out of the total who had no workshop experience. The percentages for both the first and second measurement are given. The respondents with prior workshop experience (69 per cent of the total sample) were similarly divided. In columns 4 and 5, the percentage reflected in each cell is the percentage of those with knowledge on that specific item out of the total who had prior workshop experience. The percentages for both the first and second measurement are given.

change in knowledge levels is insignificant (Table 3.4) and the change in opinion is significant (Table 3.5). In the case of 5.3 (community controls process), it is fair to deduce that knowledge levels increased significantly (Table 3.4) and in this case lead to a change of opinion about being in control of the process (Table 3.5). In the case of Question 6 (local authority as development agent) and Question 8 (sincerity of state) it appears that neither knowledge levels nor opinion levels changed significantly (Tables 3.4 and 3.6). It can be deduced that respondents did not gain any further knowledge on these issues or changed their opinion significantly. It appears that once the respondents have gained knowledge about the role of the local authority and the sincerity of the state, no further input will contribute significantly to change that.

The cross-tabulation of with workshop attendance and knowledge are reflected in Table 3.6.

The analysis of the influence of attendance at workshops on respondents with knowledge, indicates that those respondents, who have never attended workshops before, reverted more to 'no knowledge' answers than those who have. That explains the lower percentages (i.e. those with knowledge) in the 'no workshop' category. Subsequently, the percentage respondents with knowledge were much higher in the category of workshop attendance. In the first measurement this was the case in all the items or practically the same in the case of 2.4. In the second measurement it was evident that the percentages with knowledge of those who had not previously attended workshops were much higher in comparison with the first measurement in all the items except in the case of 6.1 (facilitation). In terms of the counts, this only represents 2-3 respondents. This was also the case with those who had prior workshop experience, although it did not occur in all the items namely 2.2, 2.4 and 6.2. The implication is that workshop information input most probably increases the level of knowledge to participate.

In what follows, the research findings are interpreted, conclusions drawn and recommendations made.

Conclusion

The theme of this paper is the practice of participatory democracy and its links to local development. The context is the current policy trend to consider the local authority as the core development agent. The mechanism for linking democracy and development is the concept of integrated development planning. South Africa, a relatively newly formed democracy, has put legislation, political and social structures in place to support the transformation it intended. The question that remains and that is the topic of this study, is whether the IDP initiative is a sincere attempt to install authentic participation in respect of the local community or is this another scheme for political expediency?

The main findings of this survey are the following:

a) Pertaining to the question of representation, the profile of the people who attended these workshops does not reflect that of the population of the region. It does however represent the language ratio and include all age groups, both sexes, all race groups as well as most of the interest groups that were indicated in the model of the PDC (1998). On face value, it appeared that a high percentage of governmental organizations (councillors included) were represented. Whether a full representation of all citizens in the region was accomplished, is, therefore, in doubt but this does not compromise the validity of the findings. It appears, however, that local authorities will have to clarify the nature of representation that will serve democracy. They might have to make a choice between the amount of effort they are going to expend to ascertain a non-elitist representation, that genuinely reflects the composition and the interests of the community, and the efficiency of the process.
b) A continued series of workshops and repeated attendance by the same participants provided the opportunity to practice local democracy in aid of development planning. A main spin-off was that a fairly high level of information and knowledge (understanding) of the process of development planning evolved among the local people. In this instance, workshops constituted the heart of public participation. Knowledge levels were found to be high about all the aspects of the IDP process, especially in cases where respondents were subjected to prior informative and interactive workshops. Knowledge levels also changed significantly on most of the aspects after the workshop, which implies that empowerment took place.
c) The workshops, however, do not necessarily affect opinions or perceptions about the development of the planning process within civil society. The aspects where the opinions changed significantly, reflected a positive attitude about their contribution and that they perceived their contribution as putting control into the hands of the community. This can be interpreted as a reflection on the fact that people feel the process is democratically sound. On other aspects, fixed attitudes apparently do not change easily. Mostly these attitudes are positive but informal observations point to the fact that cynicism prevails in certain areas and among certain groups. Attendance numbers are low and interest in the process is dwindling. In reference to observations of workshop

procedure, information dissemination was non-interactive except for clarification. This could have impacted on the fact that attitudes did not change significantly.

d) The process followed by the West Coast District Council leaves no doubt that all mechanisms were put in place to create the best possible situation for authentic public participation. This has a bearing on efforts to install sound representation through interest groups, as well as the nature of information given to empower people to participate. The results of the first round of integrated development planning must be interpreted against the background of the multiple constraints faced by all local authorities in the early stages of a newly passed policy. There is no reason to believe that the process was not democratically sound and it is considered as being valid. This does not mean that the next (and further) rounds should not be pursued with the necessary caution, keeping in mind the fundamental limitations of the current local authority system to meet the requirements of policy.

Conclusions that may be drawn from this study are listed as follows:

a) Representation and participation are invariably inter-linked as civil society should participate equitably if democracy is to be served through authentic participation.
b) The workshop as an instrument of information dissemination and participation contributes to higher levels of knowledge and subsequent empowerment of participants. Together with representation, clarification is needed on the most efficient content as well as method of conducting these workshops.
c) Despite efforts to ensure the best possible for authentic participation and subsequent democratization, the policy embeds fundamental limitations that will have to be ironed out as the process evolves in forthcoming rounds.

References

Bekker, S. (December 1994, unpublished) 'The Forum Movement in South Africa – Breakthrough in the 1990s'.

Bernstein, H. (1997) *Social Change in the South African Countryside? Land and Production, Poverty and Power. Land Reform and Agrarian Change in Southern Africa*, An Occasional Paper Series, no. 4. Programme for Land and Agrarian Studies, School of Government, University of the Western Cape, Bellville.

Botes, L. (1998) 'It Takes Many to Tango: The Organisational and Institutional Dynamics of Community Participation in Development', Paper delivered at the Development Society of Southern Africa, Biennial Conference, Johannesburg: 7–8 April 1999.

Bryman, A. and Cramer, D. (1997) *Quantitative Data Analysis with SPSS for Windows*, Routledge, London.

Chazan, N. (1982) 'The New Politics of Participation en Tropical Africa', *Comparative Politics*, vol. 14, pp. 169–189.

Constitution (1996) *The Constitution of the Republic of South Africa Act* (108 of 1996).

De Beer, F. (1996) 'Reconstruction and Development as People Centred Development: Challenges Facing Development Administration', *Reconstruction and Development*, vol. 26, pp. 65–80.

Du Toit, P. (1995) *State-Building and Democracy in Southern Africa*, HSRC Publishers, Pretoria.

Groenewald, C.J. (1997) 'Constraints in the Running of Local RDP Forums', In P. Styger, S. Meyer, and A. Saayman (eds), *Conflicting Challenges in Development*. Selected Proceedings of the Biennial Conference of Development Society of Southern Africa, Stellenbosch, 25–27 September 1996, pp. 379–399.

Huntington, S.P. (1986) *Political Order in Changing Societies*, Yale University Press, London.

Levin, R. and Weiner, D. (1996) 'The politics of land reform in South Africa after apartheid: Perspectives, problems, prospects', In H. Bernstein, (ed.), *The Agrarian Question in South Africa. The Journal of Peasant Studies*, vol. 23, pp. 93–119.

Levin, R. and Weiner, D. (1997) 'Towards the development of a popular and participatory rural land reform program in South Africa', in: R. Levin, R. Weiner and D. Weiner (eds), *'No more Tears ...' Struggles for Land in Mpumalanga, South Africa*, Africa World Press, Trenton, NJ.

Midgley, J., *et al.* (1986) *Community Participation, Social Development and the State*, Methuen, London.

MPA and CD (Ministry of Provincial Affairs and Constitutional Development) (1998) *The White Paper on Local Government*, Department of Constitutional Development, Pretoria.

PAWC (Provincial Administration of the Western Cape) (1997) *Voorgestelde Proses vir die Opstel van Geïntegreerde Ontwikkelingsraamwerke en Geïntegreerde Ontwikkelingsplanne*, PAWC, Cape Town.

PDC (Provincial Development Council) (1998) *Development Through Partnerships*. First Annual Report of the Western Cape Provincial Development Council, November 1996–March 1998, PDC, Cape Town.

Pillay, D. (1996) 'Social Movements, Development and Democracy in Post Apartheid South Africa', in J.K. Coetzee and J. Graaff (eds) *Reconstruction, Development and People*, Halfway House, Cape Town, pp. 324–352.

Pycroft, C. (1998) 'Integrated Development Planning or Strategic Paralysis? Municipal Development During the Local Government Transition and Beyond' *Development South Africa*, vol. 15, pp. 151–163.

RSA. WPJ (1994) 'White Paper on Reconstruction and Development', *Government Gazette*, vol. 353, no. 16085, Government Printer, Pretoria.

Ul Haq, M. (1995) *Reflections on Human Development*, Oxford University Press. Oxford.

United Nations (1975) *Popular Participation in Decision Making for Development*, UNESCO, New York.

WCII (West Coast Investment Initiative) (1997) *West Coast Investment Initiative Appraisal Document*, Department of Trade and Industry, Cape Town.

Wessels, D. (1998) 'Die Heropbou en Ontwikkelingsprogram: 'n Analitiese Perspektief'. *Acta Academica*, vol. 30, pp. 65–109.

Chapter 4
Tlalpan Neighbourhood Committees: A True Participatory Option

Arturo Flores

Introduction

When the left wing PRD won the 1997 Mexico City governor election there was hope that the new administration was going to impose a different way of doing politics. Citizen involvement was assumed as a priority by the new government and neighbourhood committees were conceived as a mechanism to prevent unilateral decision-making by local authorities, corruption and abuse of power. Neighbourhood committees were supposed to be a true democratic option for neighbours, authorities and social organizations interested in working as community mediators between official and public interests. But what were some of the main problems faced during the first stage of the implementation process? Were the people of Mexico City and its surroundings prepared for taking part in such a participatory initiative? What are the main strengths and weaknesses of this mechanism? The aim of this chapter is to analyse how this participatory initiative has been carried out. Providing firstly a background of different participatory initiatives previously implemented in Mexico, the second part of the chapter analyses how the PRD implemented the 1998 participatory law. The chapter continues with the presentation of the social composition of one municipality, Tlalpan, and a brief analysis of the main problems affecting each of the social groups. The next section is dedicated to comparing previously established social organizations to the newly created structures, finalising by highlighting the strengths and weaknesses of the whole implementation process.

Background of Participatory Initiatives in Mexico

The background of participatory forms of local democracy in Mexico dates from 1917, when President Carranza[1] visualised the importance of having local initiatives of citizen participation, although it was not until almost thirty years later that the first real participatory projects were put into practice. One of the first experiments was launched in 1940 in the southern state of Veracruz, where Governor Adolfo Ruiz Cortines created the groups for moral, civic and citizen improvement. The scheme consisted in promoting mutual co-operation between authorities and citizens. Neighbours would provide either labour or materials and for each peso saved authorities would provide another one. This project proved to be successful, as to day some of these structures still remain. Despite this successful story, most citizen organizations of later creation were used as vehicles for political control or social blackmailing.

During the administration of Mayor Hank Gonzalez (1976–1982) in Mexico City, the structure of what is known as jefes de manzana (block representatives) was established. This structure was supposed to work as a channel of communication between local authorities and citizens, informing local officials about the major problems faced by each neighbourhood and advocating for possible solutions. Despite the good intentions, block representatives were used as a mechanism of political bargaining and control. As stated by Lazurtegui, these representatives have been used as an apparatus of political approval and as a group of 'distinguished' citizens who accompany politicians throughout their visits (cited in Zermeno, 1997). Another negative element of this initiative is the fact that none of these representatives has been democratically elected (see Safa, 1997), as all of them were appointed by a few non-representative 'communitarian leaders'.

In an attempt to improve the way in which participatory mechanisms operated, President de la Madrid created in 1983 the Sistema Nacional de Planeacion Democratica (National System for Democratic Planning). The aim of the SNPD was to promote social and governmental co-operation in all matters concerning municipal and regional development (see Rodriguez, 1997). Although the initiative seemed logical in stopping or at least diminishing corruption and political control which local caciques[2] comfortably exercised, it was never fully put into practice and it failed.[3]

A sad incident triggered informal social participatory initiatives in Mexico. When, a vast area of Mexico City was destroyed by the 1985 earthquake, neighbours,[4] students and a large number of 'normal' citizens led the city's reconstruction. As a result of this informal effort, an abundant number of spontaneously created neighbourhood or social associations with communitarian interests came into existence. The difference of these organizations, when compared with those structures or initiatives promoted by the government, was that these organizations had true leaderships and not imposed leaders like those present in previously promoted official schemes. The proliferation of such associations contributed to strengthening Mexico City's political culture and as a result of these efforts it has become one of the most politically active cities in the country. Some of these associations were the bases of what became one of the most successfully implemented participatory projects, SOLIDARIDAD or solidarity.

SOLIDARIDAD, the core social project of President Salinas (1988-1994), worked as an initiative that proved that if the citizenry was offered the possibility of working in specific integrated and well organised communitarian structures, then government officials could expect to have a positive response from the population. Neighbourhoods and neighbours were grouped into solidarity committees that would engage as workers, especially in those projects aiming at the provision of such basic infrastructure services as sewage or piped potable water. Solidarity was remarkably successful in motivating community participation and in delivering services that otherwise would not have been provided; furthermore, SOLIDARIDAD became a symbol of unity and progress, and proved to be one of the best means of political control.[5] It was only after the 1994 crisis[6] that the success of SOLIDARIDAD came to grief. After the economic crisis, the programme became a synonym for catastrophe and a reminder of one of the most hated administrations this country has had in recent years – the Salinas administration.

Meanwhile as the official party, the PRI, promoted SOLIDARIDAD as the only possible way of achieving social progress, opposition parties were also interested in promoting their own participatory initiatives in the states or municipalities where they ruled. The PAN (National Action Party, right wing) under the administration of Carlos Medina Plascencia (1989-1991) as mayor of Leon, Guanajuato established the *Direccion de Integracion Ciudadana y Educacion* (Department of Citizen Integration and Education). This department aimed to work as a link between authorities, neighbourhood Organizations or any other types of citizen group; the idea was to avoid traditional priista structures of dominance. In San Pedro, Nuevo Leon, the administration of Rogelio Sada (1994–1997) created the Consejos Consultivos Ciudadanos (Citizen Consultation Councils) where citizens had the chance to participate and advise municipal authorities in policy matters and communitarian projects.[7] Also, locally elected Juntas de Vecinos (Neighbourhood Boards) were established as a channel of interaction between authorities and citizens.

Regarding the other major opposition party, the PRD, (Democratic Revolution Party, left wing) under the mandate of Cuauhtemoc Cardenas as mayor of Mexico City (1997–2000) some participatory initiatives were also promoted. The main project launched by the PRD was the promotion of a Citizen Participation Law, where such participatory forms as the referendum and the plebiscite were given a legal status. The PRD was also trying to get rid of pre-existing clientistic practices. This initiative will be analysed in the next section.

The PRD and the new Citizen Participation Law[8]

Since the 1997 governor campaign, the involvement of the citizenry was perceived by the PRD as a strategy for gaining confidence and legitimacy within the Mexico City electorate. After experiencing administrative deficiencies, high degrees of corruption and urban insecurity from precedent priista (official party) administrations, the PRD offered a political scheme where the population, would play a more active role. Empowering the 'average' citizen was projected as a core element of their government programme.[9] The result of the 1997 Mexico City governor election favoured the PRD and reforms to give more power to neighbourhood Organizations were soon promoted. It was in 1998 when a new Citizen Participation Law was approved by the Mexico City Congress. The Citizen Participation Law set the legal basis which permitted the population to participate more actively in decision-making processes and although it is true that the law did not proved to be a perfect document, it proved to be an action in the right direction.[10] The importance of participation is conceived as an invigorating, personally fulfilling strategy to pose an alternative to a 'mechanised, bureaucratised, dehumanised society' (Lasch, cited in Hain, 1980, p. 16). Greater participation would contribute to individual empowerment and, as a consequence, increment governor's legitimacy.

The CPL gave for the first time a legal status to such participatory forms as the plebiscite and the referendum; it also regulates what is known as iniciativa popular or popular initiative, which allows citizens to create, modify or reform laws. The CPL also supports other types of communitarian initiatives, such as the consulta vecinal or neighbourhood consultation, and other neighbourhood co-operation projects.

A second step taken after approving the citizen participation law was to promote the initiative within the different municipalities or delegaciones to enact the new legislation.[11] Government officials faced some problems during this stage of the implementation process as political or personal interests were being threatened by the enforcement of the law; as a result of this dispute, in some neighbourhoods, the reforms were received with joy, while in others were totally rejected.[12] In the case of Tlalpan, which is the municipality or delegacion to be presented in this paper, a mix of both took place.

Although the intentions of the law can be defined as positive, it did not consider such important aspects as the fact that in Mexico City there are still some rural areas that cannot be divided as neighbourhoods. The law did not foresee the possibility of creating such alternative structures as rural forums or other forms of organising the citizenry in those areas, or maintaining pre-existing forms of citizen organization like caciques.

Tlalpan

Tlalpan is a delegacion situated in the south of Mexico City. It can be defined as a municipality of contrasts, there are zones occupied by members of the upper classes, a vast area inhabited by members of the middle class, a considerable section outnumbered by members of the lower classes, and it even possesses some rural areas. In most of the areas above-mentioned what is known as 'natural leaders' existed before the approval of the Citizen Participation Law and communitarian work was not new for them. Although each of these groups has different objectives and priorities, we can say that they are perfectly aware that their involvement in the matters that affect their community is very important for solving their respective problems. The aim of the new legislation was to strengthen and legitimate neighbourhood organizations, something that we can say it has partially achieved, as in most cases previously established communitarian structures were used as a base for the development of the new neighbourhood framework.

Neighbourhood elections should have been held in each of the 140 territorial units or neighbourhoods in which Tlalpan was divided, but voting did not take place in all of them. There were several reasons for this, lack of information, apathy of the population or confronted political interests, were some of the main justifications provided by neighbours and authorities.[13] An issue worth highlighting is that certain groups preferred to continue operating as 'independent' organizations and not as neighbourhood committees, as they think they might lose some of their negotiating power. They feel that the CPL would deprive them of their capacities, or that they would be subordinated to a legal framework under which their influence would be reduced. An example of this is the organization headed by Socorro Jimenez,[14] who stated that they preferred to remain as an independent organization and not to join the new scheme as they have been operating with positive results for more than fifteen years. Socorro and the people she represents did not find any advantages in the new scheme, as according to their view, the new scheme does not contribute to increasing their decision-making power.

An aspect to emphasise is that Tlalpan is a quite politically active municipality. This political activity has lead to the identification of political affinities within the members of the recently created neighbourhood organizations. The delegacion or municipal authority has openly accepted that political interests or parties have 'corrupted' the neutral essence of the neighbourhood committees. According to the CPL political parties should not have been involved in the election of neighbourhood committee leaders, but this did happen.[15] Political parties supported community leaders to become neighbourhood representatives, or vice-versa, neighbourhood leaders offered their services to political parties with the promise of working for those organizations in the future. This has proven to be one of the main difficulties affecting the consolidation of the committees, as for example neighbours belonging to the PRD would not participate with a 'priista' (official party) communitarian leader, or vice-versa. This type of dispute has caused the withdrawal of citizens who were interested in participating and who now are sceptical about the whole raison d'être of the neighbourhood committees. As each of the committees is identified with a political ideology (see table one below for some examples), municipal authorities have been practically 'forced' to accept the existence of a political party, NGO or social group behind, most, neighbourhood committees.

Table 4.1 Community Representatives and Political Preferences

Name of representative	Neighbourhood location	Political preference
Jeronimo Valdez Garcia	San Miguel Topilejo	PRI
Miguel Pichardo Galindo	Santa Cruz	PAN
Benjamin Torres Becerra	San Pedro Martir	PRD
Maria Guadalupe Morones	Cruz Xochintepec	PRD
Jose Alfredo Moreno	Los Angeles	No political affinity

The majority of committee leaders interviewed perceive the neighbourhood structure as a way of gaining a political position, maintaining their influence over the zone where they live, or keeping a status as a community negotiator. We cannot generalise, but that is the trend detected.[16]

The views of the Rich and the Poor in Tlalpan

The diversity of the neighbourhoods that compose Tlalpan provides a contrasting perspective of the problems faced by each of them, as it is not the same to live in a middle or upper class neighbourhood as to live in a lower class one. Middle and upper class neighbourhoods would try to protect their environment (i.e. they are concerned about such issues as ecology or keeping certain living standards) and mostly would not have any further political interest. These sectors of the population (upper and middle) have already covered their primary needs (infrastructure wise and materially speaking) they can struggle against political parties and would not accept the imposition of certain ideas by dominant leaders.

On the other hand, lower class neighbourhoods are mostly led by someone with very specific political interests. The mediator role of the neighbourhood leader puts him/her in a privileged position, as he/she is going to have the possibility of asking for political favours as a condition to maintaining the stability of the neighbourhood. From the authority's viewpoint, the groups basically enables the authority to deal with one leader and not with 50 neighbours.

This social difference represents one of the main elements that has caused problems in implementing the new legislation. Firstly, according to the law all neighbourhoods are the same, which is definitely not true. The contrast between those areas inhabited by the upper classes and those by the lower classes is a primary disparity, for the needs of the people in the different areas are going to vary widely. The law also does not consider a large area which can be considered as being rural and where the citizen participation law could not be applied as in an urban area.[17] Secondly, the customs neighbours have in urban areas cannot be compared to those people have in rural areas. There is greater solidarity between members of rural areas contrasting with the 'coldness' prevailing in urban regions. Thirdly, the way in which the neighbourhoods were divided left out 'natural' pre-established territorial divisions, and this has meant that certain neighbours do not show any interest in joining a communitarian organization or forming a neighbourhood committee.[18]

So far we have spoken about the difficulties for implementing this initiative faced by neighbours, but what about the official structure in charge of consolidating it? What role do the bureaucrats behind the implementation of the new CPL play? Do they facilitate or obstruct its implementation? Do they favour certain political or social interests? A view of how Tlalpan's bureaucratic structure operates is presented in the next section.

The Bureaucratic Structure

The municipal or official structure that operates the neighbourhood committees is the subdelegacion de enlace territorial. The subdelegado is the citizen participation director and he has under his command the co-ordination of the five territorial zones in which Tlalpan is divided. The subdelegacion de enlace territorial channels all public demands to the governmental area that can best solve the public issue under consideration. This area plays a key political role, as it 'filters' all community demands, prioritising them and assisting all groups, in theory, without regard to their political affinities.

The Subdelegacion de Enlace Territorial lies on five sections (Centre of Tlalpan, Villa Coapa, Padierna-Miguel Hidalgo, Ajusco Medio and Pueblos Rurales). Each of these areas has a subdelegado territorial or citizen participation co-ordinator. The function of these offices is to receive all the demands from the population, this could be either via neighbourhood committees, through NGOs or by using other types of organizations. This section is constantly interacting with neighbourhood committees, and if possible, subdelegados-territoriales would solve certain problems before sending them to the subdelegacion. Subdelegados-territoriales operate different schemes to offer solutions for community problems. For example, let us say that some neighbours would like to know the cost of introducing piped water to their neighbourhood; after analysis, the area authorities find that unfortunately costs are too high and that there are not enough funds for the project. The subdelegacion territorial could offer this community the possibility of funding the cost of the majority of the project, but neighbours would assume the cost for the rest of the project. In some schemes neighbours also have the option to co-operate with their labour.[19] Each subdelegacion territorial has a project leader, who is going to prioritise each community demand. Project leaders also have the responsibility of following every case, and within a determined period of time must give feedback about the final outcome of all demands.

Below the project leaders are all the neighbourhood committee leaders. Neighbourhood committees have the opportunity of organising their groups as they wish, meeting as often as they consider. Most committee leaders meet on a monthly basis, and if something urgent arises between meetings they would organise an emergency meeting to deal with the issue. Committee leaders do not receive a salary or have access to a budget, they work in a purely altruistic way, and in some cases they receive economic support from neighbours, just to cover certain paper-work expenses.

The relationship of each committee leader with his/her neighbours is going to vary depending on the social circumstances surrounding each neighbourhood. For example, neighbourhood leaders living in a middle/upper class neighbourhood are more demanding towards authorities (they would expect that authorities would solve immediately their demands, leaving no space for negotiation) and more open to listen to each other. Meanwhile neighbourhood leaders from lower class neighbourhoods would be more dominant towards their neighbours, and could leave a space for negotiating with authorities. It is due to this factor that their demands are not placed in a primary position, unless they do something radical.[20]

The way in which local authorities deal with public demands is a crucial factor in determining whether the public problem is solved. Facilitating people's access to local authorities and having an appropriate system of communication between departments are two elements which are crucial for solving community problems. In the case of Tlalpan, the structures mentioned above seem to be working fine in the 'opening' issue (meaning facilitating people's access), but sometimes bureaucrats seem to stop or obstruct the solution of some projects.[21] There is also competition instead of co-operation between certain departments of the delegacion contributing to stagnation in the resolution of certain problems.

According to Eliseo Moyao, who is the Citizen Participation director, fifty percent of the neighbourhood forums created in Tlalpan are working properly. By working properly he means that approximately seventy committees are still meeting on a regular basis and that without regard to their political preferences they are still dealing with community issues. From the point of view of the authorities, in this primary stage of implementation, it is important to try to keep the groups united and to consolidate them as a true alternative when compared to other social groups or to isolated leaderships that previously existed.

Formal Forums vs Other Types of Organizations

In theory, the initiative to create the neighbourhood committees is to reform local leaderships, to promote democratic values, and to involve the public in decision-making processes, but has this really happened? It is certainly true that the Citizen Participation Law provides, although not entirely, the legal framework to establish neighbourhood forums with an official status which promote local initiatives and get involved in social issues. But it is also certain that independent organizations can have more informal power than those associations grouped under the formal scheme. An example we can mention is Julieta's informal association.[22] For three generations her family has fought for the construction of basic infrastructure projects in her neighbourhood. They decided not to group as a neighbourhood committee because from her point of view, the only way to achieve progress is by 'pushing' local authorities directly and not through neighbourhood committees. Today, Julieta gives advice to some neighbourhood group leaders in order to show them the best ways to proceed in order to be listened to by local authorities.

The example above mentioned could contribute to jeopardising the whole sense of the neighbourhood committees, as this type of informal or traditional organization is considered by many interviewed to be more effective than the newly created structures. It is also true that neighbourhood committees' performance could be improved in the future, once neighbours get used to the advantages available in the new legislation. Authorities also have an important role to play in strengthening the potential of the committees, as if they continue giving preference to pre-established organizations, then the forums would not be perceived as having the necessary weight to be officially used as the best channel for problem solving. Local authorities have to ponder to which groups they give preference for solving social problems. The first stage of the implementation process is certainly going to be longer than expected, as it is not that easy to consolidate this new alternative of citizen participation.

Another element to take into account when comparing other organizations to neighbourhood committees is the economic factor. Most community organizations have a budget to promote the solution of certain social demands, a budget which neighbourhood committees do not posses. Although the aim of social groups is not to make profits, the truth is that maybe neighbourhood committees need authorities' economic support to motivate people to take a more active role. But also if provided, economic support could become a negative element for the committees, as the struggle for this position could be perceived as valuable for the economic revenues it offers and not for the social benefits that could be achieved when occupying it.

The involvement of political parties has also negatively affected the implementation of the core principles presented in the participatory initiative. In some areas, neighbourhood committees have been transformed into a strategic position for doing local politics. This has happened when community leaders use the Citizen Participation Law for personal interests instead of for public ones or vice-versa, when political parties support certain candidates for achieving political positions.[23]

Strengths and Weaknesses of the Initiative

In the case of Mexico, it can be argued that the fact that participatory initiatives are still considered a novelty has affected considerably the way in which this initiative in particular and others previously put into practice have been instrumented. Participating as an average citizen in discussions that are directly related to how policies would be adopted and implemented in any community is something that still has not become a tradition or a common practice. Many Mexicans are still used to accepting any decision made by local or federal authorities, highlighting the importance of public involvement for the success or failure of this and other initiatives. Community involvement, accepting each other's (political, social and even ethnic) differences, is a practice that needs to be accepted by most of the people interacting in these community groups.

The fact that most neighbourhoods committees have adopted a political position makes these organizations the centre of a dispute for political power. If political institutions continue operating, especially in the less well off, or less educated areas, then maybe it would be better to openly accept this fact, letting political parties compete for these positions as well, as happens in other countries. An example that can be mention that is directly related to the point mentioned above, is the way in which neighbourhood leaders got involved in the 2000 presidential election. The 2000 presidential election affected the functioning of the neighbourhood committees, as some leaders were tempted by political parties to influence their neighbours' vote. Off the record,[24] I was told that certain neighbourhood leaders accepted receiving a salary or some type of concession for defending determined interests. The issue of controlling neighbourhood leaders has highlighted the relevance that these organizations have at the local level. Furthermore, it foresees an increase of their political importance in the future.

Another point to consider is the fact that caciques continue operating, offering two challenges for the authorities. Firstly, although Tlalpan's neighbourhood committees proffer citizens the opportunity for taking an active community role, this possibility has not been fully put into practice, as in certain neighbourhoods (especially in those inhabited by the lower classes) caciques do not respect the new scheme and carry on doing things their way.[25] Regarding this issue, if the authorities want to involve the average citizen, then, they will have to find the way to convince caciques to respect and implement the new scheme. This is certainly not an easy task, as diverse sectors of the population[26] openly accept the role that caciques play, leaving little space for change and practically abolishing all democratic hope.

From the opposite perspective, as long as the authorities continue to use caciques as an instrument for keeping political stability,[27] then this or any other participatory initiative is never going to be consolidated. If authorities, on the one hand, give citizens the possibility to participating and occupying positions as community representatives, then they should also forget about using caciques to solve certain social problems, leaving all the responsibility on citizens.

One of the aspects that can endanger this neighbourhood initiative is the fact that in some cases informal organizations are more successful than the 'official' ones. This can certainly have a negative impact on neighbourhood leaders as they could feel that the work they are doing is not worth it, as other organizations could be more influential than the officially created neighbourhood structures. Without diminishing the impact of previously established social organizations, the authorities have to find the balance between neighbourhood committees and this type of organization.

The main area in which the authorities are going to have to focus their attention is on how to deal with such a different socially composed community without favouring a group in particular. We can say that the way in which these participatory forums organise is going to depend on their income and education, at least in Mexico City it has proven to be like this. Meanwhile the upper classes organise by themselves without any advice, and they sometimes even ignore those structures created by their municipal authorities, (i.e. neighbourhood forums). At the opposite end, the lower classes are dependent on authorities as they do not have enough economic resources or they are not able to organise by themselves.

Notes

1. It was in the 1917 constitution that Carranza stated that the place where democracy starts is the municipality and that the population should participate in decision making processes at this level.
2. These totalitarian leaders play a primary role in the success or failure of local initiatives. Their role is to act as 'lobbyists' between governmental institutions and their neighbours. This informal type of leadership can be more real than that exercised by elected officials, as he/she is normally perceived as a figure of respect and someone who is concerned about his or her community. The methods used by *cacique* are not necessarily going to be in accordance with human rights. A *cacique* is going to try to keep power over the community, using any necessary means. Especially in rural areas, *caciques* can be associated with terror, murder, rape and commit all sorts of barbarities (see Grindle, 1977).
3. According to Rodriguez (1997) this experiment failed because neither citizens nor authorities were ready to interact under such schemes. As will be shown later in this chapter, due to Mexico's diverse social composition, even today there are difficulties and scepticism when implementing participatory initiatives.
4. A breakthrough that Patricia Safa (1997) and other researchers of citizen participation (such as, Zermeno, 1997) highlight is the way in which neighbourhood organizations erupted weeks after the 1985 earthquake (where approximately 100,000 people died). When official authorities proved unprepared to handle the emergency, these informally established social groups became the bases for social organizations of later creation (i.e. Xochimilco, Santa Fe, La Merced and Tepito).
5. It is important to mention that SOLIDARIDAD was directly associated with the PRI (official party). The party used the programme as its political banner and the government used the programme and all its structure to motivate the population to get involved in the initiative. At election times, the public was reminded of all that SOLIDARIDAD had done for them (see Rodriguez, 1997).
6. The 1994 economic crisis is known in Mexico as the 'mistake of December' or in Latin American, the 'Tequila effect'. For more than six years, the peso, was kept artificially strong due to large amounts of short-term speculative foreign investment. In December 1994, after the new administration (the Zedillo administration 1994-2000) took office, an adjustment of the peso-dollar exchange rate had to be made. The result was a near complete loss of confidence, the peso free-falling to half its pre-crisis value, inflation averaging 52 per cent, interest rates peaking at 80 per cent and a seven per cent contraction of real GDP in 1995 (Doyle *et al.*, 1999).
7. For more examples of opposition to participatory initiatives see Rodriguez (1997).

8. It is important to mention that for the elaboration of this chapter, a series of interviews were held during the summer of 2000. I would like to thank all the people in Tlalpan (authorities and neighbours) who agreed to be interviewed, especially to those in charge of the office of Dr. Sergio Zermeno. Without their help, it would not have been possible to write this chapter.
9. Under the slogan 'a city for all', the RDP visualized an active citizenry, one which would have the possibility of being involved in decision making processes and who also would participate as an observer and evaluator of the administration.
10. According to Goodman, Clark and Katznelson (cited in Hain, 1980, p. 15) and Kotler (1969), it is by organizing the citizenry into groups to tackle urban problems that positive results can be achieved, results that the established system cannot deliver.
11. It is important to mention that under an atmosphere dominated by a strong federal government, the implementation of public policies becomes a difficult task for lower levels of government, such as state or local authorities. Federal authorities exercise an absolute political and economic control over states and municipalities. The plans developed in Mexico City are going to be given priority over those elaborated within states or municipalities. The presence of personnel from the capital can also contribute to policy failure, as confrontations with state and municipal officials can take place (see Grindle, 1977).
12. In some neighbourhoods, 'traditional' community leaders, more commonly known as *caciques*, opposed its implementation or obstructed the promotion of the CLP within their neighbourhoods of influence.
13. This information was collected in the summer of the year 2000. During this period I held a series of interviews with official authorities and some of Tlalpan's main community leaders (e.g. Socorro Jimenez, Julieta and Mr. Rosas).
14. Socorro Jimenez is a community leader who represents around 300 families and who operates in a semi-rural area of Tlalpan.
15. Article 94 of the Citizen Participation Law states that it is not allowed to use any colours when competing in a neighbourhood election. It is also stated that neither political parties nor official authorities will be allowed to participate in these elections.
16. After speaking to more than 20 community representatives, most of them openly admitted the political implications of being a neighbourhood leader. According to those interviewed, being a neighbourhood committee leader could be used as a platform by people searching for a political post, as there is constant interaction between community leaders, authorities and political parties.
17. Although Article 80 of the CLP states that in each urban or rural area a neighbourhood committee would be created, the law does not consider what would happen in case the population did not find the structure of the neighbourhood committees as the most effective one.
18. Some neighbourhoods had to join communities or attend meetings in places far from previously determined locations. According to some of the people interviewed, such issues as travelling long distances and differences between the needs of each neighbourhood contributed to the lack of interest.
19. In a scheme called *fideicomiso* neighbours have this possibility.
20. It is also important to consider that most demands coming from lower classes are projects which are harder to solve as they are mainly basic infrastructure projects with a high economic cost for official authorities. Meanwhile, middle and upper class demands are simpler to work out, as most of them would be linked to keeping certain living standards, the architecture of a zone, fixing a park or a street etc.
21. According to a neighbourhood committee leader who asked me to omit his name, some

government officials gave preference to those projects led by PRD community leaders and not to those presented by a leader belonging to a different political organization.

22. Julieta defends the interests of around 1,500 families. She is recognized, by local authorities, as one of Tlalpan's most charismatic informal leaders.
23. A case that can be mentioned is the one of Mr. Rosas, who is directly linked to the PRI and who has been constantly criticising for opposing initiatives promoted by the party in power, the PRD.
24. As part of the interviews held this summer in Tlalpan.
25. We can mention the way in which Mr. Rosas's social organization continues working as before the 1998 Citizen participation law was approved.
26. A good example is how people keep on supporting Mr. Rosas, who has been working as a 'social benefactor' for more than thirty years. Although in practice he has not acted as a very democratic leader, people still thank him for acting as a mediator achieving all sorts of social actions (e.g. introducing basic infrastructure services).
27. Under certain circumstances the role of *caciques* could be perceived as positive. *Caciques* could be used by authorities as an instrument of political control, especially when dealing with problems from lower income areas, as they know better than local officials how to negotiate with the population and in some cases they are more trusted than authorities (i.e. Julieta or Socorro Jimenez). We also have to distinguish between different types of social leaders or *caciques,* as not all of them would put their interests before those of the community. For a more complete explanation of this love-hate relationship between authorities and *caciques* see Grindle (1977).

References

Doyle, R., Scott, D. and Crimmins, C. (1999) 'Was The "Tequila Effect" Rational?', *Student Economic Review 1999*, vol. 13, University of Dublin, Trinity College. [Online]Available at http://www.tcd.ie/Economics/econ_review.htm, 8 December-2000.

Grindle, M. (1977) *Bureaucrats, Politicians and Peasants in Mexico: A case Study in Public Policy*, California University Press, Berkeley, CA.

Hain, P. (1980) *Neighbourhood Participation*, Temple Smith, London.

Kotler, M. (1969) *Neighbourhood Government*, Bobbs Merrill, New York.

Rodriguez, V. (1997) *Decentralization in Mexico*, Westview Press, Boulder, CO.

Safa, P. (1997) *Noticias Locales Problemas Metropolitanos: Democracia y Organizaciones Vecinales en la Ciudad de Mexico*, Centro de Estudios Sociales de la UNAM, Mexico.

Zermeno, S. (1997) *Movimientos Sociales e Identidades Colectivas*, Centro de Estudios Sociales de la UNAM, Mexico.

Chapter 5

Decentralization and Citizen Participation in Barcelona

Georgina Blakeley

During the 1980s Barcelona city council embarked on a dual process of decentralising its organizational structures and enhancing citizen participation. Neither of these processes can be understood without reference to the other: decentralization was key to improving citizen participation in Barcelona by bringing the administration closer to the citizen, whilst citizen participation was seen as an integral part of, and justification for, decentralization. Commitment on the part of the city council to both these processes has been clear during the last two decades, which suggests that liberal democracy can contain within it more instances and experiments of participation than it does at present. However, it is also the case that citizen participation in Barcelona has gradually declined, which suggests that there are difficulties in sustaining participation within liberal democracies over time.

The Macro-Context

The impetus behind decentralization and citizen participation in Barcelona was connected to the wider process of democratization at the level of the national polity following the death of General Franco in 1975. The transition to democracy at the national level provided the context within which decentralization took place in Barcelona and gave the latter its markedly political character. Decentralization and citizen participation were key political values articulated by the various social movements which had formed the backbone of the anti-Francoist opposition. Despite their varying agendas, all these movements demanded the democratization of local government and they all agreed on what this implied: decentralization and citizen participation. Given the strength of these social movements, the local political elites, many of whom had themselves come from associations and social movements in civil society, were anxious to translate the social movements' demands into government action. Thus, the aims of decentralization, both territorial and functional, and the creation of mechanisms and spaces for citizen participation, appeared in nearly all political party manifestos in the first democratic elections at the local level in April 1979.

Second, decentralization in Barcelona was framed by a wider process of devolving power from the central state to the regional level. The extreme centralism of the previous authoritarian regime meant that democratization necessarily implied a concomitant process of devolving power to the regional level. Decentralization of local government in Barcelona was seen as a natural extension of this process of devolving power from the central state to the regions and was as much a reaction against the centralist and uniform design of local government under the Franco dictatorship as it was a restoration of local democracy. Decentralization in Barcelona involved reaffirming Catalan national identity and a Catalan vision of self-government.

Third, decentralization was framed by a severe urban crisis. The large number of immigrants[1] who came to Barcelona from the 1950s onwards exacerbated what were already dismal living conditions, resulting from the lack of state investment in basic public services under the Francoist dictatorship. These new immigrants generally lived in hastily constructed shanty towns on the outskirts of the city where most of the streets and roads were unpaved and where there were no basic services such as electricity, running water and sewerage facilities. The few council flats which did exist were generally of bad quality and were built in areas which lacked basic public services and facilities such as transport, schools, health centres and markets.

This urban crisis was aggravated by the paralysis of local government. First, local government lacked financial resources given that public spending was both centralised and inadequate. According to Borja (1986, p. 47), public social expenditure in Spain represented only 10 per cent of the GNP and only 10 per cent of this was allocated to the local administration. Second, local government was essentially an administrative body with no political powers to tackle the acute crisis it faced. Moreover, in an authoritarian context, urban decisions frequently reflected the private interests of powerful economic groups rather than the needs of the public. Real-estate interests pressured city councils into changing land use to their advantage, whilst simultaneously turning a blind eye to planning permission rules and health and safety requirements.

Moreover, this political crisis at the local level went unattended whilst priority was given to democratization and decentralization at the national level. Whilst the first democratic elections at the national level took place in June 1977, the life of the Francoist municipal councils was prolonged artificially until April 1979, almost four years after the death of Franco. This delay accelerated the crisis at local level and acted as an obstacle to democratization at precisely the level of government closest to the citizen.

The Neighbourhood Movement

The resulting vacuum of power at the local level was filled by the various urban social movements such as the labour movement, the feminist movement, Catalan nationalist and cultural movements and the neighbourhood movement, which had formed the anti-Francoist opposition. Out of all these various social movements, however, the neighbourhood movement became the vanguard in the democratization process. In its strongest moment, estimates suggest that 70,000 people were members of a neighbourhood association whilst 80 per cent of the population were aware of the existence of the neighbourhood associations (Huertas and Andreu, 1996, p. 22).

A key factor to explain the predominant role played by the neighbourhood movement is that neighbourhood associations were virtually the only legal associations tolerated by the dictatorship. This had several consequences: first, they frequently assumed a wide variety of tasks and provided an array of services which, in a democratic context, would have been assumed either by local government itself or by other organizations such as trade unions or political parties. The role of the neighbourhood movement was thus exaggerated and strengthened by the authoritarian context within which it was forced to operate.

Second, the media provided extensive coverage of the different campaigns and activities carried out by the neighbourhood associations, not just because of the severity of the urban crisis in Barcelona, but also because they were often not subject to the same level of censorship as were labour disputes. In this way, the neighbourhood movement achieved a far greater political resonance than would otherwise have been the case. In addition to the commercial media, the neighbourhood associations also had their own press. In 1977, it is estimated that there were 39 neighbourhood publications which added up to an average of 26,673 copies each month (Huertas and Andreu, 1996, p. 27).

Finally, political parties took advantage of the legal coverage provided by the neighbourhood associations to oppose the dictatorship. Nevertheless, what stands out in this respect is the ideological plurality within the neighbourhood movement rather than its capture by any one political force. According to Martí (1981, p. 53), a total of 34 different political groups were present, either directly or indirectly, in the neighbourhood movement. It is also important to bear in mind that people without any party affiliation, the Independents, were involved in the creation of 86.4 per cent of the associations.[2]

This ideological plurality was indicative of another key strength of the neighbourhood movement, namely, its ability to embrace all the various strands of opposition to the dictatorship. This was achieved partly because of the legal coverage provided by the neighbourhood movement, and also because the demands that the neighbourhood movement put forward were global and collective.[3] The global nature of the neighbourhood struggle enabled it to mobilise the population around several key issues, namely, democratic town halls, political amnesty, civil rights, regional autonomy and the defence of Catalan language and culture, and questions associated with the cost of living. In this way, the neighbourhood movement successfully united the urban struggle for better living standards with the political struggle for democracy and became the key space from which to oppose the dictatorship: demands for better living conditions could only be answered by a democratically elected and decentralized local government.[4]

In March 1979, one month before the first democratic local elections, the Barcelona Federation of Neighbourhood Associations (FAVB) published a manifesto detailing their demands which reflected almost a decade of neighbourhood struggles.[5] First, it demanded a model of urban planning to improve the quality of life in the neighbourhoods. In terms of culture, the FAVB requested the strengthening of popular forms of culture such as the street festivals, rather than the large-scale acts and festivals promoted by the city council. It demanded that local government take responsibility for promoting council housing, especially in terms of rented accommodation. It also demanded more centres for senior citizens, more public school places, more health centres in the neighbourhoods and better public transport. Finally, the manifesto demanded an authentic decentralization and citizen participation: 'We don't want to be consulted only once every four years because we build the city, our lives in the city, every single day' (Huertas and Andreu, 1996, p. 29).

The 1979 manifesto shows that the neighbourhood movement played a key role not just in demanding democracy, but also in defining the nature of that democracy. Right from the beginning, the neighbourhood movement wanted democracy to mean more than a vote every four years. It did not want to restrict democracy to the formal political sphere alone, but posited a wider definition of 'the political', demanding an 'advanced political and social democracy' (Borja, 1986, p. 83).

Decentralization: 1979–1988

Within this context of a highly mobilised citizenry, the first democratic elections took place at the local level in April 1979. As in most other major cities, the left-wing was the main victor in these first local contests in Barcelona. The two largest parties in the city council were the Socialist

Party (PSC) with 16 councillors and the Communist Party (PSUC) with nine councillors. The first step towards establishing the framework for decentralization was the territorial division of the city into ten districts. Behind the division of the districts lay the political belief that decentralization was the key instrument to achieve participation and a more efficient administration. To this end, a Decentralization Commission was created, formed by the ten District Presidents (seven Socialists and three Catalan Nationalists (CiU)), and presided over by the mayor Pasqual Maragall. At the same time, one of the PSUC councillors, Jordi Borja, was nominated both President of the Working Group responsible for elaborating the proposed territorial division as well as Vice-President of the Decentralization Commission.[6] In addition, a Citizen Commission was established in 1983 to advise the local authority on the decentralization process in general and the territorial division of the city in particular. This Commission was made up of about sixty people and included many social movement representatives. The local authority also encouraged the participation of individual citizens by organizing a series of Public Hearings during December 1983 and January 1984 which were designed both to inform and consult the ordinary citizen before the territorial division of the city was finally approved unanimously by the city council in 1984.

The main characteristics of this initial phase of decentralization were as follows: first, the high degree of consensus not only amongst the totality of political parties but also amongst the social movements and the citizenry. The need to revise the territorial division of the city in order to decentralize the administration and create mechanisms for citizen participation was uncontested. Moreover, according to Borja, citizen consensus contributed to building a greater degree of consensus amongst the political parties themselves and ultimately pushed the parties towards unanimity (Borja, 1998, p.13). In other words, even if some parties did not wholeheartedly embrace the principles of decentralization and citizen participation, they were unable to find valid reasons to oppose them, particularly in public (Interview, Vintró 16/6/99).

The second defining characteristic of this first phase was the political context in which it took place, namely, the wider context of democratization and decentralization of the national polity. Decentralization and citizen participation represented a political choice in the sense that both were seen as necessary elements of democratization. In the 1983 Socialist Municipal Manifesto for Barcelona, decentralization was one of the four basic ideas[7] which defined the kind of city council the Socialists wanted to achieve:

> Decentralization is the application, within the city, of the political principles that Barcelona City council believes are valid in both Catalonia and Spain. Participation,

> democratic control and, efficiency will only be complete when many of the services and functions which affect the daily life of citizens are decided, managed and controlled by [...] the District Councils (PSC 1983, p. 2).

In addition, the high level of citizen participation not only in the process of creating the territorial division of the city, but also more generally, served to give political meaning and legitimacy to the process.

The third characteristic was the composition of the political class which oversaw the whole process. During the first mandate, the PSC had won in nine out of ten districts whilst the PSUC was the second party in six out of ten districts giving a clear left-wing majority in Barcelona town hall. This left-wing majority was repeated in the second mandate when the PSC had 21 councillors and the PSUC had three.[8] Moreover, as mentioned above, many of those elected and many of those who joined the new town halls as technical staff were people drawn principally from the social movements which had formed the core opposition to the Francoist regime. This meant that many of those who entered the town halls in 1979 were shaped by their activities in social movements and associations and thus carried with them the values and demands of civil society.

Finally, the dual nature and aims of both decentralization and citizen participation were clear from the beginning. The criteria informing the territorial division of the city were both managerial and political: 'The districts have to be functional in terms of political participation (sociocultural meaning, internal cohesion, medium size), but also in terms of the management of services and the taking of decisions (...)' (Borja, 1987, pp. 235–36). In turn, both concepts were related to the twin aims of enhancing local democracy and improving service delivery, as illustrated by the Municipal Action Plan for 1984–1987, which defines the aims of the decentralization process as follows:

a) to decentralize decisions and to deconcentrate functions;
b) to fight inequalities and imbalances;
c) to increase and improve services and to make their delivery quicker and more flexible;
d) to introduce new technology and to contribute to the rationalization of the Administration;
e) to develop the participation, the communication and the co-operation of entities and all citizens (Ajuntament de Barcelona 1984–1987, p.25).

These aims show that, from the beginning, decentralization was both a political tool, in the sense that it was an instrument designed to democratize local government, as well as a managerial tool designed to improve service delivery (Amorós, 1995, p. 7). Decentralization was a way of bringing both politics and management closer to the citizen, making both more democratic as well as more efficient.

Following the initial territorial division, the second step in the decentralization process of transferring functions, and human and material resources from the central town hall to the districts was initiated by the approval of the basic law regulating local government (Ley de Bases de Régimen Local) in 1985 and that which was subsequently approved by the Catalan Parliament (Llei Municipal i de Regim Local de Catalunya).[9] Two key aims influenced the type and extent of functions to be decentralized: first, the improvement of welfare services in order to reduce inequalities in the city and to make service delivery more responsive to the particular needs of each district. The area of welfare services, such as social services, public health, youth, sport and education, was thus the first to transfer many of its functions to district level.[10]

Second, the transfer of urban programmes and municipal services considered particularly suitable for delivery at district level. It was envisaged that the central council would maintain overall strategic control especially in those areas which required economies of scale or a global strategy, whilst giving the districts considerable autonomy in terms of implementing policy. In the words of one administrator: 'Barcelona has one policy but ten different executions' (Interview, Fernández 25/11/97).

Finally, during this second stage, the formal framework within which citizen participation would take place was established following a process of elaboration and debate lasting two years. In December 1986, the Regulatory Norms of the Organization of the Districts and Citizen Participation were approved which laid out the various mechanisms and channels which would enable citizen participation. These mechanisms included: public hearings at the city and district level, which may be called either by the town hall or the citizens; the right to oral intervention in the district council plenaries; the right to information and the right to petition; and the establishment of various sectoral or territorial advisory councils, particularly in the area of social welfare.

Out of all these various mechanisms, the latter have become the mechanism most regularly used by both the city council and the associations themselves. The following advisory councils currently exist at either city level or district level, or often both: the Municipal Council of Social Welfare which was the first to be created in 1988, the Senior Citizens' Advisory Council, Barcelona Women's Council, the Council of Health and Safety at Work, the Municipal Sports Council, the Municipal Council of Associations and Volunteers, the Economic and Social Council, the Council of 100 Young People, the Advisory Council of Foreign Immigrants and the Municipal Schools' Council. Within these advisory councils associations are consulted on, and have the opportunity to influence, the design of municipal policy. As such, they represent spaces of dialogue and interaction between the local administration and the associational fabric of the city. Moreover, despite their lack of formal decision-making powers, it is unlikely that individuals would continue to participate in these different councils unless it was felt that their recommendations and proposals were incorporated, at least to some degree, into municipal policy, especially given that such participation entails devoting considerable time and energy on a voluntary basis.

Consolidation of the Process of Decentralization and Citizen Participation: 1988–1999

The period from 1988 onwards marks the consolidation of the districts as decentralised administrative and political units as the increase in staffing levels and financial resources at district level testifies. From receiving only 7.11 per cent of the total city council budget in 1988, the districts received 12.32 per cent in 1998. In terms of staffing levels, in 1986, staff at district level represented 5.03 per cent of the overall city council staff. By 1997, this percentage had risen to 26.46 per cent.[11] The volume of competencies attributed to the district level is also proof that the degree of decentralization which has taken place is substantial. As one of the city council's jurists maintains, it is probable that today the districts now have more competencies than were ever originally envisaged at the start of the process (Interview, Galofre 17/6/99). Moreover, the political character of the districts is also clear due to the existence of a President who is an elected councillor, chosen by the district council and confirmed by the mayor.[12] The council itself is made up of 15 councillors nominated from the party lists in proportion to the electoral results for each particular district. This is the district's organ of collective representation.

By 1988, all functions had been transferred and the districts were increasingly accepted by the citizens as their main, and often only, point of contact with the local government. As one councillor maintained, the value of the districts has continually increased for two reasons: first, they have real decision-making powers, such as deciding their own budget within the limits prescribed by the central town hall, and second, they can resolve the majority of a citizen's problems at the district level itself (Interview, Narváez 01/12/97).

The increased legitimacy and visibility of the districts has also been aided by several mechanisms such as the creation of Information Points – *Barcelona Información* – in the central offices of each district council as well as the establishment of the PACs (Points for the Attention of the Citizen) in every district where the citizen can resolve any administrative matter without going to the central town hall. In addition, most districts have a number of civic centres and other cultural/sports centres, often either self-managed by local groups or by joint partnership between the local authority and local organizations, which help to structure social life in the district and to create a sense of belonging to a particular area. This 'creation of community public space' has been particularly important for the consolidation of the districts.

The Municipal Charter

The Municipal Charter, approved by the city council at the end of 1997 and awaiting approval by the Catalan and Spanish Parliaments, has been interpreted positively by many councillors as the formal legal guarantee of the achievements of the past decades in terms of decentralization and citizen participation. With the approval of the Municipal Charter, it is argued that Barcelona's model of decentralization and citizen participation no longer depends solely on the willingness of politicians, civil servants and social movement activists, but now has a firm legal basis. The Municipal Charter elevates the Norms of Participation approved in 1986, and any further norms which have been established over the years since then, to the status of law. Moreover, Article 30.2 of the Charter declares that: 'citizen participation informs the whole of the Municipal Charter' (Ajuntament de Barcelona, 1997a, p. 27). The Municipal Charter also introduces new innovative elements of participation such as the recognition of the civic management of municipal competencies and the establishment of the 'City Advisory Council' as a mechanism of participation in which representatives from economic, social, cultural, professional and neighbourhood organizations will meet to discuss the Municipal Action Plans, which guide municipal policy from one election to another, the municipal budgets and large city projects. Other areas of innovation relate to the move towards the direct election of district councillors and the concept of Municipal Justice, designed to deal with minor offences at the district level.[13] To conclude, in theory at least, the Municipal Charter creates the potential for experimentation with new channels and mechanisms of participation.

Limitations to Participation

Despite the success of Barcelona city council in creating a decentralized city which provides spaces and mechanisms to facilitate citizen participation, the latter has declined over time. Whilst, many factors can be put forward to explain this decline in participation, three will be highlighted here.

First, there are difficulties inherent in promoting citizen participation around a local government project, defined and promoted 'from above'. One of the key aims of local government in Barcelona has been to build a more egalitarian city using social welfare and service delivery as the two key instruments to correct inequalities in the city. Given the difficulties of overcoming the inadequacy of welfare provision inherited from the previous authoritarian regime, the context of economic recession and welfare cutbacks during the 1980s, and the continuing shortfall in terms of resources and functions at the local level,[14] the city council was clear that it needed the co-operation of associations and social movements in civil society if it wished to fulfil its aim of building a more egalitarian city.

It is, therefore, no coincidence that the first advisory council to be created was done so in the field of social welfare policy as this was precisely where the need to enlist the co-operation and support of associations was considered paramount. Not only because social organizations are frequently more efficient and rapid in detecting and in responding to social needs than the administration, but also because it was recognised that in the above context of economic recession and welfare cutbacks, the city council alone would not be able to maintain adequate levels of social welfare. As Pindado points out, 'If associations did not exist, the social cost would be extremely significant' (Pindado, 1997, p. 64).

This reflects the view held by those in the city council working within the Department of Decentralization and Citizen Relations where participation is seen as a 'strategic question'. The relationship of participation and collaboration between associations and the local administration, which the city council has tried to promote, is viewed as an essential mechanism for maintaining or advancing the standards of social welfare which the city has achieved. According to one council worker: 'We have gone through a period where we [in the city council] have worked *for* the people and now we have to put more emphasis on working *with* the people. If we want to maintain our welfare state we either do so with the people or not at all'(Interview, Osan 4/11/97). Participation is, therefore, increasingly viewed in terms of involving associations in the 'co-management' of projects and services with the administration.[15] The establishment of this kind of collaborative relationship between local administration and associations is also viewed as part of a long-term political strategy, of maintaining Barcelona as a city with certain standards of social welfare whether or not the Right or the Left is in government.

However, mobilizing citizens around a local government project, based on building a more egalitarian city, implies defining participation in a way that is congruent with that project as well as a certain degree of control over that participation, especially where it is seen to run counter to, or to jeopardise that project. In particular, associations have been drawn into fulfilling a role as implementers and validators of municipal policy. Whilst this role does not necessarily have to be problematic, it can be so. If associations become preoccupied solely with managing or delivering services, one consequence may be to push to one side their alternative roles of holding the city council accountable, of offering alternative projects to those of the local government or of promoting their own autonomous projects. Without these autonomous projects the associations may end up simply shadowing the local administration and becoming a sort of auxiliary of local government action' (Pindado, 1997, pp. 98–99).

The role of associations as implementers of municipal policy has influenced the way in which participation is understood by both the city council and the associations themselves. This is evident in the dominance of the advisory councils as the key spaces of citizen participation understood in terms of the relationship between the city council and associations, often to the neglect of the autonomous activities of the associations themselves and to the neglect of participation in spheres of society other than local government such as the workplace, for example. Other authors agree that participation is increasingly located within the administrative sphere of service delivery rather than in the political sphere, a split reflected in the internal division of the city council itself into a political structure which defines policy and a management structure which applies policy, as well as the emphasis of the city council on its social welfare role.[16] Amorós is typical in emphasising the definition of citizen participation 'as an important device to improve the local policy-making: citizens would be consulted on some matters in order to be able to elaborate "better" policies' (Amorós, 1995, p. 38). This definition is confirmed by the 1996–1999 Municipal Action Plan, which refers to citizen participation under the rubric of service delivery and defines it in terms of the creation of advisory councils. The Plan states that citizens 'have to be consulted, [they] have to be able to influence the services delivered by the city council and to intervene in their management'. With those aims in mind, the city council intends to 'create citizen participation councils' and 'to develop the co-management of services' (Ajuntament de Barcelona, 1996–99, p. 37).

The fact that the city council needs associations to perform this role as implementers of municipal policy also implies some degree of control on the part of the city council over the process of participation. The logic of 'managing' liberal democracy, by definition, implies some degree of control to limit the number of extraneous factors that can arise to disrupt that management. In this respect, it is axiomatic to say that the council will see participation as an instrument to aid governance and will channel and shape it accordingly. Whilst it is possible for the council to be both 'controlling' as well as progressive in its commitment to citizen participation, the preponderant role of the local government in encouraging associationalism and in facilitating and promoting mechanisms and spaces of participation can be counter-productive, particularly in a context where associations become excessively dependent on the local government for their survival or where citizens' sense of ownership of the process of participation is reduced. As one activist pointed out, in many instances, the protagonism of the local government reduced the incentive for people to participate. As the administration now appeared to do everything, there appeared to be little left for the citizens to do themselves (Interview, Moreno 26/11/97).

The protagonism of the city council with regard to the promotion of participation contrasts with, and is partly responsible for, the gradual decline of the social movements' protagonism. This is the second factor to explain the gradual decline of participation in Barcelona. Following the first democratic elections in 1979, the associational movement faced a difficult transitional period. Both parties and movements had participated in the common struggle of opposition to the dictatorship, but, following the transition to democracy, the close relationship between parties and movements came to an end and each struggled to adapt to their new role and to different ways of doing politics. Owing their origin to the struggle against the Francoist town halls, many associations found it difficult to change their conflictive stance and to adapt their aims and their way of operating to the demands of the new political framework. One neighbourhood activist claimed that with the arrival of the democratic town halls 'the simple world of either you're with me or against me came to an end' (Martí Gómez and Marcè i Fort, 1996, p. 31).

From the point of view of the neighbourhood movement, in this initial transitional period, there was a certain amount of disorientation as they tried to adjust to a new political situation in which their old demands had to some extent been deactivated via their translation firstly into the government programmes of the PSC and the PSUC, and secondly, into government action itself. In some ways, the neighbourhood associations were simply overtaken as government action began to respond to the historic demands of the movement. Whilst the town hall extended its scope of activity to take on many of the roles previously assumed by the neighbourhood associations, the latter lost many of their functions, not to mention many of their militants, to the parties, the unions and other new associations. The neighbourhood associations lost their protagonism and their leadership role and became simply one organization amongst many others within which politics could take place.

Moreover, the relationship between the neighbourhood movement and the city council was made particularly difficult due to the fact that many of those elected and many of those who joined the new town halls as technical staff were people drawn principally from the urban social movements which had formed the core opposition to the Francoist regime.[17] This haemorrhage of personnel, not just from the neighbourhood movement but also from many other movements, led many to claim that these movements entered into a period of crisis as they lost their protagonism to the town halls. Not only had many associations lost some of their key participants to the town halls, specifically those professionals such as the architects, the lawyers etc. which had given the movements much of their strength and expertise, some also allege that this transfer of personnel left the movements open to extreme left-wing groups which had not gained electoral representation thereby contributing further to the isolation of these social movements.

In addition, those who remained within the social movements were disappointed precisely because although it was their former colleagues who were now in charge of the town halls, the kind of changes they demanded in terms of decentralization and citizen participation appeared to happen very slowly and the feeling that the council effectively ignored the demands for decentralization and participation which the social movements had articulated became widespread. The FAVB, for example, made public a document in July 1979 which: 'accused the council of marginalizing the FAVB from municipal life, of not carrying out the promises on decentralization and citizen participation as well as denying the right of citizens to have voice in the plenaries' (Barbeta 1983, p. 69). As evidence of the fact that the city council was not convinced, in its totality at least, of the desirability of participation, neighbourhood activists point to the considerable gap between the first democratic elections (1979) and the approval of the Regulatory Norms for Citizen Participation (1986).

Following this initial period of adjustment, other factors have also served to weaken the associational fabric. First, the majority of advisory councils are heavily dependent on the financial support of the local government to survive. According to a recent survey, the key source of finance for the majority of associations comes from the public administration, which represents an average contribution of 36.3 per cent of the associational sector's income. Moreover, if the largest associations, those which have an annual budget of more than 1,000 million pesetas, are omitted, the contribution from the public administration represents 44 per cent of the associations' income.[18]

The second key weakness relates to the lack of personnel in many associations. In general, associations tend to be quite small with almost half – 43.4 per cent – having less than 100 members, whilst 75 per cent of associations surveyed had less than 500 members. The lack of personnel can be a significant shortcoming given that the majority of mechanisms and spaces of participation created by the city council are labour intensive. In particular, participation in either public hearings or in the advisory councils represents a significant drain on an association's resources both in terms of time and available personnel. One interviewee estimated that participating in the Municipal Council of Social Welfare, which was only one of twelve advisory councils in which the Barcelona Youth Council was present, required him to monitor 90 meetings each year alone (Interview, Tort 05/12/97). Moreover, many associations simply do not have sufficient personnel, let alone with the kind of expertise needed to participate effectively, to send representatives to all the advisory councils.[19] It tends to always be the same minority of people attending the advisory councils, often in the name of different associations, which raises the question of their representation. It is difficult to establish whether participants are representing their own individual opinions or those of their association, let alone the degree to which they are representing the opinions of the wider population. In addition, those who attend the advisory councils are generally unable to feedback from these meetings into their own organizations, which reduces the effectiveness of their participation.

Moreover, evidence suggests that, particularly within the city-level advisory councils, and the Municipal Council of Social Welfare in particular, what takes place is a type of 'participation of the notables' whereby experts or professionals in the field take part rather than the ordinary citizen. Advisory councils at district level are where associations can really participate given the closer proximity of the district to the average citizen, but, of course, the impact of the district councils on municipal policy is far less given that the district councils have less decision-making capacity than the central city council.

Another key shortcoming of many associations is the lack of internal democracy. In the case of the neighbourhood associations in particular, the turnover of leaders has been far less than that in the city council continuously governed by the left since 1979.[20] If associations call assemblies, they are little more than a formal procedure attended by a reduced minority of members. The percentage participating in electing representatives within the associations is very low and the mechanisms for holding associational representatives accountable are, in many cases, simply non-existent.

The final factor to take into account when explaining the decline of participation in Barcelona, is the relationship of political parties with associations and movements within civil society. As mentioned already, the relationship between civil society and political parties was initially very close, given that the latter were illegal during the Francoist dictatorship and were, therefore, forced to act within civil society rather than the institutional sphere. Moreover, this closeness was strengthened as a result of the common struggle to establish democracy and by the fact that most party leaders, militants and activists came from struggles within social movements and associations.

Yet maintaining the close relationship established between parties and the associational fabric as a result of their common struggle against the dictatorship proved difficult once the former were legalised and therefore no longer obliged to operate solely within civil society. Once the parties were legalised they turned their attention to the institutional sphere and the need to win elections, often at the expense of neglecting their ties with civil society. Given their scant resources, both financial and organizational, parties had to choose between conquering the institutional sphere or maintaining their grassroots activity. Moreover, the left-wing parties tended to continue with their strategy, established during the years of transition, of discouraging overt signs of protest and participation by the social movements in order to demonstrate responsibility to the right in general and to the military in particular (Hipsher, 1996).

Furthermore, once in power, following the 1979 local elections, the parties felt the need to differentiate themselves from other associations within civil society and the need to make a clearer separation between the two ways of 'doing politics': representative democracy and grassroots democracy.[21] As seen already in the case of the associational movements, it was a difficult process of adjustment for all involved. In some cases, those now in the administration entered into direct competition with civil society and questioned whether or not the direct participation of social movements and associations was still necessary given that they, their former comrades-in-arms, were now in charge. Having cut their political teeth in the social movements, many of the newly elected representatives felt that they knew what civil society wanted. One ex-neighbourhood activist and current Socialist district councillor claimed that, in order to differentiate themselves clearly from the Francoist councils, those in the new town halls wanted to prove that they could do everything and provide everything, some of which, such as the civic centres, they could have left to the social movements (Interview, Moreno 26/11/97). Moreover, some of those in the neighbourhood movements concurred with this interpretation and were content to sit back and let their newly elected representatives do their job, at least during the 'honeymoon period'. Many activists abandoned the associations, happy in the knowledge that they could leave the work to those they had elected, especially given that they were 'their' people (Martí Gómez and Marcè i Fort 1996, p. 38).

This kind of behaviour was often a reflection of the party elites' desire for protagonism and the need to assert their new role. The parties wanted to reclaim their role and activities which had necessarily been carried out by the neighbourhood movement during the latter years of the Francoist dictatorship. Part of the difficulty in adjusting to their new role came from the fact that the parties were aware of their weak roots in civil society, a perception which often resulted in attitudes of defensiveness and mistrust towards civil society.[22] The parties were not mass-movement parties but rather were institutional forces with often weak roots in civil society. As a result, they have chosen to build on their key asset – electoral strength – and concentrated throughout the 1980s on becoming consolidated within the political-institutional sphere, often to the detriment of party activities in civil society. The distance between the parties and civil society increased and reflected their clear option to be institutional rather than social forces. The abandonment of civil society by the parties coincided with the crisis of many of the social movements, particularly those which were left bereft of the leaders and activists who had opted for either a role within the parties or within the town halls themselves. In this sense, it is difficult to establish whether or not there was a deliberate strategy on the part of the parties to deactivate social movements, or whether this tended to happen as a result of social movement activists taking on new roles as councillors or party appointees within the town halls. Nevertheless, the parties did not do anything to halt this process of deactivation, even if they had not deliberately initiated it.

In addition, the abandonment of civil society by the parties coincided with attempts by most parties to control civil society and use associations for their own electoral purposes. This tendency has been exacerbated by the continuous round of elections in Catalonia which has frequently made the relationship between parties and associations difficult, with the latter accusing the former of instrumentalist attitudes.[23] The neighbourhood associations in particular have been the battleground between the PSC and the CDC (Democratic Convergence of Catalonia) for electoral supremacy, understood in the context of the competition between Barcelona town hall, governed continuously by the left since 1979, and the *Generalitat* continuously governed by the centre-right nationalists (CDC) since 1980.

In the case of the CDC, particular difficulties have arisen due to the close identification between the party and the *Generalitat*. It is claimed, for example, that the *Generalitat* has preferred to create its own autonomous network of offices and associational structures in Barcelona's districts, rather than working through those already established by the city council, in order to strengthen its own presence within the territory and to combat the influence of the city council which it sees as its main electoral threat.[24] For example, the *Generalitat* established a Confederation of Neighbourhood Associations to counteract the strength of the one that already existed which was seen to be controlled by the Socialist and Communist parties.[25]

The CDC has also been accused of using clientelist strategies in order to strengthen its position within civil society, particularly amongst the neighbourhood associations and other associations in municipalities which were seen as a redoubt of left-wing support. Whilst the CDC has quite strong links with nationalist and cultural associations and the professional colleges, it has experienced difficulties in establishing contacts with the neighbourhood movement, especially in the larger cities where it is largely dominated by the left-wing parties. The PSC has criticised the CDC's attempt to combat this weakness by what it has labelled 'the promotion of associationalism via the electoral work of the "welfare offices"'(PSC 1996b, p. 16). This refers to what has become known as the 'Comas phenomenon', which involved the targeting of public funds to those associations known to be sympathetic to the CDC. Antonio Comas, the former Minister of Welfare, was accused by several of the neighbourhood leaders interviewed of going 'cheque book in hand' to buy votes and support from different associations. However the *Generalitat*'s 'interventionist' policy is judged, neither the Ministry of Welfare's 'cheque book policy' nor that of establishing parallel organizations to counteract the strength of those that already exist has translated into increased electoral support for the CDC.

In sum, the initial period following the 1979 elections was replete with tensions and mutual accusations on both sides. Those left in the social movements accused the parties of a deliberate strategy of demobilisation vis-à-vis civil society, as well as in some cases a strategy of co-opting via the parties' newly acquired municipal power. In this sense, the problem of associational autonomy is not just with respect to political parties, but is also with respect to the administration, especially with reference to public grants.[26] Socialist party workers stressed that: 'There has been a temptation when in power to try to control conflict' (Interview, Martí, Navarro and Martínez, 19/11/97). Pindado also qualified the policy carried out by some town halls towards the neighbourhood associations as being one of 'keeping them quiet and keeping them happy' (Interview, Pindado 10/10/97). On the other hand, those newly elected to the town halls accused those left in the social movements and associations of being anchored in the past and therefore unable to change their combative attitude towards the town halls to one of collaboration. In the summer of 1981, the PSC formally communicated its abandonment of the FAVB (although no PSC member was part of the FAVB's board at that time) due to, what the PSC qualified as, a policy of 'resistance and systematic attack' carried out by the FAVB towards Barcelona's town hall (PSC 1996, p. 37).[27]

Conclusion

The experience of Barcelona highlights both the possibilities and difficulties of moving towards a more participatory democracy. Following the left-wing victory in the 1979 municipal elections in Barcelona, those who entered the town halls, many of whom had come from the social movements themselves, made serious efforts to protect and build upon Barcelona's legacy of civic activism by creating spaces and mechanisms of participation. This shows that in a context where there is a history of radical associationalism, and where the political will exists to facilitate citizen participation, liberal democracies can sustain greater levels of participation than democratic elitists such as Schumpeter would have us believe.[28] Nevertheless, the active role of the local government in facilitating participation can be a double-edged sword. Mobilizing citizens around a project which is defined and promoted from above, necessitates a particular kind of participation congruent with that project and a certain degree of control to ensure that participation does not run counter to that project. Moreover, the active role of political leaders in facilitating participation, even when these leaders are progressive and where their actions respond to the demands of civil society itself, can be counterproductive: the initiative and protagonism passes to local government and away from the self-organization of activists in civil society, which can reduce the incentive for people to participate.

Notes

1. Compared to an increase in population of 16.5 per cent in Spain as a whole between 1960 and 1975, Catalonia's population increased by 44.1 per cent as a result of the attraction of full employment and above-average salaries. The majority of this population increase, consisting of immigrants mainly from the impoverished south, was concentrated in Barcelona's metropolitan area, which absorbed 70 per cent of that increase, and other industrial zones along the coast (De Riquer, 1999, p. 389).
2. These percentages do not add up because the creation of neighbourhood associations always concerned the joint efforts of several political forces.
3. Indicative of the global nature of the neighbourhood struggle were the Popular Plans, developed in each neighbourhood as an alternative to the official urban development plans. These included aspects such as health, education, culture and quality of life and they united professionals – lawyers, sociologists, journalists, architects – with the working class in the struggle for better living conditions. The College of Architects, for example, created the Office of Urban Information, manned by architects and a lawyer, as an advisory and information service for the neighbourhoods.
4. It is significant, for example, that the Madrid neighbourhood movement began to fade after the first general elections in 1977, whilst the Barcelona neighbourhood movement continued to be a key political protagonist at least until the late 1970s because until that

point democracy for Catalonia at the local and autonomous level had not yet been achieved.

5. The FAVB created a typology of 18 different forms and mechanisms of struggle which testify to the breadth of the neighbourhood struggle as well as to the innovative and imaginative forms which that struggle took. These are as follows: collection of signatures; exhibitions; neighbourhood assemblies; posters; occupation of public buildings; use of sport as publicity or to make concrete demands; popular festivals and shows; human barriers; civil disobedience; pacts with those in power; denouncements to the press; symbolic inaugurations; collective murals; protests in the Plaza Sant Jaume (in front of the main city council); competitions; demonstrations; kidnapping of buses and buildings; alternative urban plans (Huertas and Andreu, 1996, pp. 21–22).
6. The working group was made up of a sociologist (Anna Alabart of FAVB), a geographer (Lluis Cassasas) and two municipal technicians, both economists (Josep Maria Canals and Ernest Maragall). Halfway through the mandate, Borja submitted Maragall as President of the Decentralization Commission.
7. The others were austerity, the need to continue the reform and improvement of the administration and the need to improve the city council's information policy and relations with the citizenry in general.
8. Barcelona City Council has continued to have a left-wing majority throughout the whole of the democratic period.
9. At the same time as the proposal for the territorial division was being prepared a 'very detailed and analytical study' had been undertaken to determine which policy areas and functions could be decentralized (Borja, 1998, p. 9). This study was co-ordinated by Jordi Borja and was carried out by two teams, one external and one internal to the city council. The internal working group was led by a jurist, Manuel Palomar, and the external working group was led by an economist, Jaoquim Clusa (Borja, 1998, p.10).
10. Today 23 per cent of the total expenditure of the Department of Personal Services is decentralized (Castiella and Serra, 1998, p. 143).
11. Source: Barcelona City Council, Department of Decentralization and Citizen Relations.
12. The figure of vice-president, appointed by the Mayor, was created in 1991 following the elections of that year in which the CiU party won in four out of ten districts. The figure of the vice-president was seen as a tool to counterbalance the power of the opposition party in those four districts.
13. Municipal judges will be nominated for each district and a Municipal Tribunal will be established at city level as a central organ.
14. Far from achieving the 50–25–25 split which local authorities have long demanded, the distribution of public funds in Spain is currently 62 per cent for the central state, 26 per cent for the Autonomous Communities and still only 12 per cent for the local Authorities (Castiella and Serra, 1998, p. 140).
15. Examples of co-management include the 'Barcelona Youth Project' elaborated in 1985 by the city council with the co-responsibility of the Barcelona Youth Council; the Barcelona Strategic Plan 2000; the Integral Plan for the Development of Social Services elaborated in 1995 by the city council with more than 130 social entities; and lastly, the Municipal Institute for the Handicapped where 50 per cent of those on the governing body are elected from amongst the associations themselves, whilst the other 50 per cent are made up by political representatives from the city council.
16. See in particular Amorós (1995) and Gomà and Brugué (1994).
17. Seven out of 43 councillors elected during the first mandate were key leaders from the neighbourhood movement. In addition, the majority of those elected had been active in one or more of the social movements.

18. Source: Radiografia de les Associacions de Voluntariat de Barcelona, consell Municipal d'associocions de Voluntariat de Barcelona, 1997, The response rate for the survey was 14 per cent. Whilst this is quite low, it is about a standard rate of return for postal surveys. Moreover, it is the first of its kind to be undertaken in any kind of systematic fashion.
19. For example, there is approximately an 80 per cent overlap in personnel between the Municipal Council if Associations and Volunteers' Working Group of the Municipal Council of Social Welfare according to one of the participants (Interview, Tort 5 December 1997).
20. One interviewee commented wryly that the key neighbourhood leaders had worked with all of the mayors from the last years of Francoism throughout the whole of the democratic period (Interview, Galofre 17 June 1999).
21. Whilst these were seen as complementary, parties have always been clear on the need to keep the boundaries between the two well defined.
22. It is interesting, for example, that in many areas, it is still generally the neighbourhood association which fulfils a 'constituency surgery' role rather than the local branch party. This reflects the former's more visible presence in the districts compared to the relative invisibility of the latter.
23. Between 1979 and 1999 inclusive, there have only been four years – 1981, 1985, 1990, 1997 – when elections have not taken place! Moreover, in some years more than one election has taken place.
24. The circumscription of Barcelona represents approximately 50 per cent of the Catalan electorate.
25. The fact that all the neighbourhood associations now belong to both confederations, has meant that this policy has not been particularly successful.
26. This is particularly pertinent when, as in the case of Catalonia, the two key parties have become virtually permanent structures within the administration.
27. Not until 1985 would the PSC declare publicly its willingness to return to working with the FAVB. Once this happened, however, the FAVB gained access to public grants, began its involvement in service delivery and consolidated its organizational structure by hiring personnel (PSC, 1996, p. 37).
28. Schumpeter (1992, p. 269) defines democracy as 'That institutional arrangement for arriving at political decisions in which individuals acquire the power to decide by means of a competitive struggle for the people's vote'. Within this definition there is little room for citizen participation other than voting. He even argues that activities such 'bombarding' representatives with letters are unacceptable (Schumpeter, 1992, p. 295). The lack of emphasis on participation is partly due to his negative view of human capabilities. According to Schumpeter (1992, p. 283): 'The electorate is incapable of action other than a stampede'.

References

Ajuntament de Barcelona (1984–1987) *Programa d'Actuació Municipal.*

Ajuntament de Barcelona (1996–1999) *Programa d'Actuació Municipal.*

Ajuntament de Barcelona (1997a) *Carta Municipal. Anteproyecto de Texto Articulado de la Ley Especial de Barcelona.*

Amorós, M. (1995) *Decentralization and New Governance: A Comparison between Barcelona and Birmingham*, Working Paper, no. 110, Institut de Ciències Polítiques i Socials, Barcelona.

Barbeta, J. (1983) 'Crónica del Primer Ajuntament Democrátic del Postfranquisme', *L'Avenç*, no. 58, pp. 68–73.
Borja, J. (1986) *Por Unos Municipios Democráticos. Diez Años de Reflexión Política yMovimiento Ciudadano*, Instituto de Estudios de Administración Local, Madrid.
Borja, J. (1987) *Descentralización y Participación Ciudadana*, Instituto de Estudios de Administración Local, Madrid.
Borja, J. (1998) *Els Districtes de Barcelona*, Barcelona, Unpublished paper.
Castiella, T. and Serra, A. (1998) 'The Local Welfare Policies. The Case of the Barcelona City Council', *Barcelona Societat*, no. 8, pp. 140–152.
De Riquer, B. (1999) 'Franquisme, Transició i Democràcia', in M. Risques (ed), *Història de la Catalunya Contemporània*, Pòrtic, Biblioteca Universitària, Barcelona, pp. 337–456.
Gomà, R. and Brugué, J. (1994) *Public Participation in a Decentralised City: The Case of Barcelona*, Working Paper, no. 84, Institut de Ciències Polítiques i Socials, Barcelona.
Hipsher, P.L. (1996) 'Democratization and the Decline of Urban Social Movements in Chile and Spain', *Comparative Politics*, vol. 28, pp. 273–297.
Huertas, J. and Andreu, M. (1996) *Barcelona en Lluita*, Federació d'Associacións de Veïns de Barcelona, Barcelona.
Martí, J. (1981) 'Relación entre Asociaciones de Vecinos y Partidos Políticos. Barcelona 1970-1980', Unpublished Thesis, Barcelona.
Martí Gómez, J. and Marcè i Fort, J. (1996) *Centre Social de Sants. Una Experiència Asociativa*, Fundació Jaume Bofill, Bacelona.
Pindado, F. (1997) 'La Participació Ciutadana a la Vida de les Ciutats', *Informe de Treball*, Barcelona.
PSC (1983) *Perquè Guanyi Barcelona*, Election Manifesto for Barcelona, 1983 Municipal Elections.
PSC (1996) *L'Associacionisme Ciutadà i Els Socialistes de Catalunya*, Textos de les Cinc Conferències Nacionals de Moviment Veïnal, Barcelona.
Schumpeter, J.A. (1992) *Capitalism, Socialism and Democracy*, Routledge, London.

Interviews

Fernández, Antoni – Director of the Quality Office for Citizen Relations, Barcelona City Council, PSC – 25.11.97.
Galofre, Jaumé – Director of the Central Judicial Staff, Barcelona City Council, Professor of Administrative Law, University of Barcelona – 17.6.99.
Martí, Carlos; Navarro, Pep and Martínez, Pep – Responsible for the Citizen Movements' Section of the Socialist Party – 19.11.97.
Moreno, Custodia – Former President of the Carmello Neighbourhood Association and local councillor for Horta-Guinardó district, PSC – 26.11.97.
Narváez, Francesc – Local councillor for the district of San Martí, PSC – 01.12.97.
Osan, Francesc – Co-ordinator of the Department of Citizen Participation, Barcelona City Council – 04.11.97.
Pindado, Fernando – Lawyer and activist in Nou Barris Neighbourhood Association – 10.10.97.
Tort, Xavier – President of the Barcelona Youth Advisory Council – 05.12.97.
Vintró, Eulalia – Councillor for Barcelona City Council, IC, and President of the Municipal Social Welfare Advisory Council – 16.6.99.

Chapter 6

Metropolitan Governance and Democracy: How to Evaluate New Tendencies

Daniel Kübler and Sonja Wälti

In most western industrialized countries, cities can no longer be considered in the traditional Weberian sense of territorially integrated entities.[1] Rather, they must be described as metropolitan areas, that is multi-centred urban regions created by the social, economic and cultural dynamics of the modern societies, and held together by powerful systems of communication and mass transportation (see for example Leresche *et al.*, 1995). Metropolitan areas extend and develop mainly along functional social and economic networks, more or less independently from institutional boundaries of communities or other sub-national entities. In most European countries, metropolitan areas are characterised by a high degree of 'governmental fragmentation' (Dente, 1990, p. 60). Their territory is split up into multiple political and administrative units (communes, cantons, provinces), leading to difficulties regarding the management of metropolitan problems. Throughout Europe, there have been attempts at institutional reforms, aiming at the creation of encompassing political institutions for metropolitan areas (e.g. creation of urban provinces of Amsterdam and Rotterdam, merger of Berlin and Brandenburg, etc.) (Jouve and Lefèvre, 1999). However, these reforms have repeatedly failed. In spite of multiple initiatives in many countries, 'metropolitan governments', i.e. political institutions encompassing metropolitan areas, are exceptional (Lefèvre, 1998). This is also true for Switzerland: institutional fragmentation of metropolitan areas is high (Schuler 1994),[2] and almost no territorial reforms have taken place since the beginning of the 20th century (Joye and Leresche, 1999).

The absence of encompassing metropolitan institutions does evidently not mean that policy making in metropolitan areas is necessarily confined to the boundaries of single municipalities. Indeed, in most places there exist mechanisms of co-ordination and co-operation that allow territorial fragmentation to be over come in the formulation and implementation of policies in metropolitan areas. They are best described by the term '*metropolitan governance*' (Lefèvre, 1998), i.e. various types of flexible, purpose-oriented co-operational arrangements, involving municipalities, different governmental agencies at various levels as well as private service providers. Because they are heterogeneous conglomerates of actors and agencies from various backgrounds and with various legal competencies, they can conduct public policies in metropolitan areas in a way that is relatively independent from the territorial boundaries of local institutions. Hence, such network-like mechanisms of 'governance'[3] appear as a major thrust to metropolitan policy-making.[4]

However, these mechanisms of governance appear as a mainly managerial answer to the issue of metropolitan problem-solving. The rationale behind associating actors or institutions to form metropolitan governance networks appears as an incremental mixture of criteria such as technical know-how, financial resources, and diffuse impressions of concern. The main idea is to 'get things done', and metropolitan governance does indeed represent a possibility of formulating and implementing coherent and encompassing policies in metropolitan areas in spite of their institutional fragmentation. It is however unclear what this signifies for the connection of public policy-making to democratic procedures, since both representation and participation are strongly structured by territorial boundaries. In other words, if, thanks to governance, metropolitan policies are no longer confined to institutionally defined territories, metropolitan democracy still is. In the light of the well-known tension between efficiency and democracy, there is thus reason to think that metropolitan governance profoundly affects the relationship between policies and politics in (Joye, 1995, Hendriks and Tops, 1999). This issue is even more important given that the connection of policy-making to democratic politics is one of the key features for the deliberative quality of public policies.

The aim of this chapter is to provide an empirically informed conceptual framework to evaluate issues of democracy with respect to metropolitan governance arrangements. The first part is dedicated to a brief discussion of theoretical propositions on how issues of democracy in the context of transitions from government to governance could be examined, and the ways in which these theoretical propositions can orient research in the field of metropolitan governance. The second part then discusses these propositions in the light of empirical evidence drawn from an ongoing research project on issues of metropolitan governance and democracy. In particular, we will examine the links between policies made through mechanisms of metropolitan governance and traditional democratic procedures, as well as the emergence of new spaces of deliberation in the context of such governance mechanisms.

Theoretical Propositions in Examining Issues of Democracy in Metropolitan Governance

When it comes to questions of democratic legitimacy of public policies, scholars of governance have viewed the transition from government to governance with a somewhat uneasy feeling. In western democracies, the legitimacy of the state and state policies is generally seen to rest upon transparent procedures that give good reasons to believe that decisions made and policies implemented are, ultimately, the result of public deliberations among free and equal citizens (Habermas, 1992). This is the *raison d'être* for mechanisms assuring democratic accountability and citizen control over state activities and public policies (Ingraham and Romzek, 1994). From that perspective, it becomes clear that, when looking at the transitions from government to governance, one must keep an eye on eventual consequences that new mechanisms of governance may bear not only at the 'output-side' of policy implementation, but also at the 'input-side' of formulation and democratic control of public policies. This point is evidently not overlooked in the governance debate. As Rhodes, for example, points out, governance is likely to pose a considerable 'challenge for democratic accountability' (Rhodes, 1996, p. 53). In our view, in the ongoing intense debate on this point, two main lines of reasoning can be distinguished, which we propose to term the *pessimistic* and the *optimistic view* on governance and democracy.

The Pessimistic View

One line of reasoning mainly rests upon the classic argument of democratic theory, according to which democratic political systems are structured by an intrinsic tension between the authenticity and effectiveness of policies (Scharpf, 1970), i.e. quality of inputs versus quality of outputs. In the extent to which governance mechanisms are mainly concerned with 'making things happen', i.e. to increase the effectiveness of policies on the output-side, there is reason to think that this will happen at the expense of authenticity at the input side. Supporters of this line of reasoning thus argue that transitions from government to governance threaten democratic quality and legitimacy. More precisely, they have considered that mechanisms of governance could be a menace to two important fundaments of democracy: democratically elected bodies, as well as the political community itself.

First, they argue that governance relativizes the weight of instances of democratically elected bodies in the policy process. Governance relies on self-governing networks associating various public and private actors and agencies, which, by the same token, leads to a dispersal of political power and to a loss of importance of traditional elected bodies in making decisions that are relevant to a policy field. More precisely, some observers have pointed out that the increasing participation of non-government organizations ('quangos') narrows the responsibilities exercised by formally elected authorities thereby modifying the relationships between voters and the government: lines of accountability become murky (King, 1996, Deleon, 1998). Some claim that networks of governmental and non-governmental actors where the main criterion for membership is technical know-how, leads to a technocratic style of policy making where elected bodies increasingly loose their grip (Gaudin, 1995, Gaudin, 1996). And, referring particularly to structures of multi-level governance, others have observed that networks associating governments, public administration and non-government from different state levels in a non-hierarchical way, contributes to a disenfranchisement of parliaments and councils at all levels (Scharpf, 1993).

Second, they argue that governance may affect the very fundamentals of community-identification. Networks of governance are mostly concerned with and structured by single policy issues, thus contributing to societal fragmentation and altering the ways through which the legitimate version of the common interest is identified and negotiated (Gaudin, 1999). As some researchers have noticed (Rose, 1995, Duran and Thoenig, 1996), governance conceives the citizen primarily as a taxpayer and a consumer of various public goods, whereas his/her role as a political subject seems somewhat in retreat. In their view, this fosters a conception of the political as just another sphere for the pursuit of individual goals, thereby calling into question the idea of the political community as a collective being with a public interest that is different from the sum of particular interests. In other words, governance would tend to make us forget that citizenship in the democratic state rests not only on the republican ideals of liberty and equality, but also fraternity (Hill, 1994, p. 3).

To us, this line of reasoning seems basically a pessimistic perspective in the sense that its thread is the willingness to examine threats to democracy and legitimacy by mechanisms of governance and to ring alarm bells if necessary.

The Optimistic View

A second line of reasoning, with respect to the implications of governance for democracy, rolls up the issue from another end. Instead of centring around the tension between quality of inputs versus quality of outputs put forward by classic democratic theory, the second line of reasoning focuses on another key feature of democratic politics: the relationship between the state and civil-society, seen as the 'nexus of associations through which people organise independently to manage their own affairs and which can also be a channel of influence upon government and a check on its powers' (Beetham, 1994, p. 29). It emphasises the idea that popular control over public policies is not only exercised by elected bodies in a top-down way, but also directly by citizens and their associations. Supporters of this perspective insist on the prospects of governance with respect to direct citizen involvement and participation in public policies, independently from representative elected bodies. Two main elements have been examined with respect to how transitions from government to governance affect the relationship between civil society and the state: the pluralization of policy-making by the pluralization of policy-networks, and the emergence of new instances of deliberation and dialogue between state and citizens.

First, drawing on the tenet of 'associative democracy' (Hirst, 1994), it is argued that self-governing networks, that include not only state agencies but also varieties of non-government organizations and associations, are an important vector of pluralism and civic culture. The presence of associations in these networks increases the influence of civil society on public policies and fosters civic culture. The involvement of non-government organizations and associations in the enforcement and administration of policies would result in increasing the points of view and the interests served by a particular public policy. Thus, recruiting the energies of citizen's organizations into public governance could be a step away from an oppressive state and towards a more egalitarian-democratic order (Cohen and Rogers, 1992, p. 465). In that sense, through the link of association involvement in public policies, transitions from government to governance can be an opportunity for empowering the citizen and pluralizing the state (Bang and Sørensen, 1998).

Second, it is argued that governance structures may foster discursive processes and thus increase the deliberative quality of public policies. The reason for this lies in the augmentation of interdependencies due to the great number and variety of actors and agencies involved in governance structures. Hierarchies are mostly absent, and when they are not, the veto power of single actors and agencies are often considerable. Hence, negotiation and compromise, or deliberation and consensus, appear as the only ways of achieving agreements on the course of collective action in self-governing networks. In this sense, the emergence of new spheres of negotiation and deliberation, such as neighbourhood forums, citizens' juries, user boards etc. has been interpreted as showing the increased importance of discursive processes in the formulation and administration of public policies as consequences of the transition from government to governance (Burns *et al.* 1994, Donzelot and Estèbe, 1994, Khan, 1999).

The central tenet of this second line of reasoning is thus to emphasise the potential for democratic renewal 'from below' which resides in the new mechanisms of governance. This view can be termed *optimistic*, in the sense that it sets out to examine whether the transition from government to governance opens up the state towards civil society and, if so, where the new openings occur and what their potential is for reinvigorating democratic civil society.

Implication for Research on Metropolitan Governance

In the light of this theoretical debate, the assessment of issues of democracy with respect to metropolitan governance, which we set out in this chapter, needs to concentrate on four major points:

a) the role of democratically elected bodies: is it relativized by structures of metropolitan governance?
b) the conception of the political community: does metropolitan governance put forward a vision of fragmentation?
c) associations as vectors for empowerment and pluralization: does metropolitan governance mobilise the energy of citizens' organizations?
d) new discursive processes: does metropolitan governance favour the emergence of spaces of deliberation and negotiation?

These four elements of analysis could inspire discussions of governance structures of any type. The particularity of *metropolitan governance* is the strong spatial component that is attached to it. Hence, when examining the four above mentioned points of assessment, we need to bear in mind this supplementary spatial element of metropolitan governance structures. We need not to only discuss the effects of governance with respect to all the four elements (elected bodies, political community, associations, new discursive processes), but discuss them particularly with respect to the new territorial scope that resides within metropolitan governance. In other words, the general question 'how does metropolitan governance affect these four key elements of democratic politics?', with respect to metropolitan governance, needs to be specified into 'how does metropolitan governance affect these four key elements of democratic politics and their territorial scope?'.

Metropolitan Governance and Democracy in Switzerland: The Case of Drug Policy

In the second part of this chapter, we would like to discuss these theoretical arguments in the light of empirical evidence on mechanisms of metropolitan governance.[5] The aim is not only to provide a theoretically guided assessment of recent tendencies of metropolitan governance with respect to the democracy issue, but also to test the pertinence and usefulness of these theoretical arguments to examine this issue.

Before doing so, however, we need to briefly outline the context of the metropolitan governance mechanisms examined here, i.e. metropolitan co-operational arrangements that have emerged in urban drug policies in Switzerland since the 1990s. In our opinion, they indeed provide excellent grounds for studying issues of governance and democracy.

Metropolitan Governance in Swiss Drug Policy: Basic Problems, Structures and Tendencies

In Switzerland, as in most other countries, problems related to the use of drugs tend to appear as a mainly urban phenomenon, concentrating especially in the core cities of metropolitan areas. Indeed, modern metropolises best provide the contextual conditions and the infrastructure necessary to the functioning of the drug market. They are places of anonymity, which is important to both users and dealers of illegal drugs. They are the centres of the international trade of goods and services, hence also of the trafficking of drugs and the financial transactions linked to it. Moreover, efficient metropolitan transportation networks facilitate encounters between the actors of the drug market; throughout Europe, central railway stations increasingly become focal points for the sale and redistribution of drugs. The laws of supply and demand mean that these focal points are at the same time the places where prices are comparatively low. It may thus be profitable for drug users to travel long distances. Last but not least, metropolises provide secondary economic opportunities for drug users who are in need of money (precarious jobs, prostitution, begging, theft, hold-ups, etc.). Like many other markets, the drug market is driven by a tendency to concentrate its activities to the large urban centres.

Harm Reduction Policy and Metropolitan Spillover Effects

Until the mid 1980s, the political response to drug-related problems in Switzerland did not differ between urban centres and other regions. Policy was guided by the 'abstinence paradigm' (Clémence and Gardiol, 1993), based on primary prevention to promote life without drugs, therapy to help drug users to quit, as well as heavy police repression of dealing and consumption. The appearance of the Human Immunodeficiency Virus (HIV) in the early 1980s, rapidly spreading among intravenous drug users through the then widely common habit of needle sharing, radically altered power-relations among competing 'advocacy coalitions' (Sabatier and Jenkins-Smith, 1999) in the drug policy subsystem, thereby leading to significant policy change. In Switzerland as well as in other European countries, *harm reduction services*, such as syringe exchange schemes, were set up, in order to promote health-protective behaviour among drug users who were not willing or able to quit. Since then, primary prevention, therapy, as well as repression of drug trafficking coexist side by side with harm reduction in most European drug policies.[6] Generally however, the implementation of the harm reduction principle is mainly left to local authorities, and they were mainly set up in places where public visibility of drug-related problems was high, i.e. in the big cities. This is as true for Switzerland (Malatesta *et al.*, 1992), as it is for other European countries (Bless *et al.*, 1993).

In the Swiss context of a high degree of governmental fragmentation at the local level, this has resulted in a quite unique picture when it comes to the geographical distribution of harm reduction facilities in metropolitan areas. Until the early nineteen-nineties, such facilities were set up almost exclusively in the core cities, whereas fringe municipalities usually did not provide any. The explanation for this lies in two types of territorial spillover effects.[7] First, the existence of harm reduction facilities intensified the pull-effect of core cities on actors of the drug market. It produced a significant increase in the number of drug users and their length of stay in the core cities, since they did not only come there to buy drugs, but also to use health and social services provided to them. The massive concentration of drug users in the core cities started to produce serious worries about public order, which were, in the political debate, often seen as an inherent by-product of harm reduction facilities (Kübler, 2000). The refusal of fringe municipalities to set up such facilities can thus be seen as a deliberate strategy of externalising public order problems related to drug use onto the core cities. Second, setting up and operating services for drug users has important financial implications. Since there are no mechanisms of financial compensation between local authorities in Swiss metropolitan areas, strategies of externalising monetary costs are another factor that explains the concentration of harm reduction facilities in core cities. In many ways, drug policy appeared as just one of the many spillover issues that there exist in Swiss metropolitan areas (Frey, 1988): fringe communities get many advantages from economic, social and cultural infrastructure provided by the core cities that are somewhat left alone when it comes to bearing the costs involved – be these monetary or otherwise.

Metropolitan Co-operational Arrangements for Service Provision in the Drug Field

As in other metropolitan spillover-domains, such as cultural policy or public transportation, core city governments started to pressure fringe communities to take their responsibility: either 'take back' their drug users and provide harm reduction facilities also on their own territory, or participate in the financing of facilities placed in the core cities. However, peripheral municipalities were generally not very keen on getting involved. They usually denied that there was a need for such services on their territory ('we do not have drug problems') and tended to consider that drug users should be looked after by the core cities where they dwelled ('you created services to attract them, so you're responsible for your own mess'). In fact, governments of fringe communities could plausibly pretend not to *see* any drug problem, for it was only really visible on the territory of the core cities. From the mid-1990s, core city governments, increasingly pressurised by their electorate to do something about public order problems and financial burdens linked to the drug issue, started to take action in order to 'sensitize' fringe communities to their responsibilities in the drug issue. Standard measures included statistics on the clientele of harm reduction services, showing high proportions of non-resident drug users, as well as billing 'user-fees' to the communities of residence. Some cities started to systematically refer non-resident drug users to the social work departments of their home communities, or even close access to harm reduction facilities to residents only. Such measures of metropolitan 'foreign policy' – as the mayor of Zurich put it – had an undeniable effect: fringe communities agreed to start negotiation and co-operational arrangements emerged, generally involving fringe communities, core cities as well as, sometimes, cantonal governments. According to the two spillover mechanisms to which they responded, two basic types of co-operational arrangements should be distinguished. A first type of co-operational arrangement is principally driven by the aim to unify and co-ordinate the approaches to the drug problem among all the communities, and to set up a decentralised network of harm reduction facilities covering the whole metropolitan area. The goal is to reduce concentrations of drug users in the core cities and thus to reduce public order worries. A second type of co-operational arrangements mainly aims at pooling financial resources of communities in metropolitan areas in order to compensate core cities for monetary costs incurred by harm reduction facilities provided by and placed in the core cities. In most metropolitan areas covered by this study, co-operational arrangements seemed to correspond to this second type. In addition, the empirical observations also pointed to the existence of mixed types, aiming simultaneously at financial compensation of core cities and at unification of approaches in the drug field.

There are two main features that characterise all the metropolitan co-operational arrangements that we observed in the drug field, independently from their aim: this is 1) the absence of hierarchical relationships between the actors involved, and 2) the significance of non-government organizations and voluntary associations to whom service provision is devolved and who participate in the planning and design of services. The reason for the absence of hierarchical structures is straightforward. In the territorial hierarchy, municipalities are placed on the same level, independently of their size. Communities of a metropolitan area are totally free to enter or to exit co-operational agreements with each other. Equality of treatment and rights among communities is thus an important element of holding such co-operational arrangements together. This does not even change when cantonal governments are involved in such arrangements – although they are hierarchically superior to municipalities – since legal competency to provide services for drug users is mainly devolved to communities, and no legal coercion can be exercised by the cantonal government. The reason for involving non-government organizations and associations in these co-operational arrangements is twofold. On the one hand, non-government organizations have important knowledge necessary to the design and implementation of services for drug users. Indeed, NGOs have ever since played an important role in social service provision in Switzerland (Bütschi and Cattacin, 1993; Kissling-Näf and Wälti, 1999), and particularly so in the drug field where militant non-government organizations had acquired experience and know-how about the ways to approach and work with a population that was difficult to reach and highly diffident to state intervention (Malatesta *et al.* 1992, Kübler, 1993). On the other hand, and this is particularly interesting in the context of metropolitan governance, the devolution to non-government organizations also represents the most flexible, non-bureaucratic and non-constraining instrument to associate various local governments in the provision of services. Non-government organizations that are formally responsible for operating facilities simply 'sell' their services, or parts of them, to various communal or cantonal governments. For instance, the syringe exchange scheme in the city of Lucerne is operated by an NGO close to the catholic church; the costs involved for the scheme is covered by the city of Lucerne (33 per cent of the budget), the canton of Lucerne (33 per cent) and 10 municipalities of the metropolitan area (about three per cent each). For the municipalities involved, this only needs a budgetary decision, whereas any other form of inter-communal collaboration would require complicated legal schemes of public-public collaboration. Hence, non-government organizations facilitate co-operation across territorial boundaries and thus play a crucial role in the de-territorialization of service provision in metropolitan areas.

But be that as it may, these two features undoubtedly qualify these co-operational arrangements as mechanisms of metropolitan *governance*, i.e. as self-governing networks involving actors and agencies from various levels of government and from beyond government, who co-operate in order to provide services in a given metropolitan area.

Metropolitan Governance and the Democracy Issue

We will now turn to the discussion of the four theoretical arguments previously identified with respect to the metropolitan governance mechanisms just described.

Role of Elected Bodies

The first theoretical argument put forward refers to the question whether democratically elected bodies are relativized by structures of metropolitan governance in making policy-relevant decisions. This leads us to examine the connections and lines of accountability between democratically elected bodies and metropolitan governance structures in the field of drug policy. Our case studies show that there are two ways in which democratically elected bodies are linked to decisions that are made within the governance mechanisms studied here.

First, it is generally elected local officials who represent the various communities in the strategic bodies of these governance mechanisms (e.g. co-ordination committees, boards, etc.). Thus, for the point of view they defend in these strategic bodies, they are accountable to their (local) electorate in the same way as for other decisions or actions affecting their constituency. Theoretically, the lines of accountability are thus very clear. Nevertheless, it is true that decisions made within these strategic bodies are generally not very transparent. They are generally not open to the public and it is often unclear who defended which positions in the discussions preceding these decisions. However, this is nothing peculiar to governance mechanisms: also in fields where services are entirely administered by the public administration – thus through mechanisms of 'government' rather than 'governance' – transparency of decision-making among elected officials can be low. This is particularly so in Switzerland, where local executives are mostly coalition governments, and where positions of single members in decision processes within the executive count among the best kept political secrets.[8]

A second link between local elected bodies and the services implemented through metropolitan governance structures is budgetary decision making. As described above, services implemented through metropolitan governance structures usually involve financial transfers between the governmental bodies that participate and an NGO which operates the facilities. Generally, local constitutions stipulate that credits must be approved by the executive, by the local parliament (or citizen assembly in small communes), or that they can even be submitted to a referendum when they exceed a certain amount. Thus, if members of local elected bodies want to interfere in the ways services are provided through metropolitan governance mechanisms, approval of credits given to these NGOs provides an excellent occasion to do so. Our case studies show that this occasion has been seized quite often: many times, debates about drug policy in local parliaments and councils were triggered off by a proposal to vote an NGO-credit (see also Kübler, 2000). Again, we do not see any difference to the occasions local elected bodies have to interfere between mechanisms of 'governance' and 'government'. Also when services are provided entirely by the public administration, budget approvals are often the only occasion for local elected bodies to trigger off a debate and to interfere.

In other words, our case studies do not show evidence that metropolitan governance structures in the drug field would inherently lead to a relativization of local elected bodies in making policy relevant decisions. Local elected bodies do indeed retain an important role in conducting metropolitan drug policies – or at least continue to have possibilities to influence it in a significant way.

Conception of the Political Community

The second theoretical argument points to the influence that mechanisms of governance may have on the conception of the political community. In particular, it is contended that in a context of governance, the ways in which community issues are publicly debated promotes identification with particular interests rather than to the common interest. Relating to *metropolitan* governance, the issue that is basically at stake here is the territorial scope of the community identification, i.e. whether the metropolitan area is seen to encompass a single political community, or whether the political community to which citizens identify is first and foremost limited to the boundaries of the various municipalities. The very aim of structures of metropolitan governance is to provide services for the whole metropolitan area. As far as *policies* are concerned, the territorial scope clearly goes beyond municipal boundaries, and it can be said that the inherent community conception is one that encompasses the metropolitan area. But this is not the point here. Referring to the issue of democracy, the question is, whether *politics* related to metropolitan governance structure further or diminish a conception of the metropolitan area as a single political community. In order to answer this question, it is necessary to take a closer look at the political debate that is taking place about these governance structures in the principal loci of metropolitan politics, i.e. the public sphere as well as local parliaments and councils.

Concerning the public sphere, an assessment of the influences of governance mechanisms on metropolitan community building is not easy on the base of our empirical evidence. This is principally due to methodological limitations of our study design, resting mainly on qualitative material.[9] Nevertheless, some suggestions can be made on the basis of the media coverage on metropolitan drug problems and the governance structures set up as a response. In this respect, the coverage by the main media appears clearly driven by a discourse that puts forward the idea that solidarity of all metropolitan municipalities with core cities is a necessary prerequisite for effectively solving major problems linked to drug use. However, it is highly unclear how a causal relationship can be established between this media discourse and the setting up of governance structures.

Conceptions of metropolitan communities also crystallise in the political sphere at the occasion of debates in local executives, councils, parliaments and citizen assemblies about measures of drug policy governance, especially during discussions on the credit that the municipality would give to an NGO to operate harm reduction facilities. Our case studies show that the question on which these debates appear to focus is whether the local community has an interest to participate (financially or otherwise) in the setting up of services to drug users in the metropolitan area. In core cities, the main argument put forward is the hope that costs and negative externalities incurred by the presence of non-resident drug users will be reduced. And in the fringe communities, the debate often concerns the issues of what the participation in metropolitan drug governance structures means in financial terms for the community, and what the expected consequences may be in terms of public order problems. In core cities as well as in fringe communities, the political debate about metropolitan drug governance seems thus to be structured mainly by the will to protect and maximise the interest of the particular constituency. Hence, the underlying conception of territorial community that crystallises in these debates seems to be quite the opposite of the vision of a metropolitan community with a common interest. Rather, the single communities are seen to be the most important entities whose particular interests must first and foremost be served in the discussion on metropolitan issues. However, it must be emphasised that such a fragmented conception of the metropolitan community is much more the effect of the traditional, territorially defined political institutions than it would be an outcome of metropolitan governance structures. In other words, it is not metropolitan *governance* but local *government* that influences the conception of the metropolitan community. In that respect, it is interesting to note that in discussions among community representatives *within* metropolitan governance mechanisms, the idea of metropolitan solidarity does indeed seem to be a thriving one. But only rarely do the very same representatives use this vision to justify 'at home' the participation of their community to the governance mechanism.[10]

In the end, our empirical evidence concerning the second theoretical argument does not support the pessimists' view, according to which governance would promote a fragmented vision of the community. On the one hand, one can tentatively argue that mechanisms of metropolitan governance may have fostered a sense of metropolitan community and identity by stimulating the public debate. On the other hand, the conception of the metropolitan area as an aggregate of single local communities that does indeed crystallise in the local political arenas is not so much a produce of governance mechanisms but rather of the traditional local government structures.

Associations as Vectors for Empowerment and Pluralization

The third theoretical argument points to the potential of governance mechanisms to 'bring the state closer to the citizens' by the involvement of civil-society associations and organizations in state activities, thereby promoting citizen empowerment and pluralism in public policies. With respect to *metropolitan* governance and the special attention to the territorial dimension involved, this issue includes the question of the territorial scope of non-government organizations and associations participating in governance mechanisms. As we have seen above, NGOs and private associations are *the* central feature of metropolitan governance mechanisms in the field of drug policy in Switzerland. Not only are they involved in drug policy making because of the undisputed know-how and experience they had acquired in long years of working with drug users, but also because they represent a receptacle for organising inter-community co-operation in metropolitan areas in a flexible and unbureaucratic way.

Concerning NGO autonomy towards the state, important change has occurred in recent years in the drug field in Switzerland. It is due mostly to the sophistication of New Public Management tools (especially contractualization) combined with deliberate efforts by public authorities to restructure the NGO sector in the drug field. In most metropolitan areas, public authorities nowadays have included the support of policy principles as clauses of contracts regulating financial transfers to NGOs. Depending on state money to cover most of their budget, NGOs in the drug field can nowadays not afford any more to defend points of view and policy principles that are different or even in opposition with the official drug policy. Whereas a myriad of radical and militant associations animated the political debate about drug policy in the nineteen-eighties, this is much less the case nowadays. For instance, there is no single association left which would advocate illegal drug use as an alternative way of life to the dominant values of society – a point of view that was remarkably present in the early 1970s and in the 1980s. Public authorities have increasingly exercised pressure and forced NGOs into line with the official drug policy. Linking public subsidies to the conditions that state policy be supported has sometimes resulted in the disappearance of militant associations, and even more frequently lead to intense conflicts within associations, mainly resolved by lay-offs of the dissenting staff. However, it would be unfair to say that civil-society organizations have been completely colonised by the state and that their points of view have been lost. Indeed, some of the major militant claims of the past are nowadays part of the official drug policy, such as the various types of harm reduction interventions. Nevertheless, there is a clear tendency for the state to limit the autonomy of NGOs only to management questions, whereas positions to substantial policy issues are to be taken by the state alone. Today, many NGOs and associations in the drug policy field in Switzerland do not grandly differ from state bureaucracies, except perhaps when it comes to questions of job security and salaries – which are generally higher in the public administration.

Concerning more particularly the relationships between NGOs and various local communities in metropolitan areas, the impression of a very limited autonomy of NGOs from the state is further confirmed. Indeed, for NGOs, the receipt of subsidies from various governments often goes along with an increase in the membership of community representatives on the NGOs' boards, thereby strengthening the point of view that government institutions may defend in decisions made within the NGOs. Through the involvement of NGOs in metropolitan governance structures, their autonomy from the (local) state can be further restricted. However, in the extent to which these NGOs are accountable to several local communities, they cannot prefer some over others and must thus have a scope that goes beyond single community boundaries. By responding to the aggregate demands of single communities, NGOs generally take a stance that is more metropolitan in scope than that of any other actor. This can also be seen as a somewhat autonomous point of view, all the more so in that our case studies have shown that executive officials of such NGOs clearly are important promoters of encompassing metropolitan views of drug problems in the public debate.

Hence, metropolitan governance structures in Swiss drug policies do not really appear as a vector for citizen empowerment and the pluralization of the state. On the contrary, the involvement of civil-society organizations into governance structures seems an important leverage for colonisation of civil society by the state. However, in their role of contractors of multiple local governments, by whom they are controlled and to whose aggregate demands they need to respond, NGOs need to develop a territorial scope that is definitely not the same as the one of their governmental contract-givers. In a sense, NGOs incorporate the *metropolitan consciousness* in a way in which no local public authorities are able.

New Spheres of Deliberation

The fourth theoretical argument put forward to examine democracy issues in relation to transitions from government to governance points to the importance of discursive processes of decision-making, supposedly favoured under conditions of governance. In order to address this question, we will explore the ways in which decisions were made among actors involved in metropolitan governance structures and assess the importance of discursive processes.

We have already mentioned the absence of hierarchy between the representatives of the various communities that are part of metropolitan governance mechanisms. Since their co-operation within these governance schemes rests primarily on their free will, equal treatment of communities is an important prerequisite: the exit-option is open to the communities at any time. This is reflected in the rules and customs of decision-making within the strategic bodies of metropolitan governance structures. They make sure that single communities have sufficient voice in the debates, as well as sufficient votes when it comes to actually making the decision. From a formal point of view, decisions are made by the majority of community votes, and in many cases, votes are weighted according to the degree of the community's involvement in the governance mechanism. This is most often measured in terms of financial contribution: communities which contribute much are given more votes than others. It is thus no wonder that core cities have a strong position in processes of decision making within the metropolitan governance mechanisms. They bear the lion's share in financing facilities for drug users and thus also have more votes than others.[11]

However, our observations show that the exit-option that exists for all the communities generally has a strong effect on decision-making. Only very rarely are decisions taken through majority-votes. Normally, debates and consultation of all the different points of view have an important place before the final vote, which more often expresses a consensus than a majoritarian decision. In many metropolitan governance mechanisms studied in our research, deliberation and consensus are the most important mode of decision-making. Two remarkable cases in point are the governance schemes of the Lugano and the Zurich metropolitan areas, where there have been no majoritarian decisions at all – and that during their whole existence, with a monthly meeting during ten years.

Thus, it really seems that the absence of hierarchy between the actors of metropolitan governance mechanisms strongly pushes towards deliberative and consensual modes of decision-making. In that respect, the empirical evidence does indeed support the idea of discursive processes being fostered through mechanisms of governance. It is particularly interesting to note that the mechanisms of metropolitan governance examined here, not only seem to encourage deliberation *per se*, but also between actors from territorial entities that are situated at the same level of hierarchy and that, from a formal institutional point of view, would have no reason and opportunity to engage in policy relevant discussions with each other. Hence, mechanisms of metropolitan governance do not only encourage discursive processes in general, but they also create the opportunity for *deliberation with a new territorial scope,* namely that of the metropolitan area, relatively detached from the formal institutional levels of communes, cantons and the national state.

Conclusion

In this chapter, we have tried to provide a theoretically guided discussion of the issue of democracy with respect to empirical evidence on new mechanisms of metropolitan governance in the field of drug policy in Switzerland. In doing so, we have pursued two main goals: on the one hand, to provide an assessment of the existing metropolitan governance structures, as well as, on the other hand, to test the pertinence and relevance of four particular theoretical propositions for guiding empirical research.

Assessing Existing Metropolitan Governance Structure

The above discussion of the existing metropolitan governance structures in the light of theoretical propositions found in the literature does neither completely support the pessimistic nor the optimistic line of argument. In particular, the pessimists' alarming hypothesis according to which locally elected bodies would lose importance through the advent of mechanisms of governance was not confirmed. Lines of accountability between decision making within metropolitan governance structures and the citizens appear to be rather clear: as in other policy fields, decision-makers are elected and remain liable to the electorate of their constituency, and budgetary decision-making remains a strong leverage for elected bodies to intervene in a way that is highly policy relevant. However, it also appeared clear that the optimists' view of governance structures as an opportunity for enrichment and pluralization of the state through the involvement of civil-society associations can not be upheld in the empirical context examined here. Rather than representing a new opening of the civil society to the state, metropolitan governance mechanisms seem to be an occasion for the state to impinge on the associational sector. Many of the examined governance mechanisms do indeed qualify as 'state bureaucracy with other means' which does, however, not necessarily exclude the production of a policy close to social demands.

With respect to the *territorial dimension* inherent in metropolitan governance, the above discussion yielded some interesting points with respect to metropolitan community-building. It clearly showed that mechanisms of 'traditional' local *government* are one of the main vectors of a fragmented conception of the metropolitan community. And there is reason to think that metropolitan governance structures are contributing to the emergence of a metropolitan community with a political identity of its own, in the extent to which they set off debates with a metropolitan scope in the public sphere. This conclusion needs to remain tentative for it rests on weak methodological foundations. However, the emergence of spheres of deliberation with a new territorial scope is also a strong argument in point. Governance structures may indeed nurture a vision of metropolitan community among those who take part in the discursive processes, i.e. the elected representatives of the local communities, that go on within these spheres. In answer to the question that we posed at the beginning of this paper, it now seems that structures of metropolitan governance are not only a factor of metropolitan *policies*, but that they also nurture metropolitan *politics* and contribute to the affirmation of the metropolitan area as a sphere of the political – not only of technical management.

However, the above assessment only draws on governance mechanisms found in the drug field. It is thus unclear whether its conclusions can be extrapolated to other fields of policy, where important elements of the underlying dynamics may greatly differ. For instance, drugs policy is a highly emotional issue with a high potential for politicisation. This may well affect the ways in which connections between governance structures and traditional spheres of political decision-making were constructed. In that respect, it would be interesting to contrast the case of drug policy with metropolitan governance structures that exist in policy fields with a much lower degree of politicisation – such as water supply, for instance.[12]

Assessing the Usefulness of the Theoretical Framework

Throughout this chapter, it appeared that an assessment of the empirical evidence through a theoretical framework based on four main propositions proved possible and feasible. In particular, although taken from a line of argument that we felt to be normatively oriented – pessimistic or optimistic – the confrontation with empirical evidence produced quite differentiated results. We thus conclude that these four propositions have a certain usefulness as working hypotheses for structuring and orienting empirical research on issues of democracy with respect to metropolitan governance.

However, in our view, not all of them were equally easy to confront with empirical evidence. In particular, the second (pessimistic) argument about how governance affects political community and identification did seem a bit foggy, at least in the way it was used in this discussion. Indeed, in the review, it is unclear which the elements of political community are – as a simplification, we chose to define it on the basis of territorial criteria – and how these elements are supposed to be affected by transitions from government to governance. In order to increase its potential for providing guidance in empirical research, this second theoretical proposition certainly still needs a considerable effort at operationalization.

Looking back on the above discussion, there is another point with respect to these four theoretical propositions which, to our minds, needs further reflection. This is the interrelations and intrinsic connections that there are *between* elements of governance and democracy pinpointed by each of the four theoretical propositions. For instance, our assessment has shown that the governance mechanisms under scrutiny are still strongly linked to traditional loci of democracy, such as elected bodies. In the pessimists' view, this can be seen as a positive case in point, in the sense that it guarantees democratic control and accountability between decision-makers and citizens. On the other side, the absence of autonomy of civil-society associations within these governance mechanisms seems as a negative point when considering that the potential for empowering citizens and pluralizing the state is annihilated by efforts of the state to control contractors who receive public money. However, this may well be two sides of the same coin. In the constitutional framework of western democracies, the institutions of the state still are the main channel and leverage for democratic control and accountability in public policies: the legislature controls the executive, both control the public administration and are at the same time accountable to the electorate. Thus, from the point of view of democratic control and accountability, it is adequate for the state to give the least autonomy possible to associative contractors. This somehow points to an intrinsic tension between democratic principles underlying procedures of checks and balances within the state institutions on the one hand, and the propensity to be open to the civil society and its associations on the other hand. There is thus reason to think that strong mechanisms of democratic control intrinsically reduce the potential of associative democracy. In other words, this would mean that in western democracies, there is a choice to be made between democratic accountability and democracy 'from below'.

Notes

1. This paper draws on two research projects funded by the Swiss National Science Foundation, in the context of its Priority Programme 'Switzerland Towards the Future', conducted at the Institut de recherché sur l'environnement construit of the Swiss Federal Institute of Technology Lausanne and at the Institut d'études politiques et internationales of the University of Lausanne (Grant numbers # 5004-047870/1 and # 5004-058522/1).
2. For instance, the metropolitan area north of the lake Geneva (roughly 0.9 million inhabitants) comprises 143 municipalities located in two different cantons. The metropolitan area around Zurich (roughly 1.5 million inhabitants) comprises about 160 municipalities, located in four different cantons.
3. The generic term 'governance' as it is used throughout this paper, describes a kind of public policy making that is no longer based on authority and the sanctions of government but relies on self-organizing networks of institutions and actors, drawn from but also beyond government (cf. Le Galès, 1995, Rhodes, 1996, Stoker, 1996).
4. The argument is supported by research on metropolitan areas throughout Europe (Dente, 1990, Van den Berg *et al.*, 1993, Healey *et al.*, 1995, Bagnasco and Le Galès, 1997, Klöti, 1997, Kübler and Wälti, 2001).
5. The empirical evidence consists of case studies on the nine major urban agglomerations in Switzerland (Basel, Bern, Fribourg, Geneva, Lausanne, Lucerne, Lugano, St. Gall and Zurich), based on newspaper reviews and about 60 qualitative interviews with various stakeholders.
6. On this paradigm shift in Switzerland, cf. in particular Boggio *et al.* (1997), Kübler (1999, 2000), for other European countries, cf. Bless *et al.* (1993), Cattacin *et al.* (1995), Rhodes and Hartnoll (1996), Bergeron (1998).
7. For details on these spillover effects, see Kübler and Wälti (2001).

8. According to the so-called 'collegiality'-principle, each member of government must defend a decision that has been made, even if that means to defend a point of view that he/she was ferociously opposed to during the discussions with his or her colleagues but was out voted in the end.
9. In spring 2001, a quantitative inquiry on the issue of whether there is something like a metropolitan community feeling among residents of these areas is planned in order to overcome this limitation.
10. This has been confirmed in many interviews with elected members of fringe community governments, contending that these communities had indeed a vital interest that drug users were addressed in an efficient way in the core cities and in the metropolitan area as a whole. However, they had the feeling that this argument would not be convincing in the political debate within their community.
11. As a telling illustration for this, the case of the Lucerne agglomeration can be mentioned. The Lucernese metropolitan governance mechanism involves roughly 70 municipalities from the agglomeration plus the city of Lucerne. The annual budget is about 1.5 million Swiss francs, of which 43 per cent is covered by the city of Lucerne alone. In decision-making, the Lucerne representative has 10 votes, bigger municipalities have three and smaller municipalities have one.
12. This is what we actually plan to do in the remainder of our research project, where we set out to examine issues of democracy with respect to metropolitan mechanisms in the fields of public transportation, water supply, as well as cultural policy.

References

Bagnasco, A. and Le Galès, P. (eds) (1997) *Villes en Europe*, La Decouverte, Paris.

Bang, H.P. and Sørensen, E. (1998) 'The Everyday Maker, A New Challenge to Democratic Governance', Paper delivered to the ECPR Joint Sessions, University of Warwick.

Beetham, D. (1994) 'Key Principles and Indicies for a Democratic Audit', in D. Beetham (ed), *Defining and Measuring Democracy*, Sage, London, pp. 25–43

Bergeron, H. (1998) 'Soigner ou prendre soin des toxicomanes: anatomie d'une croyance collective. Analyse du champ de la toxicomanie en France de 1970 à 1995 ou l'histoire de la domination d'un paradigme', *IEP de Paris*, Paris.

Bless, R., Korf, D. and Freeman, M. (1993) *Urban Drug Policies in Europe 1993*, O+S, Amsterdam.

Boggio, Y., Cattacin, S., Cesoni, M.L. and Lucas, B. (1997) *Apprendre à gérer: la politique Suisse en matière de drogue*, Georg, Genève.

Burns, D., Hambleton, R. and Hoggett, P. (1994) *The Politics of Decentralisation*, Macmillan, Basingstoke.

Bütschi, D. and Cattacin, S. (1993) 'The Third Sector in Switzerland: The Transformation of the Subsidiarity Principle', *European Journal of Political Research*, vol. 16, pp. 362–379.

Cattacin, S., Lucas. B. and Vetter, S. (1995) *Modèles de politique en matière de drogues*, L'Hartmattan, Paris.

Clémence, A. and Gardiol, N. (1993) 'Le prises de position de jeunes face à la drogue en Suisse, *Déviance et Société*, vol. 17, pp. 19–32.

Cohen, J. and Rogers, J. (1992) 'Secondary Associations and Democratic Governance', *Politics and Society*, vol. 20, pp. 393–472.

Deleon, L. (1998) 'Accountability in a "Reinvented" Government', *Public Administration*, vol. 76, pp. 539–558.

Dente, B. (1990) 'Metropolitan Governance Reconsidered or How to Avoid Errors of the Third Type', *Governance*, vol. 3, pp. 55–74.

Donzelot, J. and Estèbe, P. (1974) *L'Etat animateur. Essai sur la politique de la ville*, Editions Esprit, Paris.

Duran, P. and Theonig, J-C. (1996) 'L'Etat et la gestion publique territoriale', *Revue Française de Science Politique*, vol. 46, pp. 580–623.

Frey, R.L. (1988) 'Spillovers: Ursache von Agglomerationsproblemen und Lösungsmöglichkeiten', in M. Bassand, D. Joye and M. Schuler (ed), *Les enjeux de l'urbanisation/Agglomerationsprobleme in der Schweiz*, Lang and Société Suisse d'Etudes pour l'Organisation de l'Espace et la Politique Régionale, Bern, pp. 142–155

Gaudin, J.-P. (1995) 'Politiques urbaines et négociations territoriales. Quelle légitimité pour les politiques publiques?, *Review Française De Science Politique*, vol. 45, pp. 31–56.

Gaudin, J.-P. (1996) 'Construction de la norme et négociations territoriales', *Revue européene des sciences sociales*, vol. 34, pp. 125–145.

Gaudin, J.-P. (1999) *Gouverner par contrat. L'action publique en question*, Presses de Sciences Po, Paris.

Habermas, J. (1992) *Fakizität und Geltung. Diskurstheorie des Rechts und des Demokratischen Rechstaats*, Suhrkamp, Frankfurt.

Healey, P., Camerson, S., Davoudi, S., Graham, S. and Madani-Pour, A. (eds) (1995) *Manging Cities. The New Urban Context*, John Wiley, Chicester.

Hendriks, F. and Tops, P. (1999) 'Between Democracy and Efficiency: Trends in Local Government Reform in the Netherlands and Germany', *Public Administration*, vol. 77, pp. 133–153.

Hill, D. (1994) *Cities and Citizens*, Harvester Wheatsheaf, Hemel Hempstead.

Hirst, P. (1994) *Associative Democracy*, Polity Press, Cambridge.

Ingraham, P. and Romzek, B. (eds) (1994) *New Paradigms for Government*, Jossey-Bass, San Francisco.

Jouve, B. and Lefèvre, C. (eds) (1999) *Villes, métropoles. Les nouveaux territories du politique*, Economica, Paris.

Joye, D. (1995) 'Le gouvernement métropolitain: entre efficacité technique et démocratie', in J.-P. Leresche, D. Joye and M. Bassand (eds), *Métropolisations. Interdépendances mondiales et implications lémaniques*, Georg, Geneve.

Joye, D. and Leresche, J.-P. (1999) 'Pouvoir local contre gouvernement métropolitain: l'exemple du bassin lémanique', in B. Jouve and C. Lèfevre (eds), *Villes, métroples.Les nouveaux territoires du politique*, Economica, Paris, pp. 133–162

Khan, U.A. (ed) (1999) *Participation Beyond the Ballott Box*, UCL Press, London.

King, D. (1996) 'Conclusion', in D. King and G. Stoker (eds), *Rethinking Local Democracy*, Macmillan, Basingstoke, pp. 214–223

Kissling-Näf, I. and Wälti, S. (1999) 'Der Vollzug öffentlicher politiken', in U. Klöti, H. Kriesi, W. Linder and Y. Papadopoulos (eds), *Handbuch der schweizer politik/Manuel de la politique suisse*, NZZ Verlag, Zürich, pp. 651–691.

Klöti, U. (1997) 'Stadpolitik als Zusammenarbeit', in HSSV/uus (ed), *Die Stadt Morgen – Demain les villes*, Geiger AG, Bern.

Kübler, D. (1993) *L'Etat face à la toxicomanie: action publique et contrat social*, Université de Lausanne, Lausanne.

Kübler, D. (1999) 'Ideas as Catalytic Elements for Policy Change. Advocacy Coalitions and Drug Policy in Switzerland', in D. Braun and A. Busch (eds), *Public Policy and Political Ideas*, Edward Elgar, Cheltenham, pp. 116–135.

Kübler, D. (2000) *Politique de la drogue dans les villes suisses entre ordre et santé. Analyse des conflits de mise en oeuvre*, L'Harmattan, Paris.

Kübler, D. and Wälti, S. (2001) 'Drug-Policy Making in Metropolitan Areas: Urban Conflicts and Governance', *International Journal of Urban and Regional Research*, vol. 25, pp. 33–53.

Le Galès, P. (1995) 'Du gouvernement des villes à la gouvernance urbaine', *Revue française de science politique*, vol. 45, pp. 57–95.

Lefèvre, C. (1998) 'Metropolitan Government and Governance in Western Countries: A Critical Review', *International Journal of Urban and Regional Research*, vol. 48, pp. 9–25.

Leresche, J.-P., Joye, D. and Bassand, M. (eds) (1995) *Métropolisations. Interdépendances mondiales et implications Lémaniques*, Georg, Genève.

Malatesta, D., Joye, D. and Spreyermann, C. (1992) *Villes et Toxicomanie. Des Stratégies Urbaines de Prévention du Sida en Suisse*, IREC-DA/EPFL, Lausanne.

Rhodes, R.A.W. (1996) 'The New Governance: Governing Without Government', *Political Studies*, vol. 44, pp. 652–667.

Rhodes, T. and Hartnoll, R. (eds) (1996) *Aids, Drugs and Prevention. Perspectives on Individual and Community Action*, Routledge, London.

Rose, L. (1995) *Consumers, Taxpayers, Citizens: An Inquiry into Democratic Citizenship in the Context of Local Government*, University of Oslo, Department of Political Science, Oslo.

Sabatier, P.A. and Jenkins-Smith, H.C. (1999) 'The Advocacy Framework: An Assessment' in P. A. Sabatier (ed), *Theories of the Policy Process*, Westview Press, Boulder, CO, pp. 117–166.

Scharpf, F.W. (1970) *Demokratietheorie Zwischen Utopie und Anpassung*, Universitätsverlag, Konstanz.

Scharpf, F.W. (1993) 'Versuch uber Demokratie im Verhandelnden Staat', in R. Czada and M. Schmidt (eds), *Verhandlungsdemokratie Interessenvermittlung, Regierbarkeit*, Westdeutscher Verlag, Opladen.

Schuler, M. (1994) *Die Raumgliederungen der Schweiz/Les Niveaux Géographiques de la Suisse*, Bundesamt für Statistik, Bern.

Stoker, G. (1996) *Governance as Theory: Five Propositions*, Université d'ete Transfrontalière, Uriage.

Van den Berg, L., Van Klink, A. and Van der Meer, J. (eds) (1993) *Governing Metropolitan Regions*, Avebury, Aldershot.

Chapter 7

Decentralization: New Forms of Public Participation or New Forms of Managerialism?

John Diamond

Introduction

Decentralization initiatives by some UK local authorities in the 1980s can be viewed as innovatory and radical. At a time when the Conservative New Right government focussed its attention on what some regarded as bastions of 'local socialism' the twin aims of decentralisation (improving service delivery and enhancing local democracy) can be seen as the high watermark of independent local government.

This paper is one attempt to revisit the history and experience of that period and to explore the reasons why decentralisation failed. The contention of this paper is that the failure stemmed, largely, from a failure to engage sufficiently with concepts of power within the local and central state. The absence of an agreed theoretical understanding of what was (and not) possible resulted in policies which enhanced service delivery at the expense of local democracy. The reasons for this failure are set out below.

To draw lessons from the decentralization experiment it is important to identify the consequences of the experience. The newly found enthusiasm for inter-agency working and the 'partnership' approach of the New Labour Government can locate its 'roots' in the attempts of urban Labour run local authorities to reform their organizations and working practices. The emergence of 'new managerialism' in the early 1990s comes out of the decentralization experiment and the Tory Government reforms in health, housing, education and Compulsory Competitive Tendering. It is now commonplace in both local government and central government programmes. It is suggested that this managerial change provides a new paradigm with which to assess the extent to which local democracy (rather than only service delivery) can be addressed.

The 'legacy' of 1980s decentralisation innovation was profound managerial and organizational change which has 'depoliticized' the language of debate at the local level. By focussing on service delivery, or service quality, issues of power have been marginalized. These are, of course, profoundly 'political' issues. The delivery (and quality) of particular services raise questions of resourcing and access; involving issues of decision making and how it is exercised; and embracing questions of professionalism and the rights of 'professionals' and non-professionals to critically evaluate the practices and assumptions of those with service delivery responsibilities.

The potential to challenge the framework of decision-making is limited, the 'agenda' for change has been set and the limits to that agenda are not open for negotiation or debate, so we need to be more sceptical about the claims made for the new managerialist revolution if we are to engage with the debate about transforming local democracy. The challenge for policy makers, practitioners and researchers is to imagine alternatives which could begin to shift the balance of power away from a managerial perspective to one which locates local democracy at the centre rather than on the periphery.

The Context: 1. Aspirations of 1980s Decentralization

The aspirations of 1980s decentralisation have been well documented. A wide range of literature has examined the overall aims of those who advocated change and of specific local authorities which embraced the changes. Assessments of the decentralization experiments can show how the focus slips from exploring the underlying ideology of change to one which examines the managerialist agenda. This provides us with a useful 'family tree' which, despite its limitations, does highlight important changes in emphasis and practice.

In the seminal paper by Gyford (1983) and the work of Boddy and Fudge (1984) we can see how the aims of those advocating change were expressed as a counter ideology to the 'new right' Thatcherism of the Conservative Government. In the early 1980s, decentralization and neighbourhood services were perceived as providing an opportunity for Labour run local authorities to provide an alternative project to the 'new right'. The claim was made that this could

> undermine the capitalist form of social relation by replacing it with the relation which we defined as socialist: to replace domination with co-operation and democratic control ... to extend participation within the supply of basic resources at the local level to those largely dependent upon them. Hence the drive to decentralization (McDonnell, 1984).

This possibility was explored further in the work of Hambleton and Hoggett (1984), the decentralization initiative was supported by their work with a number of local authorities. Their advocacy of change was underpinned by theorising which not only took account of the 'consumerist' agenda advocated by the new-right, and also argued the case for change in a critique of the bureaucratic model of the post war welfare state. Rejecting the approach to service delivery (which they saw as being dominated by the 'producers' of services and cemented by their reluctance to explore the impact of 'professionalism') they offered an approach which stressed the need for strong local democratic institutions, open and accountable to users. This model drew upon the fashionable claims of post-fordism and, in particular, the work of the managerial and organisational gurus of the private sector (Hoggett, 1991).

The impact of private sector thinking on local government should not be underestimated. It permeated the thinking and practice of local authority managers, the influential Audit Commission, Local Government Management Board and policy makers throughout 1990s.

The cumulative impact of the Conservative changes, had reduced the scope and power of local government in a variety of ways. For some, (Burns *et al.*, 1994) decentralization, provided an alternative to the negative stereotyping of local government engaged in by the Tories. It also gave support to those who were already advocating change. One influential grouping within the Labour Party at that time (Labour Co-ordinating Committee, 1984) set out their model of a reformed and 'dynamic' local authority. Their critique of local government drew upon the bureaucratic failures of the past. Identifying (as had the Conservatives for other reasons) the reluctance of both white and blue collar unions to change their working practices and the entrenched systems of local power which drew together leading elected members into a coalition of mutual interests with senior officers.

Decentralization was, therefore, one attempt to break up those vested interests. The challenges of this are well illustrated in the work of Burns *et al.* (1994) who explored the impact of decentralization on specific local authorities and from that experience sought to develop alternative models of enhancing local democracy.

The marginalization of the 'leftist' critique of both local and central government during this period is, perhaps, best illustrated in the work of Lansley *et al.* (1989) who locate the failure in what some regarded as the beginning of Thatcherism. Others, (Diamond, 1990b) saw it as related to the changed political context of the late 1980s (the failure of the Miners Strike, the move to the right by the Kinnock Labour Party, the absence of a coherent alternative to the Conservatives and a failure to reform politically 'corrupt' local Labour run authorities as the experience of the 1990s has demonstrated).

Another approach is to look at the experiences of some local authorities from the point of view of participants in the experiments. The work of Cockburn (1977) in the late 1970s was often discussed during this period as being too narrow in its application of a neo-Marxist perspective. Yet, if we do not place these changes in a wider and theoretical context we are left with particular stories about particular localities which lack any shared analysis. Whilst this may sit quite easily with a post-modern interpretation it does not provide an explanation from which we can begin to anticipate alternatives or to identify ways of working towards such an alternative.

In introducing decentralisation strategies, the local authorities selected by this writer (Diamond, 1990a) placed the emphasis upon organizational and structural changes. As the table below illustrates they sought to introduce (and consolidate) change by re-structuring their decision making and working practices. In two of the local authorities studied these resulted in relatively minor changes.

Table 7.1 Decentralization and Structural Change

Issue	Birmingham	Islington	Tower Hamlets	Manchester
Council committee for Decentralization	✔	✔	✔	✔
Neighbourhood Officer	✔	✔	✔	✔
Generic Teams	✘	✘	✔	✘
Departmental Reorganization	✘	✘	✔	✘
Local Forums	✘	✔	✔	✘

The changes introduced focussed upon improving service delivery. Only one – Tower Hamlets – claimed to have established ways of enhancing local decision making by consulting local people, and, taking account of their conflicting needs. Their experience has been well documented (Burns *et al.*, 1994, Platt, 1987) and raises important questions for all of us about how to balance competing interests within local communities when there is an absence of clearly defined policies.

The important conclusion, for this writer, was that whilst the authorities *claimed* to be about enhancing service delivery and local democracy the emphasis of the former was at the expense of the latter. These tensions and contradictions were well explored by Beuret and

Stoker (1986). They point to the failure of the 'activist left' of the Labour Party to explore what they understood by 'empowerment' and how that could be derived from the physical relocation of services into local neighbourhood offices. These contradictions were also examined by Callinicos (1983, p. 110) who argued that from the emergence of a 'new urban left' within the Labour Party, what was actually constructed was a new middle class made up of the urbanised professional public sector activists who supported the municipal road to socialism.

These particular critiques highlighted the limited conception of decentralization of those advocating change. Decentralization had the potential to alter the ways in which services were organised, administered and delivered. It did not have the potential to be a radical project which could significantly alter the social relations within communities or transfer power. The managerial agenda was one which *could* be achieved since it could be introduced independently of the state. Any transfer of power, however, was predicated upon the needs of the state at both a local and central level, and for this reason abdicated as a goal.

From the perspective of those engaged, on a daily basis, with the introduction of decentralisation, concerns were about the operationalization of service delivery. During the course of undertaking over 60 interviews with senior officers across the four authorities these concerns were quite clearly expressed. As the following extracts from the interviews highlight, they were attempting to meet the perceived requirements of elected members, take account of the resistance of white/blue collar unions and the 'vested' interest of middle tier professionals, as well as performing the sheer quantity of tasks involved is a major organisational change.

> What happens now is that the members couldn't care about the forums. All they want to know is have the repairs been done? And this links directly to the issue of committee and departmental structures ... An issue at the moment for neighbourhood officers is to have someone in the office who is a 'boss' neighbourhood officer.

These experiences are important because they identify the competing explanations for the failure of the decentralization experiment. Whilst there is an apparent overlap between participants in their account of the failure there also differences. Agreement can be found in the shared financial crisis of local government throughout the 1980s. For urban authorities this, of course, was made worse by growing social inequalities and the decline of its industrial base. Ted Kitchen (1997) has provided an 'insiders' view of how this affected Manchester and in particular how it impacted upon the policy making process. The 'resources' argument explains the decentralization failure, in part, as a function of the inability of local authorities to manage their budgets in ways other than by 'crisis management'. These problems had been a feature of the confrontation with central government over 'rate capping' and, for some, reached a climax with the introduction of the poll tax.

In a series of follow up interviews (Diamond and Speeden, 1993) in the early 1990s with some of these participants, the financial plight of local government was often cited as the major factor which had reduced the scope for innovation and change:

> I've tried to move the organisation to try and provide integration. But many of the old divisions reappear, especially when we get into contracting out. It's made it especially difficult to hang on to the idea of one single local authority. It leads to divisions and creates tension within the organisation. We need a total picture. Government, in terms of how we manage, don't recognise why we were interested in decentralization.

The agenda had by now shifted again and a number of local authorities had 'made their peace' with central government in an attempt to address these difficulties. As Stoker and Young (1993) and Bassett (1996) describe it, the new agenda was one of 'civic boosterism' in which localities competed regionally, nationally and internationally for economic investment and urban regeneration support. In their study of Birmingham, Loftman and Nevin (1992), point to the potential consequences of such strategies which provide physical improvements and an infrastructure to support the mobile middle class but little else for the urban poor and socially excluded.

A further explanation suggests that an important factor was the reluctance to engage with those professionals who advocated community empowerment and/or participation. In the late 1980s the inability of local authorities to engage with this debate explains why the neighbourhood services approach never really secured public support. In the early 1980s some argued for a twin track approach to decentralization, maintaining that it was necessary to change both service delivery and relationships with users and local communities if the experiment was to work. As one interviewee at the time put it:

> The development of neighbourhood services has been treated with scepticism by a number of workers in community education because, at the same time, the creation of large-scale tertiary colleges has increased bureaucracies and disempowered workers – never mind local people. That said, the neighbourhood services approach has been to not use existing networks and neighbourhood groups in presenting the policy. *The reality is that you can't decentralize when you are cutting. You alienate your workforce and you raise expectations amongst communities that you can't, in the end, deliver.* But the inertia of bureaucracy means that there probably isn't a good time. That seems to me to be the issue. Because there is a dichotomy between the community development/empowerment model, which is about the process by which people learn to take control and the needs of bureaucratic change, which means one system has to be replaced by another. *In that sense, neighbourhood services should have been outside, working with communities, before it went inside and worked in the system.* (My emphasis)

This explanation is reflected in the literature at the time. The key agenda priority had become service delivery. In some local authorities, community development units were closed down and staff relocated because they were seen to represent a 'threat' to local political elites (Diamond and Nelson, 1993), or community activists were incorporated and co-opted into the process (Diamond, 1991). This is in contrast with the current situation, where there appears to be a growth in 'community' based activity legitimised by the introduction of City Challenge and especially The Single Regeneration Budget (SRB) with its emphasis on the need to 'consult' locally (Fordham *et al.*, 1999).

Yet another explanation offered by senior officers is one which identifies the role of elected members in the process as well as the managerial skills of those implementing the changes.

Elected members were seen by some officers as 'interfering' in their area of expertise and being too interventionist in the policy making process. This claim is hardly new. What is interesting about it here is that it may illustrate the 'battle' for control over the management of local services which the decentralisation experiment sought to open up. It was an attempt to reduce the power of professional interests in order that local voices could be heard. In the early 1990s the steers from central government for performance review created yet another arena for debate and contest.

In terms of affecting fundamental managerial change the models being presented in 1980s of generic teams, inter-agency co-operation and flatter management systems were largely resisted. By the 1990s they were being espoused by quite a few of those who had resisted them.

> Right, I think that it's important to get one thing clear from the outset.[council named] is an officer lead authority. It's not politically led. Provided we provide the services they want within budget they do not interfere. So what I've been principally doing is to establish a new corporate culture. There is one authority. It has a view about the aspirations of the local community, it tries to meet them. It's not a collection of individual departments. That ethos is consistent with decentralization.

It is this new managerialist tendency which was, in some ways, the victor in the failures of 1980s.

The Context 2: The Arrival of New Managerialism

New managerialism is largely absent from the earlier studies and discussion papers although it was an inevitable consequence of the changes contemplated, as well as fitting with the changing context of the times.

The term has been used as a pejorative description as well as a positive one. In the work of Clarke *et al.* (1993) and Gaster (1995) we can see how it has been interpreted and reformed. Those who have traced its origins back to the 1980s (Diamond and Speeden, 1993) make the point that a key part of the attempt to implement a decentralized approach to service delivery involved an analysis of the structure and organisation of local authority service departments. Whilst, we can argue that this was not, of itself, innovatory the conclusions which were drawn appeared to require a fundamental change in thinking by workers, managers and elected members alike (Farnham and Horton, 1993, Leach *et al.*, 1994, 1996).

The issue of managerial and elected member decision making in urban authorities was subject to important changes. The pressure for reform, driven by the reductions in local authority spending was profound. Even without the push to decentralize, local authorities were addressing what some saw as restrictive labour practices and the relative 'freedom' of white-collar unions. The Conservatives (supported by the Miners defeat in 1985 and the 1987 General Election victory) increased the pressure on local government Labour run local authorities, seeking alternative ways of managing their services.

The reform agenda was underpinned by key agencies such as the Audit Commission and the Local Government Management Board. As the former evaluated local authority performance, the latter provided examples of innovation in practice which influenced the thinking of key figures in local government at chief officer and leader levels. This managerial reform was also being influenced by change in the private sector, referred to above. Key advocates of the decentralization initiative (Hoggett and Hambleton, 1987), reflected these ideas and practices promoting them in their work with local authorities.

The concept of 'equality' and the negative experiences of particular 'groups' in society were being cited as 'good' reasons to change not only the ways in which services were delivered but also how staff were recruited, retained and promoted. These reforms were seen as necessary conditions for change requiring changes in management practice too.

Finally, in many cases the means to effect change was either devolved to a separate unit of dedicated staff appointed for this purpose, or devolved to inter-departmental working parties to provide clear recommendations. Fundamental to effecting these changes was the notion that professional barriers had to be broken down and new forms of management developed.

It is from these processes that we can see the emergence of models of management which promote generic working, inter-agency practice, 'flatter' management systems, control over devolved budgets and greater internal and external accountability and scrutiny. By the late 1980s, there was an emerging consensus on the changes necessary, which includes significant numbers of Labour run local authorities, the Gover. (Thatcher/Major) and external agencies and organizations.

This was evident from undertaking interviews with chief officers senior officers involved in decentralisation in the late 1980s, as the following example illustrate:

> What that has meant is that I have the job of co-ordinating the staff within the offices, but without the necessary power. What we need – those of us who are neighbourhood officers – is the authority to enforce the policy and we haven't got it It's about using my authority. That includes being a doer, I'm not really a charismatic leader. People need to see you're doing things and also I'm prepared to use the disciplinary power I have if necessary. Having said that, I'm now part of the senior team. There at the centre of power. But you can't show weakness or indecision. So, you use that role to decide what people need to know, disseminate information. We've got a much flatter system now. But it's hard!
> (Same officer 5 years later)

The significance of these changes, is that these 'new managers' were, themselves, not only 'empowered' though their appointment and agreed responsibilities but also though a 'shared' language with other managers. This revolved around the need to ensure that the organisation met the needs of users rather than producers. Whatever the level of their commitment, the actual process of effecting such change (given the resource constraints) resulted in a more 'confident' and 'directive' managerial approach. The above is a generalisation and experience will vary but if we examine the outcomes of this in the last 10 years we can see significant changes in labour relations, contracts of employment and a public sector 'drowning' in quality audits and performance measurement.

The management approach to change is set out cogently by Gaster (1995). Consultancy work commissioned by some local authorities illustrates their managerial emphasis. For example, Diamond *et al.* (1997) identify how senior officers and councillors supported a major consultation strategy (Citizens panel) as one means of securing an alternative source of data to complement the 'professional' perspective and the lay interpretation of a locality's needs. What was of interest to the authority was the effectiveness or otherwise of a managerial strategy.

Ironically, 'managerial' initiatives developed from the decentralization agenda of the 1980s and Major's Citizen Charter (Prior *et al.*, 1995), CCT and New Labour's Best Value proposals are part of a process, designed to provide a coping mechanism for local authorities in a period of financial and service transition, opening up an agenda for public participation and involvement. They provide opportunities to reform the agenda from one dominated by a managerialist vision to one which is community led. As such they have created contested spaces within local government which raise important questions about local democracy and user/community empowerment.

The introduction of City Challenge and latterly The Single Regeneration Budget (SRB) have for some observers (Atkinson and Cope, 1997, Mayo, 1997, Schaecter and Loftman, 1997) raised important questions about how we can use these initiatives for innovation in community governance.

Models of Change

The critical question at the end of the 1990s revolves around whether or not we can effect the changes, and recent experience suggests not. Current practice suggests that we will need to highlight the weaknesses in much regeneration practice and identify the ways in which change is possible.

On the positive side we have the experience of the SRB to draw upon. As the work of Hill and Mawson (1991) and Nevin *et al.* (1997) suggests, there is a struggle over who is allowed (or enabled) to participate and on what terms. The experience of key officers and community activists suggests that whilst they may share the same language there is still a 'gulf' between them in terms of understanding:

> I think that they [forums] are more representative than before. We get about 30 per meeting. They are frustrated I have to say, because they have limited powers. For example, six years ago we had £60,000 per office to spend on environmental improvements which the Forum could decide. Now we have a borough pot of £100,000 which all offices bid into. I have to say that I do see it as another burden. Six years ago it was about 30-40 per cent of my time, now it's about 10 per cent. I've got a really good community worker who services the Forum and now I'm much more selfish. I use the Forum to support me. I don't really need it. I use it cynically to keep pressure on the services. I obtain power from it to meet my needs.

We can also look to the important changes New Labour have introduced through devolution to Scotland and Wales; the creation of Regional Development Agencies (RDA) in England; and the election of a 'Mayor' for London. These changes may be positive steps towards a more decentralised system of decision making. Proportional representation in elections to Scotland's parliament and the Welsh assembly also suggest that there will be changes in their local political processes. But the failure of the Government to legislate for a system of elected regional government calls into question their commitment to devolved regional government. This is accentuated by the centralising tendencies of the Government over resources and, in the case of the RDAs, inter-departmental conflicts over who should control resources and allocate them.

There are though, some indications that new Labour policies support community based participation, such as citizens' panels or citizens juries or local referenda.

One of the key differences between the period we are now in and 15 – 20 years ago is that many of the ideas and recommendations of decentralization advocates are now regarded as 'best practice'. The Audit Commission's report on partnerships (1998) contains models of working which were being recommended over 20 years ago. Indeed Hambleton (1978) set out one model for area management in Stockport which would now be seen as an 'ideal type' for regeneration initiatives either through the SRB or the Government's New Deal for Communities.

A second difference is the consequence of Labour's failure to win a general election between 1979–1997. In the period especially after 1992 there have been several policy reviews and papers recommending change. The Borrie Commission (1994) and the Commission for Local Democracy (1996), for instance have provided a rich mix of specific proposals informed by research and evaluations. It is here that we can see how Stoker (1994, 1996), and others have attempted to shape the *national* policy agenda. It has, also, attempted, (fairly successfully) to create a momentum for change based upon a consensus, which encompasses the 'representative' bodies (now one body) of local government; professional associations; practitioners and politicians. Indeed, one could argue that the debates (and recommendations) it has generated, (including the role of party organisations within local government), have gone further than might be expected.

Thirdly, there have been a number of reports which (pre 1997 election) focus on the need to engage with local communities and to shift power from a 'professional' elite to all the participants who have an interest in local communities (Hastings *et al.*, 1996, Skelcher *et al.*, 1996, Taylor, 1995).

This paper is not claiming that this will be an easy process, for reasons given below. The challenge for those who do advocate this approach lies in seeking to 'open up' the agenda for debate. There is a need for a more informed and critical exploration of the new consensus which has been created. Challenge to this new conformity may result in the marginalization of critics. Criticism may be seen as 'carping' or not being 'practical' about what can be delivered and how. The very construction of an agenda and the language to legitimise may make its critics invisible by defining what is possible and what is not. (The work of Bachrach and Baratz (1970) illustrate this process very effectively.) The 'practical' may become the 'norm' and the agenda viewed as apolitical. Thus pragmatism may over-ride consultation and discussion.

The Social Exclusion Unit (HMSO 1998) may be illustrative of this. The Urban poverty is described in stark terms, while the recommendations and action points lack any underlying theoretical or ideological explanation for poverty they do set out managerial tasks to be undertaken.

At a theoretical level Burns (1991) very usefully has re-drawn Arnstein's notion of the ladder of participation (1969) and the UK strategies aimed at urban regeneration or facilitating community involvement can be categorised and located here, enabling us to derive a critique either of strategies in general or specific strategies at specific points in specific places. While this is necessary, it may not be sufficient to derive a general theoretical model to explain why community disempowerment takes place. To do this we need to explore different models of power.

Fainstein and Fainstein's 1982 model (developed in the USA), may assist us here. It focuses on the idea of the city in crisis and, therefore, in transition. By applying a neo-marxist theory of power and economic crisis it provides a way into understanding the constraints on city managers, communities and 'actors' within the process. It describes how political power is derived from economic power and how in periods of economic crisis those whose economic interests are under greatest threat seek strategies for survival, so the 'accepted' strategy for survival is dependent upon economic stability and growth. The agenda to achieve this is defined by business elites and facilitated by the local (and/or national) political elites. Urban renewal strategies in the USA and in the UK to a greater or lesser extent fit this model.

At a local (micro) level the SRB process also fits the model. Participants in a number of SRB initiatives studied in Manchester, drew attention to economic renewal as a pre-condition for community participation and local regeneration. The following extract illustrates this perception:

> We need local jobs to give something back to the community – if we can't do that why should they come along.

Participants also identified the need for co-operation between local services and agencies to bring about economic renewal. At the same time they commented on their relative powerlessness to ensure that the key investors and employers would provide the investment necessary.

> The trick is to get the Airport involved in all local initiatives and to make them feel involved. But, we are one initiative and the demands on them are huge.

It might seem that the emphasis on inter-agency working and the 'partnership' approach supported by the Government and in a recent Audit Commission (1998) report, reinstate the centrality of communities in decision-making. Yet, this is essentially still a managerialist perspective. 'Need' is defined externally, and strategies are developed in isolation from local communities so the 'new' approach still constructs local communities as (relatively) passive participants in the process.

This, clearly reduces the potential for shifts in power. Creating space for change within these constraints is difficult enough for those street level professionals who are looking for opportunities to develop their own ways of working. It is (relatively) easier for them to engage in the inter/intra professional 'turf' wars over resource allocations and the setting of priorities. It is much harder for local community groups. They have neither the power nor the resources to impose their priorities on the professionals.

They have three 'choices'. They can accept the process and 'join' the strategy. We can predict that they are likely to become co-opted into the process and to reflect back to their local organisations the values and norms of the 'professionals'. Secondly, they can opt out and withdraw from the process altogether. Thirdly, they can seek to effect change from within and from outside. They can assert their needs and challenge the assumptions and practices of the model on offer.

The difficulty with all three possibilities, is the changed context of local government at the end of the 1990s. Twenty years ago when the neighbourhood/decentralization agenda was being formulated and developed, local authorities were *the* providers of local services. It was possible to think about a 'holistic' approach to service delivery and to imagine ways in which effective change within the organization it could, lead to change to the outside. The barriers to change still existed, but in the 1990s the context is radically different. The consequences of the Conservative reforms (CCT, the right to buy, local management of schools, community care and so on) and the Labour refusal to move to the status quo ante have made it much more difficult to anticipate ways in which change can be effected.

The most obvious example of the changed role of local government is that of the elected councillor. In large urban areas she/he has lost the power to influence housing and education policies, they lack the political and legal weight to define and to set policy objectives. These responsibilities (and opportunities) have been transferred to housing associations, education action zones and SRB initiatives. They still have an important role to play in setting strategic policy goals (for example planning and transport) but even these are likely to be shared at sub-regional and regional levels.

For local communities, therefore, the potential to apply localised political pressure upon their elected councillors is very limited. We are in a period of transition from a model of local government accountability based upon a separation of roles between elected members and officers to one which is based upon specific initiatives (officer dominated), negotiating the extent of their accountability between regional agencies, local authorities, partner agencies and to a greater or lesser extent local communities. Political accountability (at the local level) is being marginalized upwards to an unspecified (and unelected) regional tier. At the neighbourhood level we may see emerging locally elected members who begin to express (more openly) their sense of disempowerment and begin to form alliances with local communities.

This might create further opportunities to challenge the absence of participation in neighbourhood regeneration initiatives and to promote the debate on alternative models, but we need to explore the ways in which it is possible to reclaim models of decentralisation for a local community based approach.

In the work of Barr (1995), Craig and Mayo (1995) and Schuftan (1996) we can see ideas about ways in which this might be developed. If we identify the process and the framework with which community based strategies could be delivered, it is possible to locate them within the changing context of contemporary urban governance and regeneration. What they and others (Atkinson and Cope, 1997, Geddes, 1996, Healey, 1998 and Leach *et al.*, 1996) share is a focus on the ways in which both the concept of 'community' and 'governance' is constantly contested and redefined. Whilst this is important and relevant we should also restate the need to address the issues of the locus of the legitimacy of local democracy and how we can ensure that this is not assumed by the organizational/institutional questions of service delivery.

Prospects for Change

One of the interesting developments of the decentralisation initiatives was the way in which local government in the UK not only appropriated the language of the community action movement but also its personnel. While I was interviewing elected members and officers in the late 1980s it was evident that many of them were (or claimed still to be) community activists within the voluntary sector. Some of them were councillors engaged in the writing of policy papers for their council (in one case under the name of the chief executive) and others were recruited to implement the decentralization agenda.

It is from this activist 'core' that we can see some of the 'new managers' of the 1990s. But there were tensions and conflicts between their highly interventionist strategy and local government structure and hierarchy. Resistance to decentralization from within local government came from varying sectors. The extent to which there was resistance from community development staff and/or the voluntary sector (organized or unorganized) is hard to assess. We can say that in some cases community development initiatives were scaled down or marginalized (Diamond, 1991, Diamond and Nelson, 1993), indicating local authority reluctance to implement strategies proposed from this sector.

In the 1990s there is little evidence to suggest that the same movement of personnel referred to above has taken place. In some respects this is not surprising. By the mid 1990s the 'community' had been re-discovered and recognised by nearly every agency of the state. This broad brush use of the words 'community' and 'empowerment', by all political parties gives no hint as to the ideological underpinning from which any one party is proposing strategies.

For example, new Labour initiatives may be just as likely to close down existing fora or the name of local democracy as to develop local empowerment. In one locality which now has an SRB programme covering part of it the forum for the voluntary sector has decided to close itself down and work with the SRB initiative. The rationale for this decision rests, in part, on the fact that this is where resource decisions are taken. It has, also, been influenced by the pressures of time on activists to attend meetings, indicating not new developments but substitution.

The SRB process and structures may just as effectively *contain* discussion as extend it effectively ensuring that the policy decisions and implementation strategies secure more legitimacy is justified.

The top-down approach is unable to respond to local issues and needs which have not been anticipated by those who set the local agenda. It is not just that the timetable to submit bids explains the lack of engagement with the local community nor is it the technical and complex language which is required to complete the bid. It is the identification of need from the outside which is, at the root of the problem. We can see through the public debates generated over the past 10 years that 'needs from within' must be a pre-condition for successful community based initiatives.

Another set of concerns relates to the difficulty in identifying which 'community' we are talking about. There are communities and they have overlapping interests (and in some cases membership). This is complicated by the way in which the concept of 'representativeness' is applied to local community leaders, a much more stringent requirement which, until recently, has not been demanded of local political leaders.

Whilst it is difficult to develop ways of working with competing interests within a local community it is not impossible, though unlikely to happen without shared 'ground rules'.

The very 'core' of the decentralization experiment in the 1980s was to improve service delivery and to enhance local democracy. These aims grew out of the failure of the local government system and the political processes to engage with local communities on their own terms.

It follows from the discussion above that we need to promote a much enhanced and legitimate role for the voluntary and community sector. The potential risk of this approach is another layer of 'professionalized' community workers or community activists.

We *can* (as Holman, 1999 does), imagine a context in which what emerges is a model based upon principles of decentralisation and democratization. We need to be clear, however, about the developmental model which is being discussed. This is not about establishing local socialism but it is about attempting to occupy the terrain of 'localism' and resisting the drift towards 'corporate' localism supporting locally based organisations through direct funding. We could create a national fund for the support of local activists, involving local institutions (further/higher education for instance) in their communities by establishing local resource centres. We could use facilitators/development workers – external to the local partnerships – to work with local groups, we could 'twin' locally based initiatives to learn from each other and we could integrate already existing opportunities (such as education and training initiatives) into local neighbourhood provision. These developments should be seen as a pre-condition for enabling locally based organisations to address the absence of local democracy. They are integral to the notion of 'capacity building' but in terms of what the local state needs, not what local communities need or want.

Decentralization in the 1980s failed to deliver for a variety of reasons but its failure to begin to address the notion of local democracy and its complexities requires us to start there and to develop an approach which has the potential to enable local groups to navigate their way through the regeneration maze, to negotiate (from collective strength) with professional agencies and to campaign for the external parties to meet their obligations and responsibilities. It is about creating a model of 'dual power' within localities to act as a catalyst for change, where the 'bottom-up' demands are given legitimacy equal to that of the current decision-makers.

References

Arnstein, S.R. (1969) 'A Ladder of Citizen Participation', *Journal of the American Institute of Planners*, vol. 35, pp 216–24.

Atkinson, R. and Cope, S. (1997) 'Community Participation and Urban Regeneration in Britain' in P. Hoggett (ed), *Contested Communities*, pp. 87–104.

Audit Commission (1998) *A Fruitful Partnership: Effective Partnership Working*, Audit Commission, London.

Bachrach, P. and Baratz, M. (1970) *Power and Poverty: Theory and Practice*, Oxford University Press, Oxford.

Barr, A. (1995) 'Empowering Communities beyond fashionable rhetoric? Some reflections on Scottish experience', *Community Development Journal*, vol. 30, pp. 121–132.

Bassett, K. (1996) 'Partnerships, Business Elites and Urban Politics: New Forms of Governance in an English City?', *Urban Studies*, vol. 33, pp. 531–555.

Beuret, K. and Stoker, G. (1986) 'The Labour Party and Neighbourhood Decentralisation: Flirtation or Commitment', *Critical Social Policy*, no. 17, pp. 4–22.

Boddy, M. and Fudge, C. (eds) (1984) *Local Socialism?*, Macmillan, London.

Borrie Commission (1994) *Social Justice: Strategies for National Renewal – The Report of the Commission on Social Justice*, Vintage, London.

Burns, D. (1991) 'Ladders of Participation', *Going Local* 18, pp 2–4.

Burns, D., Hambleton, R. and Hoggett, P. (1994) *The Politics of Decentralisation: Revitalising Local Democracy*, Macmillan, Basingstoke.

Callinicos, A. (1983) 'The New Middle Class', *International Socialism*, 20, pp. 3–7.

Clarke, J., Cochrane, A., and McLaughlin, E. (1993) *Managing Social Policy*, Sage, London.

Cockburn, C. (1977) *The Local State: Management of Cities and People*, Pluto Press, London.

Craig, G. and Mayo, M. (1995) 'Rediscovering Community Development: Some Pre-requisites for Working In and Against the State, *Community Development Journal*, vol. 30, pp. 105–109.

Diamond, J. (1990a) *Local Socialism as Decentralisation: A Study of the Neighbourhood Services Initiative in Manchester 1984–1988*, University of Salford. Unpublished Ph.D.

Diamond, J. (1990b) *Neighbourhood Services in the 80s* Paper Presented to CSE Annual Conference at Sheffield Polytechnic.

Diamond, J. (1991) 'Community Co-operation or Empowerment? The role of community based work in decentralisation initiatives', *Journal of Community Education*, vol. 9, pp. 10–16.

Diamond, J. and Nelson, A. (1993) 'Community Work: Post Local Socialism', *Community Development Journal*, vol. 28, pp. 38–44.

Diamond, J. and Speeden, S. (1993) 'Look Who is Wearing the Emperor's Clothes: Rise of new Managerialism in Local Government', Paper Presented to the Urban Change and Conflict Conference, Sheffield University.

Diamond, J., Speeden, S., Cuff, M. and Loftus, C. (1997) 'Lessons from Performance Review' in *Local Government Policy Making*, vol. 23, pp. 27–30.

Fainstein, N. and Fainstein, S. (eds) (1982) *Urban Policy Under Capitalism*, Sage, Beverley Hills, CA.

Farnham, D. and Horton, S. (ed) (1993) *Managing the New Public Services*, Macmillan, Basingstoke.

Fordham, G., Hutchinson, J. and Foley, P. (1999) 'Strategic Approaches to Local Regeneration: The Single Regeneration Budget Challenge Fund', *Regional Studies*, vol. 33, pp. 131–141.

Gaster, L. (1995) *Quality in Public Services*, Open University Press, Buckingham.

Geddes, M. (1996) *Extending Democratic Practice in Local Government*, CLD Research Paper 17, CLD, London.

Gyford, J. (1983) 'The New Urban Left: A Local Road to Socialism', *New Society* 21 April.

Hambleton, R. (1978) *Policy, Planning and Local Government*, Hutchinson, London.

Hambleton, R. and Hoggett, P. (eds) (1984) *The Politics of Decentralisation: Theory and Practice of a Radical Local Government*, School for Advanced Urban Studies Bristol Working Paper 46.

Hastings, A., McArthur, A. and McGregor, A. (1996) *Less than Equal: Community Organisations and Estate Regeneration Partnerships*, The Policy Press, Bristol.
Healey, P. (1998) 'Institutionalist Theory, Social Exclusion and Governance' in Madanipour, A. *et al.*, *Social Exclusion in European Cities*, HMSO, London.
Hill, S. and Mawson, J. (1999) *Challenge Funding, Contracts and Area Regeneration*, Policy Press, Bristol.
HMSO (1998) *Bringing Britain Together: A National Strategy for Neighbourhood Renewal.* Report by the Social Exclusion Unit, Stationary Office, London, Cm4045.
Hoggett, P. (1991) 'A New Management in the Public Sector', *Policy and Politics*, vol. 19, pp 143–156.
Hoggett, P. and Hambleton, R. (1987) *Decentralisation and Democracy: Localising Public Services*, School for Advanced Urban Studies Bristol, Occasional Paper 28.
Holman, B. (1999) 'Limited Imagination', *The Guardian*, 31 March.
Kitchen, E. (1997) *People, Politics, Policies and Plans*, Paul Chapman Publishing, London.
Labour Co-ordinating Committee (1984) *Go Local to Survive*, Labour Co-ordinating Committee, London.
Lansley, S., Goss, S. and Wolmar, C. (1989) *Councils in Conflict: The Rise and Fall of the Municipal Left*, Macmillan, Basingstoke.
Leach, S., Davis, H. and Associates (1996) *Enabling or Disabling Local Government*, Open University Press, Buckingham
Leach, S., Stewart, J. and Walsh, K. (1994) *The Changing Organisation and Management of Local Government*, Macmillan, Basingstoke.
Loftman, P. and Nevin, B. (1992) *Urban Regeneration and Social Equality: A Case Study of Birmingham 1986–1992*, Research Paper 8 Faculty of The Built Environment University of Central England in Birmingham.
Mayo, M. (1997) 'Partnerships for Regeneration and Community Development', *Critical Social Policy*, no. 52, pp. 3–26.
McDonnell, J. (1984) 'Decentralisation and New Social Relations', *Going Local*, no. 1, pp. 3–4.
Nevin, B., Loftman, P. and Beazley, M. (1997) 'Cities in Crisis – Is Growth the Answer? An Analysis of the Outcome of the First and Second Round of the SRB Challenge Fund', *Town Planning Review*, vol., 68, pp. 145–164.
Platt, S. (1987) 'The Liberals in Power', *New Society* 11 September.
Prior, D., Stewart, J. and Walsh, K. (1995) *Citizenship: Rights, Communities and Participation*, Pitman, London.
Schaecter, J. and Loftman, P. (1997) 'Unequal Partners', *City*, no. 8, pp. 104–116.
Schuftan, C. (1996) 'The Community Development Dilemma: What is really Empowering?', Community *Development Journal*, vol. 31, pp. 260–264.
Skelcher, C., McCabe, A., Lowndes, V. and Nanton, P. (1996) *Community Networks in Urban Regeneration*, The Policy Press, Bristol.
Stoker, G. (1994) *The Role and Purpose of Local Government*, CLD Research Paper 4, CLD, London.
Stoker, G. (1996) *The Reform of the Institutions of Local Representative Democracy: Is there a Role for the Mayor-Council Model?*, CLD Research Paper 18, CLD, London.
Stoker, G. and Young, S. (1993) *Cities in the 1990s*, Longman, London.
Taylor, M. (1995) *Unleashing the Potential*, Joseph Rowntree Foundation, York.

Chapter 8

Rediscovering the Citizen: New Roles for Politicians in Interactive Policy Making

Erik-Hans Klijn and Joop F.M. Koppenjan

Introduction: Interactive Policy Making and its Background

In the Netherlands, as in other countries, in recent years many various initiatives have been taken by government authorities to introduce new forms of participation in policy formation and decision making (Most *et al.*, 1998, Klijn and Koppenjan, 2000). Various ministries, provinces and local governments have been experimenting with forms of interactive policy making in which citizens, consumers and interest organizations are invited to contribute ideas and discuss desirable solutions to policy problems.

Interactive policy making differs in various ways from traditional participation methods. Two differences are important. In the first place interactive policy making makes use of participation during the phase of problem definition and exploration of solutions. Most traditional participation methods concern only a phase in the process in which policy proposals have already been formulated. Secondly interactive policy making explicitly tries to incorporate participation of various actor in a search to find innovative policy proposals with generate enough support to be implemented.

In general, three motives for the introduction of these new forms of participation can be distinguished:

Creating support. Interactive policy making can be seen as an attempt to maximize support for policies and to minimize resistance by involving potential veto-groups in the process of policy formation. This motive is connected to the observation that today's modern society is complex and that public actors depend for the realization of their policy initiatives on a wide variety of private or semi-private actors or on other public actors which have different perceptions and veto power to block policy initiatives for shorter or longer periods (Rhodes, 1988, Kickert, *et al.*, 1997).

Improving quality. By involving citizens in the process of policy formation, local information, experiences and preferences are mobilized in order to improve the quality of local, regional and national policies. This motive is connected to the growing awareness that we live in a network society in which knowledge, information and preferences are widely spread over actors (Castells, 1997). Problem situations are ambiguous and there is a need for creative solution. These solutions often need the involvement and the knowledge of different actors.

Improving (local) democracy. The participation of citizens, consumers and local pressure groups can also be viewed as an attempt to bridge the gap between citizens and local governments (Andersen and Burns, 1996). New forms of participation are part of a remedy for the often perceived existing crisis in (local) representative democracy.

In this chapter we focus our attention mainly to the last motive. We first show that in modern society the preferences of citizens are hard to know. They are not so connected to the political system as they used to be due to an individualization processes. Interactive policy making can from that perspective be viewed as 'a search for the citizen' (section 2).

After this we show that in these types of processes the role of politicians appear to cause difficulties. Politicians do not participate in these processes and they claim in advance the right to deviate from emerging proposals by referring to the primacy of politics. Afterwards, participants in interactive decision-making processes often are disappointed with what politicians do with the outcomes of the interactive process. The link between interactive processes and 'normal' political decision-making procedures is problematic. This experience is not exclusive to the Netherlands. Thus Fisher and Forester (1992) point out that attempts to put 'the argumentative turn in public policy making' into practice often encounter the objection that such forms of participatory democracy are not compatible with the rules of the game of representative democracy prevalent in the west.

We illustrate this problem by analysing a case study: the restructuring of the Bijlmermeer, a high rise neighbourhood in Amsterdam (section 3). Building upon the findings of the case, we then formulate a number of suggestions to improve the connection between interactive decision making and politicians (section 4). In addition to that we try to assess the practical value and feasibility of these proposals by examining recent experiments in interactive policy making in five Dutch municipalities (section 5). We end this contribution with a summary of our findings (section 6).

Interactive Policy Making as a Search For the Invisible Citizen

An important reason for the interest in and experiment with interactive policy making is the dissatisfaction with the regular form of participation of citizens and interest groups. The standard participation methods are considered 'insufficient' because they always attract the same group of participants and fail to reach certain other groups. In much of the literature, this is attributed not only to traditional forms of participation, but also to changes in society and relations between the citizen on the one hand and administration and politics on the other.

In this context, we refer to a gap between citizen and government. Among other things, this gap is evidenced by increasingly lower voter turn out. Still, it is widely acknowledged that the gap between citizen and government as well as citizen and politics is an expression of something deeper than voter turn out.

Background: Individualization in Society

Until the late 1960s, Dutch society was characterized by a pillar system. Political and societal life was organized in ideological pillars which had relatively little contact with each other. Catholics had their own building societies, schools and other societal organizations and their own Catholic Peoples Party. The same could be said for the protestant pillar and the non-denominational pillar (in which the socialists were better organized than the liberals) (see Lijphart, 1992). This pillarized society established social and political ties in various ways. First, individuals felt connected to their pillar. This created both social connectedness (in various societal organizations) as well as political connectedness (with a political party). Furthermore, the leaders in the pillars, especially at the political level, insured that society as a whole continued to be integrated. Through consensus and debate, the political leaders assured that decisions were made in view of the well-known pacification rules described and analyzed by Lijphart: business-style politics, pragmatic tolerance, top consultation (between political elites), mutuality (distribution of means and positions), depoliticization, secrecy, and government governs (Lijphart, 1992).

This model called for a high degree of citizen passivity and a strong coherence within the pillars. The interests of citizens were represented by the political and societal elite who guaranteed their foundation in the pillarized structure. That foundation also insured that the (political) leaders kept in touch with their electorate and were aware of their desires. In the course of the 1970s, this model came to an end. Polarization and especially the development of individualization resulted in a breach between citizens and the leaders of the pillarized system. The Social and Cultural Planning Bureau – that has analyzed social and cultural trends in Dutch society on the basis of large scale surveys since the 1970s – has labelled individualization one "of the major trends of our time". The dependency of individuals on their immediate environment (family, neighbourhood) decreased and gave way to a dependency on much larger groups.

In its 1998 Report, The Social Cultural Planning Bureau formulated it in the following manner:

> In a highly evolved welfare society, individuals no longer depend upon their immediate environment for their livelihood. As a consequence, the maintenance of relations with family, political and religious organizations and associations becomes an option instead of a necessity. Ideally, cohesion at the micro-level gives way to cohesion at the macro-level (the welfare state is an expression of this), but this process stops in the sphere of individual feelings. Collectively organized solidarity at the macro-level cannot create strong moral ties. The autonomous individual is, however, not without conscience or the ability to attain solidarity with others. But, that solidarity has become optional an can lead to 'investments' in various directions depending upon the preferences of the individual (Sociaal Cultureel Planbureau, 1998, p.6).

Changes in the Relations Between the Government and Citizen: Gap or Something Else?

This is also reflected in decreased party loyalty and low voter turn out. It is no longer self-evident that citizens will vote for their pillar's party. Instead, they will select a party that fits their ideas and perceptions about government performance and promised policies (see also Sociaal Cultureel Planbureau, 1998). It remains to be seen whether this trend can be immediately translated into a hypothesis that the gap between citizen and government has widened. Interest and political involvement evidenced during the 1970-1995 period have not really decreased and feelings of powerlessness of citizens vis-à-vis government have generally decreased. In fact, the appreciation of government – including the functioning of government – has become more positive in the past several years (see Sociaal Cultureel Planbureau, 1998). Thus, it is interesting that voter turn out appears to be declining while the expressed inclination to vote has not. Non-voters often refer to non-political circumstances (lack of time, etc.) rather than to dissatisfaction with politics as a motive for not voting (Sociaal Cultureel Planbureau, 1998, pp. 744-748). While there is a clear declining tendency of political participation in party political activities, there is an increase in participation in activities outside the direct political realm (Greenpeace, nature preservation, incidental political activities).

In the first instance, available data do not point to a large or growing gap between government and citizen. If we can speak of a gap at all, it has more to do with the fact that the citizen is no longer as visible in modern society because of increased individualization and that the citizen makes his participation dependent upon a large number of (often personal) factors.

In view of the above, interactive policy making can also be qualified as a *search for the citizen*. That search is necessary because of individualization in society. On the one hand, citizens are more autonomous and outspoken to public policy initiatives. Political participation is no longer self-evident and citizens are less inclined to accept policy proposals by public organizations at face value. This may result in serious resistance when groups of citizens are confronted with the actions of public actors. To phrase it differently: the potential citizen preparedness for action has grown and can thus be activated. On the other hand, individualization has made it more difficult for public actors to find a sounding board in society while at the same time, the connections between citizen and traditional political forms of expression – such as political parties – have decreased. Interactive policy making can be seen as an attempt by government to strengthen its link with citizens along two lines. First, government attempts to enhance the meaning of participation and thus hopes to increase it and diminish the opposition to policy proposals. Second, government tries to gain insight into wishes and ideas of citizens that are otherwise hardly visible.

Models of Participation and the Role of Politicians

If the observation is correct that citizens are more difficult to trace and 'calculate' their options for participation more against other activities, but at the same time tend to be more critical about decisions that governments make, governments face a problem. Research on the satisfaction of different forms of participation in The Netherlands indicates that traditional forms of participation in which participation is organized after policy proposals have been prepared can count on much dissatisfaction. Citizens who participated in traditional participation procedures had a more negative view of governmental actors afterwards then citizens which did not participate at all (Ministerie van Verkeer en Waterstaat, 1996, Rooij, 1997). Governmental actors need new forms of participation in policy making to improve the legitimacy of their decisions.

Interactive policy making in fact assumes a different form of participation than is usually known in decision making processes. If we take a historical perspective three models of citizen participation in local government can be distinguished: the consultation model, the representation model and the discourse model (Klijn, 1998a). These models developed more or less chronologically, but are at the moment co-existent. They are presented in Table 8.1.

Table 8.1 Three Models of Participation

	Consultation model	Representation model	Discourse model
Focus of participation	Expression of opinion on policy intention	Involvement in the whoel decision making process	Involvement in the process of problem definition and design of solutions
Interactions	Incidental	Intensive during the whole process	Intensive at particular moments
Institutionalisation	Formal consultation procedures	Standing organizations (project organizations, etc.)	Ad hoc provisions (project groups, meetings, assessments)
Principle of participation	Self interest of individuals, Single issue organizations	Solidarity, often territorially organized	Interest as user or resident
Criterion for participation	Personal involvement	Representativeness	Functional involvement, information and knowledge
Motive	Protection of (legal) positions	Citizens' representation	Creating support, quality improvement, democratic legitimation
Examples	Consultation provisions in formal planning procedures	Local networks around urban renewal projects	Interactive decision-making processes: city councils

The first model represents the decision-making procedures institutionalized on the basis of the democratizing waves of the sixties and seventies. They aim at strengthening the role of representative bodies in decision making and regulating the participation of citizens, interest groups and advisory councils in these processes, by organizing opportunities for advice, objection and appeal. They organize the involvement of parties *ex post*, after a policy proposal is already in place.

The second model provides the citizen with much more opportunity to influence the decision-making process, from the very beginning to the final solution. However, there are other problems; for instance the assumptions of solidarity and representation which are seldom realized. This kind of participation requires a high degree of self organization and expertise on the part of citizens. For instance, the urban renewal policy in the city of Rotterdam could only be organized along the lines of this representation model because of intensive and costly support of the residents provided by the city government. In general it is very doubtful if the conditions of coherent and well organized citizens interests which are important for this second model can be met in modern society if we look at the remarks in the former section on the relation between citizens and governments.

Interactive policy making, characterized by the opening up of existing arenas of decision making to new actors, new interest groups, other authorities, private organizations, citizens and users, has much resemblance to the third model of participation. The third model is becoming increasingly popular, especially at the expense of the second model. This means that the way citizens are involved in decision-making processes is changing. Compared to the first model, they are involved in earlier stages of the policy formation process. The level of participation is that of co-production. Compared to the second model, participation takes place on an ad hoc basis and is less intended to achieve goals regarding representation and democratic legitimation. Improving the quality of policy proposals seems to be the most important motive.

The Position of Politicians in Interactive Policy Making

In interactive decision-making processes, various features of a more direct vision of democracy can be recognised (Pateman, 1970, Macpherson, 1977, Klijn and Koppenjan, 2000). This applies to the greater emphasis on direct participation of citizens, their responsibility and active role. But also the emphasis on interaction and achieving mutual agreement fits in this picture. This is not surprising considering that interactive policy making is meant to more actively involve social groups and citizens. Especially many local initiatives are taken from the need to narrow 'the gap between government and citizen'. One can rightly argue that, through interactive policy making, an institutional regime of roles and rules, based on views of democracy that emphasise direct participation and interaction between government and citizens, is introduced into a system dominated by representational democracy in which decision-making power is concentrated in elected representatives and where the primacy of politics is an important feature (Klijn and Koppenjan, 2000). Edelenbos and Monninkhof (1999a) speak of 'hybrid democracy'.

This mixing of two institutional regimes is not without difficulties. There are tensions between the rules of the game of representational democracy, with its emphasis on the passive role of citizens and the strong decision-making power of elected politicians, and the rules of the game of more direct forms of democracy that are oriented much more towards interaction and communication. The rules of the game of representative democracy are aimed at a procedure in which elected political institutions at the end of the decision-making process pronounce a final judgement in which they represent the general interest unhindered and without consultation. Interactive policy making is precisely aimed at settling the question of what the common interest is in and through interactions between interested parties. The question is then what can the role of elected politicians still be at the conclusion of a process of policy preparation if in that process there has been broad social participation? In the next section we investigate the tension between interactive policy making and representative democracy by analysing an interactive process regarding the formulation of a urban renewal plan for the Bijlmermeer (see Klijn, 1998b).

Interactive Policy Making: The Case of the Bijlmermeer

'Even God does not love the Bijlmermeer', a resident despaired after an El Al plane crashed into the high-rise estates of Kruitberg and Groeneveen in the Bijlmer (an abbreviated form of the name) on October 4, 1992. Indeed, the Bijlmermeer has never been very popular since its completion in the seventies. Built according to 'modern' architectural principles, the Bijlmermeer was thought of as a 'city of the future', with clusters of ten-storey buildings separated by large grassy areas. Car traffic was led on elevated roads to spacious parking garages. It all looked beautiful on the scale models: large, rather luxurious flats surrounded by lots of greenery, with all kinds of social and recreational activities taking place in the commons areas and the streets between the parking lots and the buildings. The first estates were finished in 1969 and the last in the mid-1970s. In total

18,000 dwellings were built in the Bijlmermeer, of which 13,000 are the high-rise estate type.

Bijlmermeer: An Area Riddled with Problems

From the beginning the Bijlmermeer has faced many problems: dissatisfaction by the residents, socio-economic problems among the population, drugs problems and a high crime rate. Although the flats are large and well equipped they are not in demand, and from the start there has been a high vacancy rate. Instead of the middle income groups that the dwellings had been designed for, in the eighties and nineties the inhabitants have mostly consisted of low-income groups, unemployed people and immigrants, initially from Suriname and later from a number of African countries. The costs of maintaining the dwellings is very high, and most inhabitants are difficult to reach by public and social organizations because they stay there only a short time and because of the variety of ethnic backgrounds. There is a small but active group of Bijlmer residents – mostly white, who have been living there for a long time and support the original ideals of the Bijlmer – known as the 'Bijlmer believers'. They are the most active part, politically speaking, of the inhabitants.

By the end of the 1980s, it becomes clear that the problems of the Bijlmer could not be solved without taking more dramatic measures than simply improving maintenance. Despite various measures (demolishing some of the parking lots, increasing maintenance and surveillance, improving some of the flats) the vacancy rate remained high, higher income groups continued to leave the area and the rapid influx of migrants could not be halted. An additional pressure was that the city of Amsterdam was not willing to pay the large annual losses of the housing association. Without this support, the housing association would go bankrupt. The city of Amsterdam, the New Amsterdam housing association and the district government council of Amsterdam South-East decided to undertake a drastic restructuring of the Bijlmer. A committee formulated, in 1992, the following goals which formed the basis for succeeding policy proposals:

a) improvement of the housing stock; turnover of the dwellings, around 14 per cent a year in 1992, should be reduced in ten years to 8 per cent. For that, the variety in types of dwellings should increase. The committee proposed to demolish a part of the high-rise estate (up to 25 per cent) and replace this with other types of dwellings (mostly low-rise). A number of the high-rise dwellings should be renovated and brought into a higher segment of the housing market;

b) stimulation of job creation and reduction of unemployment in the Bijlmer.The unemployment rate in the area was high (about 30 per cent of the population). The aim was to reduce the unemployment rate in ten years to 8 per cent (the average rate in the Netherlands at that time);
c) strengthen cultural and social activities.

Restructuring the Kraaiennest Area: An Interactive Approach

Experiences with renewal of parts of the Bijlmer which followed the decisions of 1992 had shown that large groups of residents, especially those of various ethnic backgrounds, were not involved in the decision making. For this reason, the political parties in the district council suggested that in the proposed restructuring of the neighbourhood and shopping area around the Kraaiennest (the so-called K-neighbourhood) new ways be looked for to involve residents in the policy-making process.

In many ways the K-neighbourhood is typical of the structure and the problems of the Bijlmermeer. It is made up exclusively of high-rise estates. There are eight of these: Kikkenstein, Kruitberg, Kleiburg, Koningshoef, Kralenbeek, Kempering, Klieverink and Kouwenoord, and together they total 4,018 flats. All the problems that have been mentioned before can be found in the K-neighbourhood.

Table 8.2 summarizes the main decisions and activities that took place during the making and discussing of the plan, between the summer of 1995 and the beginning of 1997. In the decision-making process three 'rounds' were demarcated. The first was between mid-1995 and December 1995, when problems were explored. The second round was situated between December 1995 and August 1996 and consisted of sometimes heated discussions from the different perspectives of the participants about possible solutions to the problems in the K- neighbourhood. In the third round formal decision making took place.

The restructuring process of the K-neighbourhood started in summer 1995. The project group, which took the initiative, formulated a citizens' participation plan which was accepted by the district council in December. The project group tried to involve groups of residents in brainstorming sessions and at various information meetings and tries to collect ideas in the shopping area and through mailings. In this first round of the decision-making process, the project group concluded that the lack of safety was regarded as a very important problem by the residents. The project group tried to connect this formulation of the problem to the main issues of other actors. For the housing association, New Amsterdam, the main problem was the poor market position of the housing units, because they were not in

Table 8.2 Decision Rounds in the Restructuring of the K-neighbourhood

Rounds	Mid 1995–December 1995	December 1995–August 1996	August 1996–January 1997
Character	Exploring problems and mobilizing ideas	Exploring and discussing solutions	'Official' decision making (citizen input and political decision)
Activities	Start project group, brainstorming sessions	Surveying physical surroundings/drafting various options	Discussions in the district council and official participation procedures
Ideas	Lack of safety as key issue	Exploring possibilities of restructuring physical surroundings to increase safety (remove parking garages, lower main roads, undo separation of different traffic modes)	Discussion on the measures of the restructuring plan
Residents' Participation	Information meetings Idea Contest (Bijlmer suggestion box)	Brainstorming sessions on studies about restructuring solutions (later) information meetings about ideas (in churches, shopping area etc.)	Official meetings for citizen input meetings with committee of district council

demand and the area was very unpopular. An additional problem is the high maintenance costs of the flats. The district council, meanwhile, was more interested in reducing maintenance around the high-rise blocks and creating a more desirable living area with less criminal activity.

After the first round in the decision-making process the project group started to develop alternative solutions for different sub-areas in the K-neighbourhood by assigning several urban planners the task of developing architectural solutions which met certain conditions, such as:

a) reducing the number of paths through the green area;
b) reducing the maintenance costs of the green area;
c) investigating possibility of demolishing high-rise estates to create space for low-rise dwellings;
d) possibilities for lowering several of the elevated roads.

The resulting options were discussed with all kind of actors including tenant organizations. Along with criticism there was also appreciation for the proposals, although the project leaders stated that some did not go far enough and would not solve the lack of safety problems in the K-neighbourhood.

There were some striking differences between the opinions of the well-known tenant groups that participated in the 'official' meetings and the non-organized tenants who express themselves through the more informal channels (like the Bijlmer suggestion box, the meeting in the shopping area and in the results of a survey held in the shopping area). The latter group tended to be less critical and less negative about drastic restructuring measures like demolishing dwellings. It was also clear that while many tenants were reached through the new methods of interaction and planning, it remained difficult to reach non-organized tenants, especially those of different ethnic backgrounds. The 'official' citizen participation meetings still attracted mainly the same people as before.

In all these sessions, politicians were almost entirely absent. They did not participate in the discussions on various ideas. The discussions were between the project group, civil servants from the district government, the housing association and some organized tenant groups.

In the last round, some problems occurred. The plan presented by the project group was a bit more drastic than the one developed during the brainstorming sessions. The plan proposed to demolish 1,013 dwellings (about 25 per cent of the high-rise dwellings) and to build 1,050 new dwellings (mostly low-rise). One of the major elevated roads was to be lowered so that it becomes a regular road through the neighbourhood. The strict division between different forms of traffic (cars, bikes and pedestrians) was to be ended. The reactions during the official citizen input session were rather negative, as were the reactions during the input session held by the district council. Also the political parties were critical and it seems as if most of the proposals by the project group are going to be rejected. However, after intervention by the housing association and deliberations within the executive committee of the district council, the council voted in favour of the plan.

Participation and the Role of Politicians in Interactive Policy Making

One of the important aims of the interactive process in the Bijlmer was to improve participation of tenants. This was done by a deliberate decision of local politicians who explicitly asked for a participation plan in this interactive process and agreed on this plan. Although a lot of attention was given to attracting non-organized residents, this only partially succeeded. While various 'alternative' forms of participation, like trying to elicit reactions at the shopping centre, were somewhat successful, participation in the 'official' channels remained the domain of the well-known groups. There was also a striking difference of opinion between these well-known groups and the non-organized residents, in so far as this has been voiced. The lesson is that in interactive policy making it remains difficult to attract large underprivileged groups, but that better results can be achieved. This means that it remains necessary to look for more than the classical means of participation. These classical means often assume a level of organization of residents, tenants and citizens that does not exist in reality. Findings that confirm the observation which have been made in section 3.

Although political parties in the district council explicitly asked for a participation plan and for an action programme to attract non-organized citizens to the planning process, they were largely absent during the process and in the end mostly paid attention to the official modes of participation. The involvement of local politicians definitely was a problem in this case. They were interested in solutions which had not received much attention during the policy-making process, and were rather unwilling to accept the solutions which had been developed. If they had been involved more and at an earlier stage, not only could some of the solutions they were interested in have been developed and tested for feasibility, but it would also have resulted in a better understanding by the politicians of the process and the ideas that were being developed there. That would have required at least some commitment to the process by politicians before the final decision in the city council, which they hesitated to make. So interactive policy making seems at odds with the function of politics and the idea of the primacy of politics, which is so widespread in parliamentary democracy. Interactive policy making assumes that some of the decision-making power of politicians is being shared with others and that politicians are being drawn into the process. The idea of the primacy of politics, in contrast, assumes that government makes its choices at the end in 'the general interest' and remains at a certain distance in the interactive process. Yet it is representative governments that mostly initiate these processes. An important aim they have is to 'bridge' the gap between politicians and citizens. This central problem of interactive policy making is developed further in the next sections.

Involving Politicians in Interactive Policy Making Processes: Redefining their Roles

Involving politicians in interactive policy making processes presupposes an adaptation of their usual role as substantive selector at the end of the process of policy development. In order to accomplish that, we have to realize that we do not replace one practice by another. Instead we have to reconcile elements of direct and representative democracy: a matter of institutional design (compare, Weimer, 1995, Goodin, 1996). This means we must be aware of the reasons why politicians do not participate in interactive processes. We have to find ways to reduce the political risks they perceive. Therefore, involving politicians in interactive policy making also has consequences for these processes themselves. For instance, we should not expect politicians to abandon their role as substantive selector at the end of the process, by committing them unconditionally to the outcomes of an interactive process. These outcomes may be at odds with their party programme, electoral promises or government statement. And they may be hard to sell to the politician's constituency. And such a commitment is not necessary if politicians are part of the learning process in the interactive arena. Although alternatives developed in the interactive arena will not automatically and unchanged be adapted in the phase of formal decision making, the ideas that lay behind them will become part of the argumentation process in the formal arena. In short we do not expect politicians to give up their role as selector, but to supplement it with that of initiator and facilitator. This addition to their traditional role, however, is crucial: taking the lead in interactive processes offers politicians the possibility to organize the process by which values and preferences of citizens are articulated and by which solutions for complex problem situations are generated. To sum up, the role for elected politicians in interactive policy making processes consists of the following elements (Klijn and Koppenjan, 2000):

Initiating and Facilitating Interactive Policy Making Processes In addition to taking the initiative for interactive policy making in order to guide the social debate, politicians can act as catalysts for such processes by actively supporting them, by urging those involved to participate or by acting as manager of the process.

Guarding the quality of the processes Politicians and political institutions should guard the quality of the interactive policy making process. This concerns protecting the openness, conscientiousness and representativeness of the decision making.

a) *Legitimizing the interactive process* Through their active involvement, the meaning of interactive policy making will increase for all parties, as well as their willingness to participate.
b) *Setting the agenda* At the start of the process, politicians can make statements about the problem situation, possible solutions and the values at stake. However, these must not be seen as dictates but rather as challenges and guideposts.
c) *Taking part in the substantive discussion* Politicians should participate in any fashion in the interactive process in order to share in the learning process that takes place.
d) *Correcting the interactive process during the 'ride'* Influenced by learning experiences during the process, the substantive preferences of politicians become clear. If they keep their preferences to themselves in order to select at the end of the process, this will result in a 'hard coupling'. They need to correct as much as possible *during* the process.
e) *Selection of policy proposals* At the end of the process, politicians select an option that best serves the values and interests in question. The greater the degree to which politicians have been partners in the interactive process, the greater the possibility that arguments and considerations that have gained weight in that process will make their way through the final selection.

Implementing Politicians' New role: Their Experiment

Vital for the successful involvement of politicians in interactive decision making is their preparedness to redefine their role. Such a profound redefinition of one's role will not occur easily. In this section we focus on an experimental project of the Dutch Institute for Public and Politics which was aimed at implementing this new role for politicians in interactive policy processes. This experiment may provide us with insights about the practical implications and feasibility of this new role and the problems which occur when implementing it.

The Amsterdam-based Institute for the Public and Politics aims at enlarging political and societal participation. From the start, the IPP has been involved in the development of interactive policy making in the Netherlands, for instance by acting as the process supervisor or advisor in a large number of interactive projects. The IPP initiated the experimental project with a focus on developing an overview of the various experiences with interactive policy making in municipalities and at other levels of government. The project's objective is to evaluate the potential and limitations of this approach and to further develop thc approach. In Cupertino with an inter-university research team and a number of municipalities, several experiments have been initiated: 2-year projects where an interactive work style – developed according to a process design by the IPP – is attempted and evaluated. Below we discuss how the IPP design involves citizens, members of the board of mayor and aldermen and council members in the interactive process, how this design was implemented in five local projects and what lessons can been learned from this implementation.

The IPP Design: Creating a New Division of Roles in Interactive Processes

The IPP design for interactive policy making processes is focused on establishing political-administrative commitment to the process, on the clear formulation of conditions for the process and the co-ordination between process design and political and administrative processes. The IPP includes the commitment of the mayor and alderman and of the council (committee) in their respective roles as facilitator and contractors of the process. This commitment is realized through a formal decision about a procedure proposal of the IPP at the end of a consultation and by a decision on the assignments for work projects that develop various solutions. Thus, the procedural conditions for the process have been established. The IPP approach also provides the opportunity for politics to determine substantive *conditions* for interactive policy making at the beginning of the process.

With regard to *participation* and the relevant roles, the process design assumes that citizens will be involved from the start as co-designers of policy. In this the features of the third model of participation are clearly present. This results in a new set of roles: from the very beginning, citizens and council members are involved in formulating problems and developing potential solutions. The municipal council or the council committee acts as contractor. It established conditions for the creation of variety by formulating assessment criteria for the solutions prior to the process. Meanwhile the council members express their ideas about problem formulation and solution alternatives. Thus they actively participate in the interactive process since they become acquainted with the arguments and proposals that are brought to the table. At the end of the process, the council's role changes to that of a decision maker. Decision aspects are prepared in mutual consultation with all participants and the council debates with all participants in one or more public debates in the course of decision making. The Board of Mayor and Aldermen establishes conditions but has no steering role. Civil servants serve all participants in the project, not only the council members. Together with external experts, they provide citizens with background information and make corrections if unrealistic proposals are brought to the table.

The *structuring of the interaction* in the generic IPP design is as follows. Daily co-ordination of activities is provided by a core group of municipal representatives together with the IPP. A discussion group chaired by the IPP discusses the most important steps in the process. All parties involved participate in this discussion group. It is thus possible to respond to unexpected circumstances. Hence, decision making and conflict management are regulated within the process.

The process design contains several *process steps*. In the first *consultancy phase*, meta decision making occurs: the IPP drafts a procedure proposal or process design after hearing all those involved speak on the topic and manner of working. This process design is submitted for approval to the Board of Mayor and Aldermen and to the council. In the second *agenda formation phase*, the problem is defined, partially on the basis of a telephone or written survey. This survey is conducted as much as possible by council members. During the phase of mapping the problems, the instrument of monitoring can be used, i.e. going to the problem area. In a public opening meeting the starting points for generating solutions are determined. The Board and the council amend these. In *the third phase, exploration and design of solutions*, citizens formulate solutions in so-called 'work studios', preferably together with politicians. In a public meeting, the intermediate results of the work studios are presented. In the fourth phase *the Board prepares a draft council decision*. Participants in the work studios will express their opinion about this draft. This is followed by an investigation of the support among the population at large. The Board states in a public meeting why certain proposals have not been included. Next the council makes a *final decision*. Prior to phase six, *implementation*, agreements are made about the role of citizens during implementation.

In this presentation of the process phases, the most important *working techniques* have been mentioned: the survey, the monitoring, public meetings, work studios, and support surveys. Council and Board members are assumed to participate in these activities. In the end, *process management* has to monitor the adequate fulfilment of these roles.

All and all, it is clear that the IPP design attempts to involve politicians in the interactive process from as early on as possible. In addition to an indication of a new role for council and Board members, there is attention for actions that politicians can take during the various phases in the process. There are also provisions for intermediate correction and organizational linkages are in place within which parties can shape their new role. And the design respects the traditional role of elected politicians: that of substantive selectors at the end of the process of policy making.

This design comes close to the suggestions presented in the former section about how to involve politics in interactive policy making Thus, the question to be addressed concerns the degree to which this intertwining between politics and interactive policy making has been realized in practice. To answer that question, we now turn to the experiences with the experimental projects implemented between 1997 and 1998 in five Dutch municipalities.

Project 1: The Construction of the Europe Square in Leerdam

The interactive project in Leerdam was aimed at the reconstruction of a square on the basis of co-operation between the municipality, shopkeepers and neighbourhood. Earlier attempts had been blocked by differences of interest between shopkeepers and citizens. The municipal council defined the financial, substantive and procedural conditions and committed itself to an interactive process: the responsible alderman promised to submit the plan without changes before the council. Then interaction proceeded in a consulting group between shopkeepers, neighbourhood and municipality where civil servants remained in the background so that individuals from the neighbourhood had an opportunity to present their ideas. Local businessmen also had bilateral consultations with the municipality, for instance about their financial contribution to the reconstruction. Two facts characterized the process. First, early in the process, the municipal council unilaterally decided to introduce paid parking on the square thereby intervening in the interactive process. Shopkeepers and the neighbourhood successfully protested. Second, the reconstruction turned out to be more expensive than had been agreed upon. Shopkeepers, however, were prepared to cover the extra costs. What is striking is the great willingness for compromise among all parties. Perhaps this was a consequence of the fact that the unilateral decision by the council drove the other parties (businessmen and the neighbourhood) together. Despite the IPP design, council members did not participate in the consultation group. Nonetheless, the plans were adopted by the municipality without difficulty. The intermediate conflict had in fact strengthened the co-ordination between council and interactive process.

Project 2: The Reconstruction of the Stadserf in Enschede

The experiment in Enschede was focused on the reconstruction of part of the centre of the city, the Stadserf, as a co-operative effort between the municipality, shopkeepers, homeowners and individuals living in the neighbourhood. Here, too, the municipality imposed substantive, financial and procedural conditions upon the process. The process started with difficulty. The business association desired a bilateral consultation with the municipality and did not support the participation of citizens. The municipality and the IPP initially adhered to the IPP design. Once the businessmen appeared to drop out, the organization adapted and individual citizens were no longer a part of the consultation group. They were only consulted at certain points in the design stages. The alderman exercised more steering in the process. Council members did not participate. In the phase where solutions were to be developed, the civil service working group dominated the consultation group. In the end, the project failed to result in a concrete reconstruction plan and related financial guarantees. However, a number of solutions had been formulated that had found broad support. From the viewpoint of intertwining of politics with the interactive process, success was mixed.

Project 3: Youth Problems in Hellevoetsluis

Given his responsibility for administrative renewal, the mayor of Hellevoetsluis ordered the search for a suitable experimental project. The municipal council defined a number of general conditions and committed itself in extremely vague terms: if the outcome would be concrete and if it found broad support, then the council would approach that project positively. The choice of project was determined between IPP, the municipality, societal associations, and citizens: youth problems. Two working groups were formed: 'Going Out' and 'Meeting Points/Hang-Outs'. The municipality did not set any conditions at the start of the working groups. Differences of opinion with the IPP resulted in the municipality taking the lead in process monitoring. Participants in the working groups were civil servants, council members and youth representatives as well as senior citizens who had been active in neighbourhood work. When the working group 'Going Out' noted in their discussions about locations for a discotheque that people from the neighbourhood were not represented, this was corrected. Youth participated well in the 'Going Out' working group, but had a hard time voicing their opinion amidst the senior citizens and representatives of the municipality in the 'Meeting Points' group. Finally a quarrel emerged between the municipality and the 'Meeting Points' group about the number of meeting points that should be established. Because of budgetary constraints, only seven out of the initial 21 places were realized. As in Enschede, the experiences are mixed. On the one hand the process initiated a dialogue between the municipality, council members included, and the youth, the latter not being a group that is easy to reach. On the other hand, decision making with regard to the outcome of one of the working groups became derailed because conditions for the interactive process had not been made clear prior to and during the process.

Project 4: An Integral Safety Plan for Zeewolde

The experiment in Zeewolde also began with a search for a suitable project. The project which was selected was the development of an integral safety plan for the municipality. Substantive conditions had not been set, but there was an extensive process design in place to which the municipality committed itself. During the process, the council members occupied a listening role. A planned steering group, in which council members were to guide the process, was not established. Thus, the process was steered by civil servants. This resulted in the derailment of the work studios during the phase in which solutions were developed. Instead of a plan, some 100 actions were formulated, and the council had to respond to these within two weeks. After the participants in the work studios refused to prioritize the actions, the council selected 13 actions. The process was continued for a number of other subjects. This selection resulted in disappointment among the participants in the work studios. Aldermen complained that 'these proposals never should have been made'. Council members refused a public meeting and claimed that decision making had to take place in the regular council meeting. The co-ordination between politics and interactive process was a failure.

Project 5: An Integral Zoning Vision for De Bilt

The interactive process in De Bilt was focused on developing an integral structure vision for the municipality. Earlier attempts had met with bureaucratic political conflicts and political differences of opinion. The municipality did not formulate substantive conditions, but presented its own agenda in the form of a brochure on the structure vision. Despite the council's agreement with the procedural proposal by the IPP, in practice council members and civil servants were not sure what was expected of them. Some council members participated in the work studios, but in a reluctant role. The municipal elections in the spring of 1998 also played a role. The 'old' council members did not want to rule beyond their grave. The new council members were not committed. An intermediate meeting had been planned once the work studios were halfway, but the meeting was not used to correct the process. The process design in this phase was complex. There were seven parallel work studios. It appeared to be very difficult to co-ordinate the activities and products of the work studios. In developing the final document for submission to the council for decision making, a conflict emerged between the work studio participants and the mayor. Work studio participants wanted to be involved in drafting the final document, as was envisaged in the IPP design. In the end, the products of the work studios were listed one after another in the final document, to which a rather abstract closing section written by the Board of Mayor and Alderman was added. The participants in the work studios were very disappointed about the lack of clear choices. Although the confrontation between interactive process and politics was not as vehement here as in Zeewolde, there was derailment of the interactive process during the work studio phase, so that politics in the decision making phase was confronted with a package of solutions that they did not know how to handle. Despite the existence of a council agenda, there was hardly any intertwining between politics and interactive process.

Lessons from the Experimental Projects

The five experimental projects demonstrate the difficulty in engaging politicians in the interactive process despite the existence of a process design which was explicitly focussed on that objective. A number of 'classical' problems were reproduced: absence of politicians during the interactive process and 'hard couplings' at the end of the process, resulting in politicians being confronted with propositions they can not handle and disappointed and frustrated participants of interactive workshops. Why could these problems not be prevented by the process design? A number of barriers made the implementation of the design difficult. The most important were:

a) Lack of commitment. The formal decision of the council is insufficient for realizing a factual commitment of all persons and groups involved. This is partially the result of a lack of communication about the process design. When new role definitions have been put on paper but have not been discussed with participants, it can not be assumed that participants are informed let alone that they could have internalized the new rules. In addition, the acceptance of a design with a formal decision is not a certainty. In fact, choosing an interactive process is often a hierarchical decision. An interactive process is not initiated because civil servants or council members are convinced this is the proper way to do, but because one or two board members, together with a small group of enthusiasts which are in favour of it. A formal approval for an interactive policy making process, this does not automatically mean that all involved parties are committed.

b) The lack of clear substantive guidelines and conditions at the start. This appeared to be a reason for misunderstandings and differences of opinion between politicians and participants in the interactive process at the end of the process. Especially projects that were initiated for political rather than substantive reasons are open to this difficulty. If an 'open approach' at the start implies that politicians are not really interested in the substance of the issue, it becomes difficult to engage in a process of mutual adjustment. This is asking for trouble at the end of the process, when substantive solutions will force politicians to take a stance.

c) In the IPP design Board members are supposed not steer but facilitate. This is perhaps too far removed from reality. Certainly when council members do not fulfill their role as initiators of the process, the process management would fall to the hands of the civil service, as was the case in Zeewolde and De Bilt. This strengthens the chance for a 'hard coupling' at the end of the process and is undesirable from the viewpoint of democratic legitimation.

d) The process design of the IPP contains a number of provisions which require politicians to defend their viewpoints in public meetings. If, during the process, a gap emerges between participants in the interactive process and politicians, then politicians will have a very difficult time at the end of the process. So, the process design should not only set provisions for public accountability of political decisions at the end of the interactive process, but it should also include a sufficient number of moments for mutual adjustment and corrective action during the process.

e) It is striking that the process management of the experimental projects did not succeed in being corrective when there was lack of participation of council members or lack of political steering. An explanation could be that the internal organization of the interactive process demanded so much attention that there was little time left to insure the political embedding of the process. It is also conceivable that bureaucratic process supervisors enjoyed the their discretionary powers which result form the lack of political steering (cf. Edelenbos and Monnikhof, 1999b). This development clearly jeopardizes the democratic quality of the process and should be addressed in a future process design.

f) A peculiar omission in the process design was that municipal elections were held during the interactive processes, so that the involvement of politicians in the process was disrupted. In order to guarantee the proper political-administrative context for interactive processes, it is crucial to coordinate the interactive process with predictable and not predictable developments in the broader the political and societal environment of the process.

In the end, the experiences with the IPP design were mixed. The projects did result in proposals which were developed in an interactive settings. And citizens and users were involved in a process of co-production. However the projects were not very successful in getting politicians involved in the interactive process in a constructive way. The analysis of the projects shows that this failure was for a large part due to the lack of communication about the new role politicians were supposed to assume. The design of the interactive process lacks itself a interactive approach, as result of which politicians were not committed to the process and did not have a chance to internalize their new role. In fact they often were in uncertainty about how they were supposed to behave. As experiments are meant to generate experiences from which we can learn, the IPP-projects were quite successful in that. They provide us with clear and practical clues about how to design and manage interactive processes in the future.

Conclusion

In this contribution we have analyzed one of the main stumbling-blocks of interactive policy making: the inclination of elected politicians not to get involved. We argued that this problem exists because the primacy of politics is interpreted by elected politicians as their right to make substantive decisions at the end of the policy making process. That is way they consider citizens participating in the preparation of these decisions as a threat: this reduces their possibility to make their own choice.

We suggest a redefinition of the role of elected politicians in order to reconcile practices of direct and representative democracy. A constructive involvement of politicians in interactive processes means they should not just see themselves as ex post selectors, but also as initiators and facilitators of public debates. Such a redefined role fits much better the conditions of the complex network society we live in, in which the representation of citizens can no longer be organized ex ante at a central location. Taking the lead in interactive policy making processes provides politicians with the opportunity to organize the process of articulation of values and alternatives in stead of standing aside.

By discussing the IPP experiment we have investigated the possibilities to implement these new role for politicians in practice. The results form this experiment show that at this moment we have not developed yet a strategy to successfully implement these ideas in practice. Yet the experiment provides us with some valuable and practical suggestions for further improvement of the design and management of interactive processes in order to successfully engage politicians in these processes.

References

Andersen, S.S. and Burns, T. (1996) 'The European Union and the Erosion of Parliamentary Democracy: A Study of Post-Parliamentary Governance,' in S.S. Anderson and K.A. Eliassen (eds), *The European Union, How Democratic Is It?* Sage, London, pp. 51–76.

Castells, M. (1997) *The Rise of the Network Society: Economy, Society and Culture*, Blackwell, Oxford.

Edelenbos, J. and R. Monnikhof (1999a) *Spanning in Interactie*, IPP, Amsterdam.

Edelenbos, J. and R. Monnikhof (1999b) *The Power of the Process Manager*, Paper Presented at the Conference on Public Participation and Innovations in Community Governance, University of Luton, Luton.

Fisher, F. and Forester, J. (eds) (1992) *The Argumentative Turn in Policy Analysis and Planning*, Duke University Press, Durham, NC.

Goodin, R.E. (ed.) (1996) *The Theory of Institutional Design*, Cambridge University Press, Cambridge.

Kickert, W.J.M., Klijn, E.H. and Koppenjan, J.F.M. (eds) (1997) *Managing Complex Networks*, Sage, London.

Klijn, E.H. (1998a) *Ruimte voor Beslissen. De besluitvorming over het plan van aanpak van de K-wijk in de BijlmermeerGgeëvalueerd*, Eburon, Delft.

Klijn, E.H. (1998b) 'Kwaliteit als toetsstem; de rol en positie van bewoners bij herontwikkeling', *Tijdschrift vor de Volkshuisvesting*, 4, pp. 19–26.

Klijn, E.H. and Koppenjan, J.F.M. (2000a) 'Politicians and Interactive Policy Making: Institutional Spoilsports or Playmakers, *Public Administration*, vol. 78, pp. 365–388.

Lijphart, A. (1992) *Verzuiling, Pacificatie en Kentering in de Nederlandse Politiek*, Second edition, Becht, Haarlem.

Macpherson, C.B. (1977) *The Life and Times of Liberal Democracy*, Oxford University Press, Oxford.

Ministerie van Verkeer en Waterstaat (1996) *Directorate Rykswaterstaat, Open Deuren*, 's-Gravenhage.

Most, H. van der, Koppenjan J.F.M., and Bots P.W.G. (1998) *Informatief Interacteren door Interactief Informeren. Verkennende Studie naar Eisen aan Informatievoorziening bij Interactieve Besluitvormingsprocessen, in Opdracht van Rijkswaterstaat*, RIZA, Waterloopkundig Laboratorium, Delft.

Pateman, C. (1970) *Participation and Democratic Theory*, Cambridge University Press, Cambridge.

Rhodes, R.A.W. (1988) *Beyond Westminster and Whitehall: The Subsectoral Governments of Britain*, Unwin Hyman, London.

Rooij, A. de (1997) *Drie jaar Infralab: Samen een brug Bouwen Tussen Overheid en Burger*, Hoofdkantoor Rijkswaterstaat, Den Haag.

Sociaal Cultureel Planbureau (1998) *Sociaal en Cultureel Rapport 1998*, 's-Gravenhage.

Weimer, D. (1995) *Institutional Design*, Kluwer Academic Publishers, Boston, MA.

Chapter 9

Neighbourhood Councils – Municipal Instruments or Grass-Roots Movement? Some Reflections on Results from Two Norwegian Surveys

Nils Aarsæther, Torill Nyseth, Asbjørn Røiseland

Introduction

In this paper, the merits of the emerging community council "movement" in Norway will be assessed. After an inventory of the phenomenon in question, we will discuss an hypothesis on the emergence of a new political institution in local level politics – the community council. We contend that the emerging community or neighbourhood councils (NCs) have characteristics that are irreducible to those of small scale municipal government, and that they can also be distinguished from locally based voluntary organizations, as well as from informal or *ad hoc* community development groups. Following this argument, we contend that institutional innovation will be followed or produced by the emergence of a new political role – that of the neighbourhood councillor. Finally, we will discuss the implications of the development of an NC system for municipal government and for locality development.

What do we mean by 'neighbourhood council'? We choose a wide definition: NCs we define as formal political institutions operating on a territorial basis, covering parts of municipalities. NCs may be constructed by the municipality as a response to demands from the locality level, or they may be part of a reform strategy for municipal decentralisation. They also may be initiated by people locally themselves and thereafter obtain recognition by the municipal council as at least an advocate for people in that specific geographical part of the municipality. NCs of the latter type tend to have a board elected by the people in the locality, either by ballot or by attending an election meeting. NCs of the former type tend to have a board appointed by the municipal council, often mirroring the distribution of seats between the parties in the municipal council.

Some Theoretical Considerations

The point of departure for this paper theoretically, is partly the ongoing discourse on civil society, communitarianism and social capital (Deth *et. al.*, 1997, Etzioni, 1995,1997, Walzer, 1990, Tam, 1997, Putnam, 1993) which all more or less explicitly refers to de Tocqueville's theory of democracy based on the role of voluntary organizations as micropillars of democracy. Part one of this theory states that the creation of, and involvement in, local voluntary organizations improves the ability of citizens to take part in political processes. This is the argument of democratic empowerment which constitutes the mobilising dimension of democracy. Following the communitarians, we agree with Tam (1997) that it is only where people have a sense of belonging, that deliberative communities can be established. This sense of belonging, however, need not necessarily rest on a 'feeling of community'. This is where the other part of Tocqueville's theory comes in. The importance of the civil organizations to democracy was derived from two steps: 1) engaging in a voluntary organization makes people co-operate. 2) The possibility of an individual to become a member of several organizations enhances capacities for problem-solving, both on the individual level, and on the societal level. The preconditions for this process is that people in a community will not group themselves into mutually exclusive segments by the selection of voluntary organization memberships, and therefore most likely a situation of organizational overlap will emerge. A sense of belonging results more or less as spin-off of such processes.

One of our hypotheses is that the need for a co-ordinating unit at the local level that is able to respond to local needs and communicate these towards the municipalities, still exist. The reason for this is that people still live most of their lives locally, in quarters, districts and neighbourhoods.

They are members of local communities, and some still exercise the ideals of citizenship, involved in actions in the interest to the local community as a whole. From this it follows that in construction such institutions, it is possible that social capital is being produced. By social capital we hereby understand the collective resources for problem solving created by networks of civic engagements in a locality, city or region (Putnam, 1993). Furthermore, we see social capital as a side-effect of processes with other purposes (Røiseland and Aarsæther, 1999, Coleman, 1990), from processes of co-operation and working together across interests and social backgrounds within the context of a political community, in which the NC is the central body. In this way NCs institutionalise the mechanisms of 'overlapping membership', that is so important in the theory of social capital formation.

Following the work of Robert Putnam, the registered decline for several years now, both in the level of membership in voluntary associations and in political parties in all of the Scandinavian countries, could represent a decline in 'social capital', and, as such, pose a problem for democracy (Selle and Øymyr, 1995 Gundelach and Torpe, 1997). In this context, how can we understand the increase in neighbourhood councils, and even the existence of such organizations? Beside the tendencies of the participation in party- and civic organizations, to decline there is another trend, pointing in an opposite direction. What we see in Scandinavia, is a rise in new modes of local organizing and a new wave of decentralization (Bogason 1996, Prahl 1997, Montin, 1998), including setting up more neighbourhood councils and new channels for user influence. On the other hand, the revised Local Government Act has prepared for a more centralized and elitist local government by allowing for a reduction in the number of councillors in the municipal councils and by introducing management principles and techniques inspired by ideas from New Public Management. The trends, then, are pointing at different directions and the picture is more fragmented and ambiguous than clear.

Paragraph (§) 12: Legal Framework for Neighbourhood Councils

In Norway, sub-municipal political organizations like a NC system are not mandatory, but § 12 in the Act of Municipal Government (revised 1992) makes it clear that sub-municipal organization is an option, and certain rules for NCs are laid down. The municipality may according to §12 empower NCs with municipal tasks and resources, in the same way as with sectored municipal boards. Some restrictions, however, are put on the organization of NCs: they may be established and terminated solely by the municipal council, and the people in the locality are not allowed to elect the council members or its leader.

By looking into the documents and studies used in the preparation of the §12 text, it is easy to discern a conflict pattern among the legislators. Even the Local Government Committee's recommendations to the Parliament contained formulations that paved the way for direct, locality-based elections of neighbourhood councillors. And prior to the final decision on the Law on Municipal Government, the Ministry of Municipal Affairs issued a pamphlet introducing the new Law, and here they cited the majority position on the Committee, i.e. an opening for direct election of neighbourhood councils.[1] The Parliament voted however unanimously for a text that ruled out this option.[2]

Top Down and Bottom Up

In our opinion, we think the conflict referred to in the legislative process is a salient reflection on the dilemmas related to all decentralisation reforms: How much power shall be devolved to lower levels? How can the higher level (in this case the municipality) keep control over what is going on politically within the municipal territory? If the legislators – despite of the unanimous vote in the final stage – were in doubt, how is the dilemma reflected at the local and municipal levels? In our research project, we have made a distinction between NCs created by the municipality, and NCs organized by the people themselves, but obtaining formal recognition by the municipal council – enthusiastic or reluctant – as representatives of the people in the particular localities. Although we feel that there are a lot of issues that will be common to NCs irrespective of whether initiated by the municipal or locality-based, we are also expecting differences within the population of NCs to be at least partly explained by this variable.

Our expectations in this respect is that NCs created by the municipal council will be flavoured by municipal practices, i.e. that such institutions will tend to be more of a miniature municipality, with representatives that are more party politically oriented, and who have no problems in adapting to formal rules and the informal practices that make up the municipal institution. This is partly caused by the process of initiation itself, partly because members in municipally initiated NCs are usually appointed by the municipal council. Conversely, locally initiated NCs are expected to be closely linked to the local community and its practices in the way of e.g. informal 'dugnad' work and experiences from voluntary organizations working for a common cause. This is the result of the process of initiation it self, and partly caused by the process of recruitment. In both forms, however, NCs are expected to relate both to the municipality and to the local community. It is in how the respective forms handle the dual obligations that we expect to find differences.

Mapping Neighbourhood Councils in Norway: Survey 1

In our research project, in which our basic aim is to trace the dynamics created by the dual relations between NCs and the municipal level on the one hand, and between the NCs and the grass-roots on the other, our first task was to try to define and identify Neighbourhood Councils nation-wide. We deliberately developed a broad, realist definition as outlined above, in order to capture locality-based political organization in all its facets, and we knew that formal statistics on the distribution of NCs operating according to the §12 prescriptions in the Law on Municipal Government (1992) would exclude many political creatures that were in fact operating on a territorial, sub-municipal basis.

In fact, an available statistical report from 1996 (Teigum, 1996)) showed that out of the country's 435 municipalities, only 14 had established '§12-NC'-system by 1995 (questionnaire answered by 372). The corresponding number for 1996 was 16, and only 1 municipality had reported that it planned to establish an NC system by 1999.

Reading this report, one would easily get the impression that only a negligible proportion – three to four per cent of the Norwegian municipalities – operated or planned to operate an NC system. From our own acquaintance with municipalities through project works on organizational and political themes on municipal level, and by reading newspaper articles in our region, we were confident that a much larger proportion of the municipalities had in fact established a NC system, but for some reason or other they had not bothered to establish it as 'Kommunedelsutvalg', which is the official term used in the §12. Simply by naming the sub-municipal units 'village', 'area' or 'district' councils, they evaded the collection of statistics on sub-municipal political organization completed by the Norwegian Statistical Bureau.

Our first research task was thus to prepare a postal questionnaire addressing the chief administrative officers in all Norwegian municipalities, asking them to tick off in what way their municipality related to people in the localities and districts that made up the municipal territory. The ones that reported that they operated a NC system – weakly or strongly linked to the municipal level, partly or totally covering the municipal territory – were further asked to give some information on the formal arrangements of this type, and to give their own assessments of the NC systems weak and strong sides.

In the autumn of 1997 we carried out the survey work, and by the end of the year we had obtained returned and completed questionnaires from 311 out of a total of 435 municipalities, a comfortable 72 per cent response rate. The response rate was lowest among small municipalities, and highest among the 40 municipalities with more than 20,000 inhabitants (here we got an 85 per cent response rate). This skewdness in the distribution of answers was expected, as we had envisaged that the theme of municipal decentralisation was more interesting to the leaders of big municipalities, compared to the smaller ones. In this connection, it is important to inform that only 190 municipalities in Norway have more than 5,000 inhabitants. In a very stepwise manner, the questions to the chief administrative officer started by asking them about how important they perceived the contact between the municipality and various organizations at the local level, both task-oriented and locality-oriented. We also included the municipality's contacts with 'persons with informal authority within the locality'. At the top of the list, 'locality organizations' and 'voluntary organizations' received the highest scores, closely followed by local level school/parents groups. Among the municipalities that reported that they operated a NC system, NCs received the highest rating on locality – municipal contact.

Compared to the official number of some 16 municipalities with §12 NC systems, our data show that out of the 311 municipalities that answered our questionnaire, 124, or 43 per cent reported that there was an NC system operating in their municipality. Of those surveyed 68 municipalities reported that they had NCs that were established by the municipality, 76 municipalities reported that they operated an NC system based on municipal recognition of locality-initiated councils, and 22 municipalities had both forms of NC system within their organization and territory. This means that the number of municipalities with the one, the second, or both systems present, can be computed to (68 + 78 – 22)= 124. The fact that 22 officers reported that they had both 'municipal' and 'local' councils operating within their municipality is in itself an indication that at least some of the municipalities have a flexible approach to the challenges of municipal decentralisation.

Table 9.1 NCs in Norway, Depending on Municipal Size

Number in the municipality	% top-down NCs	% bottom-up NCs	% mixed NCs
0–2499	17 (15)	19 (17)	3 (3)
2500–4999	24 (19)	28 (22)	9 (7)
5000–19999	23 (25)	30 (33)	4 (4)
20000–	50 (17)	32 (11)	18 (6)
Total	24 (76)	27 (83)	7 (20)

NB The final column contains municipalities that are included in columns 2 and 3.

From the returned questionnaires we learned that within the municipalities in question, there are a total number of 455 NC units established by the municipality, and 363 NC units of the type initiated at the local community level, but recognised by the municipality. This means that the survey has located some 800 political bodies operating at the locality level, integrated into the municipal local government system.

Why are NC Systems Established by Municipalities?

Some NC systems were established long ago in the municipalities, both by municipalities and by people at the local level, and the relatively high proportion of municipalities reporting that they had an NC system is an indication that this system is not only a product of recent discussions on municipal reform. In the questionnaire we wanted, however, to get some information on the processes which lead to decisions on whether or not the municipality should set up an NC system. We asked the chief administrative officers to report whether or not their municipality had put municipal decentralisation on the agenda in the last ten years, knowing that a lot of municipal reform models had been launched during this period, and knowing that, except for Oslo, the setting up of NC systems was not among the models or strategies that had attracted much attention among municipal level leaders. Of those answering this question, 74 municipalities out of a total of 302 (i.e. 24.5 per cent) answering this question reported that such discussions had taken place, and in more than 60 per cent of these municipalities, the discussion had led to the introduction of an NC system in some or other form. After a discussion in the municipal council 53 municipalities implemented a NC system and only two of these reported that they had later abolished the NC arrangement.

What were the decisive arguments in the discussions preceding the decisions on whether or not to construct an NC system? In the survey, we presented to the officers a list of what we thought were plausible arguments *pro et contra*, and asked if these arguments had been of importance in the proceedings. We presented three positive and six negative arguments. The three positive arguments received a higher agreement score than any of the six negative arguments:

a) NCs will increase political engagement (2.5).
b) NCs will lead to increased well-being in the local community (2.2).
c) NCs are efficient means for municipal problem-solving (1.7).

The highest-scoring negative arguments were:

a) NCs create unrealistic expectations (1.2).
b) NCs increase geographical conflicts in the municipality (1.2).
c) NCs lead to problems of governance (1.2).

The threefold arguments – civic engagement, local well-being and efficient problem-solving – are all arguments that are easy to defend within a political culture like the Norwegian one, in which political participation, a happy local life and public sector efficiency are central values. These values are hardly contested, and the question is more whether or not an NC system will fulfil the expectations created by these arguments. The critics of NCs will especially tend to question if the municipality really gives away power to the locality level.

Party Politics, Small Scale?

One central theme would be the link between municipal party politics and the NC system. In Norway, municipal affairs are run by councillors elected by party lists, with a proportionally representative system. Only in few cases do we find a dominance of non-partisan representatives, or lists made up by informal groupings of citizens. How does this system of party politics at the municipal level relate to the activities at the level of the locality?

As already mentioned, we expected to find difference between NCs created by municipalities, and NCs created by local people, on the importance of party politics. Locally created and informal community organizations, transformed into sub-municipal, formal councils, are expected to keep their grass-roots profile, putting weight on what unites, and under-communicating partisan cleavages among the local participants.

The results from the chief administrative officers' survey however showed that in both groups (Top-down NCs and Bottom-up NCs), non-partisan recruitment is dominant. Among the locally created NCs, only two municipalities report party political recruitment, while the remaining are composed of non-partisan (62 cases) or mixed recruitment (10 cases). Among the municipalities reporting NCs created by the municipality, only 11 were composed of party representatives, while 53 were non-partisan and 14 mixed.

This dominance of non-partisan composition of NCs is an indication that the NCs bear little similarity to ordinary municipal affairs, irrespective of the way they originated. The strong case for this is the small proportion of party-based recruitment to the NCs created by the municipalities.

The natural next question would be: How are they elected? Very few municipalities report ordinary elections carried out alongside the municipal elections (four cases).[3] In 29 municipalities, councillors are appointed by the municipal council, but the vast majority of municipalities (80 cases) report direct elections in open local meetings. Interestingly, there is one additional way of recruiting local councillors: They are not quite often appointed by voluntary organizations at the local level. In 54 municipalities this is the way NCs are composed.

Summing up, the people serving on NCs seem to be primarily local level activists, but from our data we do not know for sure if they are also party-members that do not activate that status in their NC affairs.

Decentraliztion of Power?

One frequent ironic characterisation of NCs is ‘street name committees’. This means that a NC is created, but it has got no mission nor has it got money or other resources, and it may serve as a retirement arena for cast-offs from party politics and municipal affairs. To determine whether this was the case, and with suspicions that many of the locally created NCs may merely be local social clubs, we asked the chief administrative officers if the NCs were involved in municipal service deliveries in some specific areas.

On a scale from 0 to 3, the respondents were asked to place NC activities in specified municipal sectors from ‘not involved’ (0), involved on a ‘sounding out’ basis (1), further on to “discussion partnership” (2), and with the top score ‘full responsibility’ (3). Mean scores were first computed, and the highest scoring area was ‘Culture and leisure activities’, which received a modest 1.6 score. Following this area, ‘business and community development activities’ got a 1.5 mean score, this was also the score obtained in ‘technical infrastructure/ communications/ environmental protection’. ‘Planning’ scored 1.4, while ‘School and day-care’ came up with 1.2. ‘Health, social and services to the elderly’ scored less than 1.0 – lowest among the listed alternatives. As an overall conclusion, we find that the municipalities engage their NCs on a wide range of municipal activities, but not ‘in- depth’.

Money: Budgets or Local Contributions?

In an attempt to find out the accurate amount of public money being distributed through this decentralized channel, we asked the chief administrative officers to state how large sums were annually appropriated from the municipal budget to the NCs. We just asked for a lump sum, and thereafter we had to compute a per-NC appropriation, by dividing the sum by the number of NCs in each municipality.

These data must be treated cautiously, as we have information from only 67 of the total of 124 municipalities that reported having NC systems. This may of course mean that the other half of the municipalities transferred no money at all to the NCs, but it may as well mean that it is difficult to assess the exact sums, as they may come from several different municipal or via the municipalities, but originating from other (county, State) sources. But we can conclude that a substantial proportion of the NCs – a total of 24 per cent – does not receive any municipal funding in money. Not unexpectedly, this zero funding practice is much more widespread among the locally initiated NCs (40 per cent).

Minimum sums – less than NOK 1,000 per year – are given to 12 per cent of the NCs. Then the bulk of the NCs receiving money seem to be in the interval from 1,000 to 10,000 NOK. This will be a sum that should enable the NCs to operate with a minimum of secretarial / office support, like stamps, envelopes and some paper copying capacities. Within these minimum-sum brackets (less than 10,000 NOK), almost 2/3 of the municipalities are located. The remaining 1/3 receives more than 10,000, but less than 100,000 NOK. This will normally make the NC a potential development actor at the locality level, if the NCs in question use their money in a strategic manner. Only four of the municipalities appropriate what we would call a substantial amount of budgetary means, enabling them to take at least some municipal responsibilities. In this 'high-income' bracket, we only find municipalities with municipally initiated NCs.

The conclusion seems to be rather simple: NCs get little financial support from the municipality level, and 'bottom-up-NCs' are worst off in that respect.

In a survey addressing leaders of NCs in nine selected municipalities carried out in 1998 (presented below), a similar question was asked, by making the leaders give an assessment of how the annual income for the NC was composed. A total of 45 NC leaders answered this question, and in the table below the results are provided:

Table 9.2 NC Expenses and Financing, as Reported by NC Leaders

	All NCs	Bottom-up NCs	Top-Down NCs
Mean expenses per NC '97	24,600 NOK	32,000 NOK	13,350 NOK
Proportion of income from:			
Municipal sources (regular appropriations)	53%	9%	88%
Other municipal sources	6%	4%	8%
Other public sources	3%	3%	4%
Income from own activities	18%	40%	0%
Membership fees	17%	39%	0%
Other sources	2%	5%	0%
Sum (N)	100% (20)	100% (25)	100% (45)

What is consistent, comparing the two surveys, is that the funding of NCs initiated by the municipalities is largely made up by municipal appropriations. The table above indicates that each NC receives 10,000 NOK per year on a regular basis, plus small extras, and 'that's it': These NCs seem unable to get any substantial funding superseding this amount, and to the extent that they succeed in getting extra funding, they obtain it from other public agencies.

The funding structure of the locally initiated NCs is radically different: According to information from NC leaders, only 13 per cent of their income emanates from municipal sources, and very little is additionally obtained from other public agencies (3 per cent). By contrast, the NCs of this type are perfectly capable of raising money themselves, by income-generating activities, and by levying membership fees. Combined with 'other sources', self-generated income amounts to a solid 84 per cent of the total income.

But even more interesting than this is the total level of income/spending in these NCs: Contrary to our expectation, locally initiated NCs have far more money than municipally initiated ones! While the latter type have to rely on 'crumbs' from the municipal chest, the former type gets even less money from the municipality, but nevertheless generates its own incomes, and ends up with twice as much money. But again, let us underline the dubious quality of the data presented in Table 9.2, which means that the information from that table should be treated as possible trends, not as facts.

Summing up, we can say that NCs have not that much in the way of responsibilities, and that the municipal level has kept control of both service responsibilities and the money. The sheer scope of NC activities however is of such magnitude that it would be wrong to label them 'street name committees'. Anticipating this, we went further by asking the chief administrative officers how they assessed or evaluated the NCs, by presenting some propositions to which they had to agree or disagree.

NCs' Performance Through the Glasses of the Chief Administrative Officer

In our first NC survey, we finally asked the chief administrative officers reporting that they had NCs in their municipality to give their evaluations of the merits of NCs, in the form of expressing agreement / disagreement to some positive and some negative propositions. The chief administrative officers were explicitly asked to answer on the basis of their role within the municipal organization, and we hope that the answers reflect their own experience with NCs, and not their ideological commitments. We selected 11 often mentioned propositions from the debate on the merits of NCs, five of them positive, and six of them negative. These were listed randomly, and the officers could express strong and weak agreement or disagreement on each item.

In the following table positive and negative propositions are listed separately, and by mean scores. A score of 4 means strongly agree, while 1 = strongly disagree.

Table 9.3 How Chief Administrative Officers Evaluate Neighbourhood Councils

	Mean	*Variance*
POSITIVE PROPOSITIONS:	3.2	.88
NCs have contributed to better co-operation across municipal sectors	2.4	1.25
NCs have led to an increased interest in municipal politics	2.3	1.53
NCs have contributed to a more client-targeted service delivery system	2.2	1.26
Interest in NCs are bigger among women than among men	1.2	.41
NEGATIVE PROPOSITIONS:		
NCs function as local pressure groups on the municipality	2.8	.83
NCs are functioning best where people are endowed with resources	2.7	1.57
It is difficult to recruit councillors to the NCs	2.1	1.49
NCs have led to greater conflicts of distribution between localities	1.4	.74
Inner strife makes it difficult to regard NCs as the people's spokesmen	1.3	.78
NCs make the municipal more difficult to govern	1.2	.30

There seems to be a potential interesting convergence between the top-scoring propositions: The number one 'positive' – NCs role in mobilization and problem-solving may be perfectly compatible with the chief administrative officer's perception of NCs as pressure groups. The strength of these two propositions is underlined by the fact that the answers to these two propositions show little variance.

Summing up, there are strong and weak sides to the NC system, but the chief administrative officers, being plagued by the increase in local demands emanating from NC activities, nevertheless are willing to credit them with empowering people at the level of the locality.

Enter the Neighbourhood Councillors: Survey II

We have already mentioned that a follow-up survey has been completed, addressing the leaders and other members of neighbourhood councils. Not able to cover the representatives serving on all of the some 800 NCs located in our 1997 survey (with an average of five members, this would have amounted to some 4,000 respondents) we selected nine municipalities that operated NC systems, four of them with NCs created by the municipalities, and five with their NCs locally initiated. Within the latter group, only NCs that are 'alive' are included. Some of the locally initiated NCs tend to dissolve, but sometimes without notice, so that the municipal presentations of NCs sometimes include 'sleeping' NCs. This is normally not the case with NCs initiated by the municipality. In total, we mailed questionnaires to the members of 43 'Top-down NCs' and 25 'Bottom-up NCs', thereby including 432 councillors. 281 of these returned the questionnaire, which resulted in a 65 per cent return rate, which is not that impressive (our first survey had a 72 per cent return rate), but acceptable for our purposes.

Who Are They?

The councillors who returned the questionnaire had answered the questions on personal background, and the following table presents this information. Background characteristics are presented for members of NCs created by municipalities, and locally created NCs. According to our hypothesis, members of the two different types of councils should differ in their backgrounds. We expected the Bottom-up NC members to reflect demographic characteristics at locality level, while the top-down NC members are expected to show background traits that are similar to members of municipal councils. The latter type can be characterised as being made up mainly by middle-aged males, well educated and often affiliated to the municipality as employees (Larsen and Offerdal, 1994).[4]

Table 9.4 Members in Municipal Councils, Top-Down NCs and Bottom-Up NCs Compared

	Municipal councils	*Top-down NCs*	*Bottom-up NCs*	*Norwegian population*
Share of female	30%	46%	51%	50%
Share below 30 years old	6%	2%	18%	20%
30–39 year	25%	14%	35%	20%
40–59 year	41%	56%	42%	31%
Above 60 years	30%	28%	5%	29%
Share municipal employees	26%	16%	17%	–
Share, university training	43%	33%	36%	8%

The number of respondents from the bottom-up NC group is rather small (77), and the results presented in the table must be treated as possible tendencies rather than general characteristics of that group. With this in mind, the table shows some interesting differences and similarities between the groups compared: As for educational level, occupation and gender, there are only small differences, few are municipal employees, the gender distribution is almost equal in both groups, and the educational level is also the same. The educational level is markedly higher than in the Norwegian adult population, but lower than among elected councillors at the municipal level where the average educational level is 42 per cent (Larsen and Offerdal 1994). The proportion of females in NC are remarkable higher (47 per cent) than at the municipal level. At the 1995-election, the female proportion was 32 per cent.

Neighbourhood councillors, by education, seem to represent a group endowed with strong personal resources. Also their mean age, people in their late forties, underline this tendency. Looking at the columns centre and right we detect some striking differences between 'bottom-up' and 'top-down' NCs. The members of locally initiated councils are definitely younger than the other group, a difference of 11 years in mean age. Knowing this, we are not surprised that the 'bottom-uppers' more often have children below the age of 16, and here the difference is marked: 61 per cent and 40 per cent.

If we move on to the neighbourhood councillors activity profiles in leisure time activities, the differences between the two groups do not disappear:

Table 9.5 NC Members' Participation in Associations and Volunteer Organizations. Share that is 'Active' and 'Very Active'

	Bottom-up NCs	Top-down NCs	Total
Economic associations	18.7%	30.6%	27.1%
Political parties	1.3%	37.3%	26.9%
User's boards	13.6%	17.6%	16.4%
Sports Clubs	28.0%	14.6%	18.6%
Church and mission	2.6%	15.7%	11.7%
Clubs for youth and children	3.9%	15.2%	11.9%
Clubs for songs, music and theatre	17.1%	11.8%	13.4%
Social and humanitarian organizations	14.3%	13.0%	13.3%
Clubs for culture, hobbies and leisure	27.7%	26.9%	27.1%
Lodges	4.0%	9.0%	7.5%
Organizations for environment and solidarity	1.3%	10.8%	7.9%
Average number of membership in volunteer org. with meetings etc. at least every month	2.0	2.4	2.3
N (min)	74	176	253

The neighbourhood councillors are engaged people, they participate 'actively' over a broad range of organizations, at the same time as they hold NC positions. Treated as one group ('All councillors' column) there is no specific activity that is worth mentioning. But analysing the groups separately, one big difference looms over the data collected: The members from top-down NCs keep up political party activities. The 'bottom-uppers' do not participate. Here the difference is really dramatic (36 per cent), and the activity rate among 'bottom-uppers' is down to one per cent! This study has no recording of party membership, and in principle, the 'bottom-uppers' may be enlisted as party members. What these data show is however that the councillors in locally created NCs do not combine councillor and party activities, while members of the other group is likely to do so.

The following picture emerges: The 'bottom-uppers' as 40-year old parents, with little contact with the local party political life, as contrasted to the 'top-downers' – 50-year olds and active in local party organizations. The natural follow-up question is whether these differences in personal traits are reflected in the workings of the NCs. Does personal background matter, or is the business to be carried out on the level of the locality so similar that personal differences are weakened? An indication that there may be marked differences between the two types of councils can be read from the financing structure, because a substantial amount of energy has to be devoted to collecting local funding in the NCs that are initiated from below.

In the following table, we have asked the councillors to assess degrees of importance of a variety of tasks that NCs may be expected to engage in.

Table 9.6 NCs Tasks. Share of NC Members that Answers 'Very Important' on Different Alternatives

	Bottom-up NCs	Top-down NCs	Total
a) Organise local activities	60.3%	8.8%	24.3%
b) Implement actions to improve the local community	70.5%	21.0%	35.6%
c) Carry out ordinary municipal tasks	8.1%	8.5%	8.4%
d) Act as a body entitled to comment on municipal business	21.1%	72.3%	57.9%
e) Promote local issues against the municipality, county and state	51.9%	79.5%	71.5%
f) Inform local community about present issues	32.4%	67.5%	57.7%
g) Business development initiatives	16.0%	11.6%	12.9%
h) Co-operate with municipality on issues like planning and development	42.9%	68.9%	61.5%
N min	74	176	250

The table illustrates substantial differences in perceptions about what are the proper tasks for a neighbourhood council, dependent on whether the NC is created by the municipality or not. Only in two of eight areas do the points of view converge: The NC should not expand their activities into the ordinary service areas (education, elderly, technical infrastructure etc.), and should neither bother much about local level business initiatives. Outside these two areas, however, the opinions differ. In three areas these differences are conspicuous:

'Bottom-uppers' put weight on 'arranging social occasions' and 'implement own initiatives for locality development' to a much larger extent than members of the other group, while the latter feel more comfortable in answering letters and responding to plans and proposals from the municipality, thus participating in the decision-making process in areas relevant to people in the locality.

In other task areas, like raising issues, informing people at the local level, and co-operating with the municipality in planning, the 'top-downers' are more likely than the 'bottom-uppers' to be active, but the differences are not that dramatic.

Two 'Regiments' in the Service of Local Democracy

From the data presented above, one is tempted to conclude that the two types of local democratic assemblies are so different in recruitment, and the respective role incumbents express so different views on what are important tasks, that it hardly gives any meaning to treat them as the same type, namely Neighbourhood Councils. The differences are also pronounced between the two groups when asked about frequencies of contact frequencies with municipal sector officers, to the chief administrative officer, and to the municipal political leaders.

But other questions are answered in a way that soften this difference. When presented with a series of propositions on the role of neighbourhood government in the local community, we find that the neighbourhood councillors, irrespective of whether they are a 'top-down' or 'bottom-up' to a large extent agree on what NC activities mean to the localities in question, and also their perceptions on the qualities of the local community is surprisingly consistent. The most striking example of this is the proposition: *In our locality, the spirit of 'dugnad' is strong*. Of those surveyed 65 per cent of the 'bottom-uppers' and 64 per cent of the 'top-downers' expressed agreement to this statement. And the two groups are also in perfect agreement that they oppose the statement that 'People in our locality have more resources, compared to people in other parts of the municipality' (agreement percentages are here 26 and 24 in the two groups). Strong agreement in both groups is expressed as for the statements: 'Our council is an important vehicle in getting "goods" to our area', 'Our council means a lot to people's well-being and welfare level', and 'Most people regard our council as their spokesman'.

Summing up, the most interesting findings are perhaps the identification of what we have called the 'Two regiments in local democracy'. Our findings seem to justify both parts of the heading – that there are two relatively different sets of NCs. There are definitely differences in perceptions of the NCs role in relation to the municipality, and in how resources should be gathered and used by the NCs. These differences may stem from the initiation phase, and they have since then been reflected in differences in recruitment patterns. Most striking are the differences in obtaining funds, and how the NCs created by the municipality find the municipal appropriation as their final financial framework ('this is it'), while on the contrary, a much smaller sum allotted to the locally initiated ones triggers off a series of income-generating activities that also are social occasions for the local community.

Table 9.7 Two Regiments in Local Democracy

	'Regiment of social activity'	*'Regiment of public inquiry'*
Model of NCs	Bottom-up	Top-down
Representatives in NCs:		
Typical socio-demographic characteristics	40 years old, children younger than 16 year	50 years old, long time living
Participation in ass. and vol. org.	Sports clubs	Political parties
Typical motivation to join NC	Interest in local community + a social need	Interest in local community + politics
NCs tasks	Local actions and local activities	Public inquiry, promote issues
Contacts with the municipality	Weak and formal	Strong and formal
Contacts with local community	Strong and direct/personal	Strong and indirect/impersonal

Obviously, some of the differences between the two 'regiments' can be explained with references to the difference between the voluntary sector, on one side, and the formal political system, on the other. And it is tempting to assume that the 'regiment of social activity' is more social capital producing than the 'regiment of public inquiry'. They also show more communitarian traits than the 'inquiry regiment'. They even control more economic resources. Those in the 'regiment of public inquiry' are probably more deeply embedded in their local communities, which means, in problem-solving activities, they are able to play different tunes with different parts of the community, e.g. initiating and encouraging participation in social arrangement and the like, which may not have any instrumental purpose, but nevertheless play an important expressive role as symbols of community unity.

The 'inquiry regiment' seems to be more integrated in the local government system, adhering to formal bureaucratic procedures set up by the municipal government, which seems to dissembled them, and prevents them from taking part in symbolic expressions of community. Extending this finding to a more general point, one hypothesis would be that setting up decentralized units run by centrally-appointed people with no input from local people would serve only to further alienate citizens from the political process. This, however, is hardly the case here. As we have shown in this last section, there is much in common between the two types, especially when it comes to perceptions of the role of the NC in the local community. Both types of NCs represent local arenas for co-operation and responses to local problems and needs. The differences between the two types of NC, then, need not be exaggerated. First and foremost, these observations call for further research, and other data, i.e. intensive fieldwork, in order to draw final conclusions.

Notes

1. Kommunaldepartmentet/Kommunenes Sentralforbund (1990).
2. Stortingsforhandlinger (1992).
3. This is hardly surprising, cf. the above mentioned ruling out of the possibility of direct (formal) elections by the legislators.
4. Larsen and Offerdal (1994, p. 72) characterize local councillors as a social elite. They have higher education and income than the average population. The average councillor is a middle aged, married man, occupied in the public sector as an officer.

References

Bogason, P. (ed) (1996) *New Modes of Local Organizing. Local Government Fragmentation in Scandinavia*. Nova Science Publishers, New York.

Coleman, J.S. (1990) *Foundations of Social Theory*, Harvard University Press, Cambridge, MA.

Etzioni, A. (1995) *The Spirit of Community*, Fontana, London.

Gundelach, P. and Torpe, L. (1997) 'Social Reflexivity, Democracy and New Types of Citizen Involvement in Denmark', in J.W. van Deth (ed), *Private Groups in Public Life*, Routledge, London, pp. 47–63.

Kommunaldepartementet/Kommunenes Sentralforbund (1990) *Ny kommunelov*, Kommuneforlaget, Oslo.

Larsen, H.O. and Offerdal, A. (1994) *Demokrati og deltakelse i kommunene. Norsk lokalpolitikk i nordisk lys*, KS Forskning. Kommuneforlaget, Oslo.

Montin, S. (1998) *Lokala demokratti-experiment*, Statens Offenlige, Utredningar, Stockholm.

Prahl, A. (1997) De tredje decentralisering og lokalsamfundsvikling I de nordiske lande – en strategi til udvikling af den nordiske velfœrdsmodel?, TemaNord, København.

Putnam, R.D. (1993) *Making Democracy Work. Civic Traditions in Modern Italy*, Princeton University Press, Princeton, N.J.

Røiseland, A. and Aarsæther, N. (1999) 'Lokalsamfunn og demokrati – teoretiske og metodiske aspekt ved begrepet "sosial kapital"' i *Norsk Statsvitenskapelig Tidsskrift*, vol. 15, pp. 184–201.

Selle, P. and Øymyr, B. (1995) *Frivillig organisering og demokratti*, Samlaget, Oslo.

Stortingsforhandlinger (1992) *Kommuneloven*, 17 September, Section 1043.

Tam, H. (1997) *Communitarianism. A New Agenda for Politics and Citizenship*, Macmillan, Basingstoke.

Teigum, H.M. (1996) Undersøkelse om kommunal og tykeskommunal organisering 1996, Norwegian Official Statistics Report 96/51, Statitisk Sentralbyrå.

Tocqueville, A. (1995) *Om demokratiet i Amerika*. Gyldendal. Oslo.

Walzer, M. (1992) 'The Civil Society Argument', in C. Mouffe (ed), *Dimensions of Radical Democracy*, Verso, London, pp. 89–107.

Chapter 10
Is Public Participation a Good Thing?

Peter McLaverty

There has been a massive increase in interest in public participation over the last ten years. A host of initiatives have been introduced to involve members of the public more fully in public affairs. Public participation has become the flavour of the day, in many countries. Public participation can be defined as 'Taking part in the processes of formulation, passage and implementation of public policies' (Parry *et al.*, 1992, p. 16). Why do people support public participation? Despite the growing consensus that public participation is a 'good thing', people support public participation for a variety of reasons. I want to try to show in this paper that whether one believes public participation is desirable, and if so why, will depend upon one's normative values and on the mechanisms that are being used to promote participation. I will consider a number of approaches to public participation and contend that for most people support for public participation will not be absolute but contingent.

From an academic point of view, there are a number of reasons why different writers have supported public participation. Rousseau, for example, argued that participation was desirable because no one is able to express the views of another. As is well know, Rousseau (1968) in *The Social Contract* argued that the people should come together in an assembly to decide the laws that would cement and govern the society. Those laws would be based on the 'general will', which would differ from the 'will of all'. How Rousseau believed the 'general will' would be achieved is not that clear in *The Social Contract*. For much of the work it appears that the people will reach the general will though their own efforts, by thinking in terms of what might be termed the 'common good'. However, Rousseau's introduction of the 'law giver' complicates the situation and can lead one to question why the people need to be involved in law making at all. Why cannot the whole process be left to the super-knowledgeable lawgiver? Rousseau's answer would be that the laws gain legitimacy from being endorsed by the people who are thus duty bound to obey them. However, drawing on the work of Plamenatz (1963), Pateman (1970, pp. 24–25) has argued that the main reason why Rousseau supports participation is because of its psychological impact. For Rousseau, participation in law making is desirable because it educates people. It is through participation that individuals learn that they are part of a society and develop a sense of justice. Pateman summarises Rousseau's position as follows:

> As a result of participating in decision making the individual is educated to distinguish between his own impulses and desires, he learns to be a public as well as a private citizen. Rousseau also believes that through this educative process the individual will eventually come to feel little or no conflict between the demands of the public and private spheres.

It can be argued, therefore, that Rousseau supports participation in decision making for two reasons: because it produces desirable outcomes and because it helps people develop as individuals, in socially desirable ways. He sees the educative effect of participation as the more important of the two benefits which come form participation. The two, however, are closely related.

The argument that public participation should be supported because of its ability to educate individuals is one that is adopted by a number of other writers, such as John Stuart Mill. Mill's approach is, in some respects, ambiguous. In *Considerations on Representative Government*, he supported the idea of plural voting. The number of votes allocated to individuals should depend upon their level of formal education (Mill, 1951). However, Mill (1873, 1982, Williams, 1976) also argued that it was through participation in public affairs, locally and particularly in the workplace, that individuals learnt how to participate. Mill argued that through participation in decision making in the workplace individuals would develop their capacity to participate responsibly in their own self-government. For Macpherson (1977), Mill's approach represented a 'developmental' approach to democracy.

Supporters of public participation for its educative consequences, would view participative mechanisms that are purely consultative with suspicion. The aim, for those who adopt positions close to that of Mill, is for individuals to be educated through participation, so that they can eventually participate at the highest level of decision making. Forms of participation which do not promote the opportunity for individual development are, therefore, flawed, on this approach. Giving people the right to vote in referendums, especially if the referendums were purely consultative, would be treated with suspicion on this approach, unless it could be shown that individuals were gaining the ability to engage in decision making. Supporters of what might be termed 'educative democracy' might react more favourably to referendums which are binding. Even in those cases, however, referendums might be seen as a limited way of increasing people's capacities to engage in public decision making, given that they are 'one-off' events, which concern a limited range of issues. Citizens' juries, while in most cases consultative, might be viewed as 'developmental', in that they involve citizens' in the detailed discussions of issues and might increase their ability to engage in democratic debate. However, in as much as the juries are single events and do not lead to opportunities to participate in decision making on public affairs, they would probably be seen as inadequate. The same might be said about user panels, though standing user panels, such as those introduced in the British National Health Service (cf. Mort, *et al.*, 1999), might be considered more favourably, though the consultative nature of such panels would be a course for concern. Where decision making powers, even if only to a limited extent, are devolved to bodies such as neighbourhood councils, mechanisms are likely to gain some support from those who take a broadly Millian approach.

The idea of democratic involvement helping to educate citizens is one that can shade into a commitment to participation in deliberative forms of democracy. For writers who support this approach, public participation is desirable in as much as it is tied into the development of deliberative mechanisms. It is the quality of the participation that is stressed in this approach. Writers, such as Offe and Preuss (1991) argue that the important factor in strengthening democracy in liberal capitalist societies in the current period is that people should have to defend their opinions against those of others and that people's opinions should be open to challenge. In that way the quality of democracy will be enhanced, as people come to question their own assumptions and positions. The argument that deliberation will produce better decisions, is one that is supported by Cohen (1996). However, other writers who want to see an extension of deliberation, or discourse, such as Habermas (1994, 1996), argue that the crucial importance of deliberation is that it improves procedures not outcomes. Habermas (1993) argues that if all opinions are given a voice and the only factor that influences the outcome is the force of the best argument, then a position will be reached in which no one will feel that his or her interests have been ignored or overrun. As a consequence, we will end up with justice. The exact outcomes of decisions is less important, on this approach, than the way in which decisions are reached.

Habermas's approach to communication and discourse, which I will not consider at any length in this paper, has been criticised from a number of angles. For the purposes of this paper, I will concentrate on criticisms that deliberation is not necessarily a good way to make decisions, for it is rarely if ever that the best argument wins through, in the way hoped for by Habermas; moreover, the best argument is never likely to win through. Two contributions to the recent publication *Deliberative Democracy* (Elster, 1998) are particularly relevant to this paper. Both Adam Przeworski (1998) and Susan Stokes (1998) argue that deliberation can result in people supporting beliefs that do not represent their best interest. In other words, Przeworski argues that people can be ideologically dominated in deliberative processes. Preworski's position is based on the types of areas in which deliberation generally takes place. He argues that most deliberation that involves the public is about means rather than ends. In such situations, if people change their beliefs, for Przeworski, it is largely on technical matters, concerning the relationship between means and ends or what he terms 'equilibrium beliefs' which concern 'the political efficacy of alternative directions of collective action' (Przeworski, 1998, p. 41). In such situations, Przeworski argues, people are easily open to manipulation by the powerful, the organized and the articulate. On this approach, Przeworski would seem to view any deliberative mechanism which is not concerned with aims, rather than simply with means, with suspicion. It is interesting to speculate how developments, such as citizens' juries, would be judged on Przworski's approach. They involve deliberation between citizens but are usually concerned with deciding, normally on a consultative basis, the means to agreed ends (cf. Coote and Lenaghan, 1997, Deniel, 1999). However, they are often restricted in the options from which they can choose and there may be some concern about the manner in which the 'experts' to which jurors have access are chosen (cf. Stewart *et al.*, 1994).

However, against the type of arguments advanced by Przeworski and others, Habermas distinguishes between instrumental and strategic rationality and communicative rationality. Instrumental or strategic rationality occurs where people try to convince others to support their aims and goals. Communicative rationality, on the other hand, exists where people are trying to reach understanding and consensus and are willing to be persuaded by strong arguments and evidence and to change their positions accordingly. In the latter case, the chances of manipulation are much lower than they are in the former case. Some criticise Habermas for either producing a false dichotomy between instrumental and strategic rationality, on the one hand, and communicative rationality, on the other, or for inadequately distinguishing between strategic rationality and communicative action (Johnson, 1998, p. 173).

Other writers, such as Elster (1998), argue that the motives of participants are not that important, for deliberative mechanisms can have an impact on decisions irrespective of people's motivations. As Elster (1998, p. 104) writes:

> Because there are powerful norms against naked appeals to interest or prejudice, speakers have to justify their proposals by the public interest. Because there are powerful norms against the use of threats, they have to disguise them as warnings. Moreover- and this is the key point from the bahavioral [sic.] point of view – the proposals will *be modified as well as disguised.*

In other words, Elster is arguing that having to defend one's positions in public forces one to take a less self-interested, more communal approach. This is not because of any specific commitment to 'communicative rationality' but because expressing oneself in terms of simple self-interest is not likely to succeed. You are more likely to achieve your aims if you try to show that those aims are in line with the general public interest. Moreover, threats are unlikely to succeed in public debate. The logic of the public debate leads people to present the consequences of not making a particular decision in terms of a warning, rather than a threat. Iris Young (1997, pp. 402–403) also sees deliberation as important because it encourages people to put forward arguments in terms of justice, rather than self-interest. On this approach, public deliberation is a good thing because the structures of deliberation lead people to act in certain ways. As such, this position is different from the Habermasian support for discourse. It has some similarities with the approach of writers like Offe and Preuss.

A similar position is adopted by Joshua Cohen. In a series of works supporting deliberative democracy, Cohen (for example, Cohen, 1989, 1996, 1998, Cohen and Rogers, 1995) has argued that deliberative participation is not only desirable because of the procedures on which it is based but because it produces acceptable outcomes. And that is because

> the deliberative conception requires more than that the interests of all be given equal consideration in finding collective decisions; it requires, too, that we find politically acceptable reasons – reasons acceptable to others, given a background of reasonable differences of conscientious conviction. I call this requirement the principle of inclusion (Cohen, 1998, p. 203).

For Young (1997, pp. 403–404), while there is no such thing as the common good, public communication can help people to understand the partiality of their own perspectives and by helping them to get a clearer understanding of the processes in which their partial knowledge resides, help to achieve better solutions to collective problems.

However, against that broad approach, one might consider the work of Jane Mansbridge on New England town meetings in the USA. Such meetings are open to members of the public. Mansbridge (1983) found that attendance at town meetings was not popular with some citizens because of the demands it made upon them. The element of disagreement involved in participating in the meetings worried some inhabitants, who were not happy having to disagree and argue with neighbours. However open and encompassing meetings may be, it can still be a daunting task to put forward one's point of view in a public forum. There is always the chance that deliberative processes, however they are set up, will be dominated by the articulate, the self-confident, those with more formal education, and who enjoy taking part in debate, as well as by those with greater social power. Moreover, engaging in deliberation can be very time consuming. The criticism Oscar Wilde made of socialism ('there are only seven evenings in a week') can also be applied to participation (though it must be borne in mind that a number of mechanisms, such as Planning Cells in Germany, help people to participate by paying them and in other ways which mean they can participate during the day). For those and other reasons, some argue that the best way to extend public participation is not through the development of deliberative mechanisms which may, even if unwittingly, discriminate in favour of some and against others.

The Italian political and legal theorist Norborto Bobbio (1987) has argued that the battle facing democracy is to extend participation through voting by increasing the spheres in which people are able to vote. In the future, Bobbio argues, it should become as commonplace to collectively elect one's boss at work as it is to elect one's member of parliament. One can imagine how the number of representatives who are elected by citizens also increasing in the years ahead. Representatives could be elected according to the groups and organizations to which we belong (see, for example, Held, 1995, who sees this as a way of moving towards cosmopolitan democracy). Electing representatives, of course, tackles the problems associated with the time demands associated with participation. It can also give everyone an equal right to participate, even if that participation is formally limited to the act of voting. However, any participation in decision making is indirect and raises its own problems of how representatives are to be held accountable to those they represent. Developments in voting, on their own, would not meet the aims of those who support public participation for its educative role or who support it for its promotion of deliberation and justice.

A number of writers have argued that social inequality makes enhanced public participation very difficult. Macpherson (1977, pp. 98-108), for example, argued that for greater participation to occur, greater social equality is required. However, greater social equality, in turn, demands greater public participation. Whether that vicious circle, where the inability to make progress in one area blocks progress in the other, can be turned into a virtuous circle, where progress in one area leads to progress in the other, which in turn leads to progress in the first area and so on, is uncertain. Held (1996) writes about 'double democratization', by which he means that the democratization of the state, through enhanced citizen participation, needs to be accompanied by the democratization of the economy, through mechanisms of industrial democracy. Of course, there are writers who argue that the main emphasis should be placed on increasing participation at the work place and in the economy (cf., for example, Bachrach and Botwinick, 1992, Archer, 1995). For such writers, increasing the opportunity for greater public participation in the activities of the state, on its own, is inadequate and perhaps inappropriate.

From another angle, some writers, such as Putnam (1993) argue that participation is desirable because it can enhance social capital. Participation can bring together people from groups which might otherwise be excluded and give them an input into public policy. It can also help to increase trust between citizens and those who run government and public sector bodies (Putnam, 1993). Putnam has also argued, from his research in Italy, that a living public sphere within civil society can help to lessen problems of social exclusion and alienation and a number of associated social problems. For those reasons, Putnam argues that public participation, in its broadest forms, can help to produce a more inclusive society and a greater sense of community and community self-confidence. It can help to prevent a large gap emerging between the 'governed' and the 'governors'.

All the above justifications are based on arguments that public participation is either good for individuals, and/or improves the quality of decision making, which is more likely to reflect the public interest. However, public participation can be approached form a very different angle. Geraint Parry (1972, pp. 19-26) has argued that as well as those who support participation for its developmental consequences (such as Mill, Tocqueville and the guild socialists), there are others who support participation for what he terms 'instrumental reasons'. Such writers believe participation is needed to protect the interests of individuals and to protect and/or to ensure the legitimacy of the state. Writers who support participation for instrumental reasons (as examples, Parry (1972, pp. 22-23) mentions writers such as James Mill, Justus Moser and eighteenth century republicans like Henry Neville) have traditionally been non-egalitarian in their outlook. They have also, Parry argues, tended to see the type of participation which was necessary and desirable as limited in scope, often involving no more than voting in periodic elections, for parliamentary or council representatives.

If one looks at public participation from the perspective of the managers of public services or those who manager public organizations today, the approach to public participation may also be seen as reflecting an 'instrumental approach'. It is not always clear why managers in public organizations support public participation. In Britain, the central government is calling on lower levels of government to increase their consultation with, and the participation of, their communities. It is also encouraging local authorities and other public bodies to work in collaboration with other organizations (private businesses, not-for-profit organizations, community groups) in the delivery of services and other activities (cf., for example The Department of the Environment, Transport and the Regions, 1998). There can be little doubt that the development of participation initiatives, by the leaders of public orgaizations in Britain, is in part a response to the agenda of the central government. Public bodies are looking at ways of improving public participation, in order to satisfy externally imposed demands. There would also seem to be little doubt that in some cases the process of public participation is being driven by a concern to ensure that support is maximized or opposition is minimized for the policies pursued by public bodies, especially in sensitive areas. It is also interesting to note that in a number of cases, participation in the National Health Service has revolved around the use of scarce resources and may reflect an effort to ensure that at a time of 'fiscal crisis' (O'Connor, 1973), decisions retain some legitimacy with the public (see Mort *et al.*, 1999 for a consideration of participation exercises in the National Health Service).

However, those are not the only explanations for management's interest in public participation. For some public bodies have been engaging in public participation exercises for a number of years and have been pioneers in the implementation of participation mechanisms. A number of pilot citizens' juries have been conducted by local authorities and National Health Service hospital trusts (see, Coote and Lenaghan, 1997, Hall and Stewart, 1996). Lewisham Borough Council in London is currently conducting a 'Lewisham listens' programme, which involves the use of citizens' juries, community forums and focus groups. In addition, the council has been involving the local community in the decision making process, using information and communication technologies. The council is working with the European Commission in this initiative. Citizens and young people have been included in internet discussions with counterparts in other parts of Europe, on a series of issues (Lewisham Borough Council, 2000).

How is one to make sense of such developments? Do they simply represent a refined effort by the political leaders and the managers of local authorities like Lewisham to improve the legitimacy of the council's actions in the local community? Is the aim to improve policy and decision making and to give members of the local community real participation in the policy and decision making within the council? To what extent do the council's initiatives represent a movement away from a purely instrumental approach to public participation, where the local community is simply consulted on how best to implement the policies and decisions which have already been taken by the council? The Lewisham approach does appear to represent some opening up and extension of the participation process. In some areas, the public is able to decide which issues and concerns will be discussed. In that sense, the process cannot be seen as simply one that is driven by the council's instrumentally existing policy agenda. Recommendations and ideas from the various participation exercises have informed council policy making and no doubt will do so in the future. However, the participation exercises are not a substitute for decision making by councillors but an adjunct to it. As such they do not provide residents with control over decision making and might not meet the requirements of 'Millians'. Many of the initiatives are deliberative in nature and do represent a move away from simply involving people through voting in competitive elections. They would, therefore, probably be supported by advocates of deliberative democracy.

The 'Lewisham Listens' exercise, which is unusual in its scope and diversity within the British public sector, raises a number of interesting and important questions about the relationship between various forms of public participation and traditional liberal representative democracy. The development of the suffrage, so that today the vast majority of citizens in advanced capitalist societies have the franchise on a 'one person one vote basis', represents a victory for the idea of formal political equality. (Whether that formal equality is reflected in the other areas of the governmental process, is, of course, a quite different question). In theory, our elected political representatives, whether at national, regional, local, or levels above the national, are accountable to the voters. As 'ordinary' citizens, we have an input into the government through our votes, our ability to lobby and pressure our representatives and our access to various means of political communication. It can be argued that our link with our representatives is the crucial element in the workings of liberal democracy. For some, participation beyond periodic voting, is seen as a threat to the successful workings of the liberal democratic system. Schumpeter (1976), for example, argued that the roles of voters and their representatives should not be confused. The task of electors was to periodically elect their representatives, who would be selected from among competing groups of elites, and should then be allowed to get on with the task of governing. If citizens tried to hold their representatives to constant account or became involved more directly in the process of governing, the benefits of representative democracy would be lost. This 'competitive elitist' view of democracy stressed the centrality of political leadership, a strong executive and an independent and well trained bureaucracy (cf. Weber 1970; Held, 1996, ch. 5).

One does not have to accept the approaches of Schumpeter, Weber or Burke, who stressed that Members of Parliament are representatives, not delegates (cf. Macpherson, 1980, p. 25), to acknowledge that not all forms of public participation may fit neatly with representative democracy, as it has been applied in liberal democracies. It may be impossible for all citizens at most levels of government in the modern world, given the problems of size, if for no other reason, to directly participate in the formulation, making or implementation of public policy, except probably through referendums. It can be argued, therefore, that participation mechanisms that delegate powers of decision making away from representatives to bodies, which are not directly elected on grounds of universal suffrage in some sense, mark a move away from formal political equality. Does that mean, therefore, that public participation, other than in referendums and similar mechanisms, should be limited to consultation and advice? Can public participation in policy and general decision making be extended without undermining the formal political equality of liberal representative democracy?

Of course, there are those, like Burnheim (1985) who argue that the liberal representative approach should be replaced by an approach to democracy that abolishes general representative politicians. People supporting that approach argue either that different areas of society should be run by people who have a particular interest in that area or that 'governing' positions should rotate between citizens. However, there are those who argue that a more direct form of democracy is not only desirable but also feasible, given developments in ICTs. There is no reason why, given the scope of computer and other technology, citizens collectively should not be able to vote on issues which are currently decided by our elected political representatives. Support for such an idea is not new and was proposed by Wolff (1970), as early as the 1970s, since when there has been considerable development in ICTs.

Whether such a development would be desirable is, however, another matter. There is, of course, a long tradition among theorists which argues that citizens are simply not capable of making responsible decisions on issues of public concern. The tradition can, of course, be traced back to Plato (1974), who argued that specialists were needed to govern, just as they were needed to captain a ship. Of course, one of the counters to that position is that people learn to govern from participating in government, if at low levels to begin with – the approach of J. S. Mill. How far 'the people', however defined, are capable of self-government in a direct and active sense is, of course, one of the perennial debates in political theory.

Conclusion

Having come full circle, what might we make of approaches to participation? Whether one supports participation, and what type of participation one supports, will in many cases be a normative matter. Your approach will depend upon what you think is desirable either for individuals and or for society. Attitudes to participation also relate to how one views the capabilities of human beings. Are people capable of engaging in collective self-government and, if so, in what circumstances? Is government best carried out by experts, who should largely be free to do what they think is best, in the public interest? Are some people, because of their knowledge, social position, or whatever simply better placed to determine and carry out the public interest than others? People's responses to these and other related questions will help to determine their approach to public participation. Answers to those types of questions have informed the current surge in interest in public participation. There can be little doubt that 'public participation' has become a trend in many countries and is viewed as something that managers of public organizations should promote, and be seen to be promoting. As a result, in some cases, public participation is seen as in a vague sense desirable or necessary, without any real connection to more philosophical debates. Public participation can be seen as simply a tool to be used by management to meet their objectives. Even in those cases, however, it is likely that the participation initiatives introduced will be informed by some notion of the extent to which people are capable of engaging successfully in public affairs, although such notions may not be clearly articulated.

There are, of course, important issues surrounding public participation which have not been addressed in this paper. No systematic attempt has been made to locate philosophical approaches to public participation within theories of social change. This is an important subject, for one may take a certain philosophical approach to participation, such as the view that people can and should be able to engage in direct self government, while having doubts about whether, in practice, such self government is achievable. In other words what a person may support ideally may differ from what he or she supports in practice. However, to consider such an issue in depth, important though it is, is beyond the scope of this paper. My aim has been more mundane: to try to show that support for public participation has a number of different and conflicting roots. As a result, there will probably always be debates and disagreements about the desirability of public participation initiatives and the forms that public participation should take. Ultimately, the issues surrounding public participation get to the heart of the type of society we want to produce and how power should be distributed within that society.

References

Archer, R. (1995) *Economic Democracy*, Oxford University Press, Oxford.

Bachrach, P. and Botwinick, A. (1992) *Power and Empowerment*, Temple University Press, Philadelphia.

Bobbio, N. (1987) *Which Socialism?*, Polity Press, Cambridge.

Burnheim, J. (1985) *Is Democracy Possible?*, Polity Press, Cambridge.

Cohen, J. (1989) 'Deliberation and Democratic Legitimacy', in A. Hamlin and P. Pettit (eds), *The Good Polity: Normative Analysis of the State*, Blackwell, Oxford, pp. 17–34.

Cohen, J. (1996) 'Procedure and Substance in Deliberative Democracy', in S. Benhabib (ed), *Democracy and Difference*, Princeton University Press, Princeton, NJ, pp. 95–119.

Cohen, J. (1998) 'Democracy and Liberty', in J. Elster (ed), *Deliberative Democracy*, Cambridge University Press, Cambridge, pp. 185–231.

Cohen, J. and Rogers, J. (1995) 'Secondary Associations and Democratic Governance', in E. O. Wright (ed), *Associations and Democracy*, Verso, London, pp. 7–98.

Coote, A. and Lenaghan, J. (1997) *Citizens' Juries: Theory into Practice*, IPPR, London.

Department of the Environment Transport and the Regions (1998) *Modern Local Government In Touch With the People*, Stationary Office, London.

Dienel, P. (1999) 'Planning Cells, the German Experience', in U.A. Khan (ed), *Participation Beyond the Ballot Box*, UCL Press, London, pp. 81–93.

Elster, J. (1998) 'Deliberation and Constitution Making' in J. Elster (ed), *Deliberative Democracy*, pp. 97–122

Habermas, J. (1993) *Justification and Application*, Polity Press, Cambridge.

Habermas, J. (1994) 'Three Models of Democracy', *Constellations*, vol. 1, pp. 1–10.

Habermas, J. (1996) *Between Facts and Norms*, Polity Press, Cambridge.

Hall, D. and Stewart, J. (1996) *Citizens' Juries in Local Government: Report for the LGMB on the Pilot Projects*, LGMB, London.

Held, D. (1995) *Democracy and the Global Order: From the Modern State to Cosmopolitan Governance*, Polity Press, Cambridge.

Held, D. (1996) *Models of Democracy*, second edition, Polity Press, Cambridge.

Johnson, J. (1998) 'Arguing for Deliberation: Some Skeptical Considerations', in J. Elster (ed.), *Deliberative Democracy*, pp. 161–184.

Lewisham Borough Council (2000) *Lewisham Listens*, [Online] Available http://www.lewisham.gov.uk/index.htm, 10 November 2000.

Macpherson, C.B. (1977) *The Life and Times of Liberal Democracy*, Oxford University Press, Oxford.

Macpherson, C.B. (1980) *Burke*, Oxford University Press, Oxford.

Mansbridge, J. (1983) *Beyond Adversary Democracy*, Chicago University Press, Chicago.

Mill, J.S. (1873) *Autobiography*, Columbia University Press, New York.

Mill, J.S. (1951) *Considerations on Representative Government*, in H.B. Acton (ed), *Utilitarianism, Liberty and Representative Government*, Dent, London, pp. 187–482.

Mill, J.S. (1982) *On Liberty*, Penguin, Harmondsworth.

Mort, M., Harrison, S., and Dowswell, T. (1999) 'Public Health Panels in the UK: Influence at the Margins?', in U.A. Khan (ed.), *Participation Beyond the Ballot Box*, pp. 94–109.

O'Connor, J. (1973) *The Fiscal Crisis of the State*, St. Martin's Press, New York.

Offe, C. and Preuss, U. (1991) 'Democratic Institutions and Moral Resources', in D. Held (ed.), *Political Theory Today*, Polity Press, Cambridge, pp. 143–171.

Parry, G. (1972) 'The Idea of Political Participation', in G. Parry (ed.), *Participation in Politics*, Manchester University Press, Manchester, pp. 3–38.

Parry, G., Moyser, G, Day, N. (1992) *Public Participation and Democracy in Britain*, Cambridge University Press, Cambridge.

Pateman, C. (1970) *Participation and Democratic Theory*, Cambridge University Press, Cambridge.

Plamenatz, J. (1963) *Man and Society*, Longmans, London.

Plato (1974) *The Republic*, Penguin, Harmondsworth

Przeworski, A. (1998) 'Deliberation and Ideological Domination' in J. Elster (ed), *Deliberative Democracy*, pp. 140–160.

Putnam, R. (1993) *Making Democracy Work: Civic Traditions in Modern Italy*, Princeton University Press, Princeton, NJ.

Rousseau, J-J (1968) *The Social Contract*, Penguin, Harmondsworth.
Schumpeter, J. (1976) *Capitalism, Socialism and Democracy*, Alen and Unwin, London.
Stewart, J., Kendall, E. and Coote, A. (1994) *Citizens' Juries*, IPPR, London.
Stokes, S. (1998) 'Pathologies of Deliberation' in J. Elster (ed), *Deliberative Democracy*, pp. 123–139.
Weber, M. (1970) 'Politics as a Vocation', in H. H. Gerth and C. W. Mills (eds), *From Max Weber*, Routledge and Kegan Paul, London, pp. 77–128.
Williams, G. (ed.) (1976) *John Stuart Mill on Politics and Society*, Fontana, London, pp. 335-338.
Wolff, R. P. (1970) *In Defense of Anarchism*, Harper and Row, New York.
Young, I. M. (1998) 'Difference as a Resource for Democratic Communication', in J. Bohman and W. Regh (eds), *Deliberative Democracy*, MIT Press, Cambridge, MA, pp. 383–406.

Index